THE GOTHIC FLAME

NEHRU of INDIA

in the western clothes he wore rarely. The photo was taken during
a visit to Ottawa in 1957, when *The Gothic Flame* was first
published.

THE

Gothic Flame

Being
a History of the GOTHIC NOVEL in England:
Its Origins, Efflorescence, Disintegration,
and Residuary Influences

By

DEVENDRA P. VARMA
M.A. Ph.D.

NEW YORK / RUSSELL & RUSSELL

PR
830
.T3
V3
C.2

FIRST PUBLISHED IN 1957
REISSUED, 1966, BY RUSSELL & RUSSELL
A DIVISION OF ATHENEUM HOUSE, INC.
BY ARRANGEMENT WITH D. P. VARMA
L. C. CATALOG CARD NO: 66—15435

For
JAWAHARLAL NEHRU
Visionary and Statesman
who in action and language embodied
the dreams of India past and present

PRINTED IN THE UNITED STATES OF AMERICA

ACKNOWLEDGEMENTS

I wish to record my grateful thanks to Professor Bonamy Dobree who introduced me to the delights of the Gothic Novel, and whose constant guidance and encouragement fostered my investigations. Dr. Arnold C. Kettle, PH.D. (Cantab) gave me much unfailing counsel and judicious help in difficult places. He spared neither time nor trouble in discussing with me, and disentangling many perplexing points, and he generously aided me with his keen scholarship and sympathetic understanding of English fiction. To that eminent critic, Professor G. Wilson Knight, M.A. (Oxon), F.R.S.L., I am particularly indebted for much real and appreciated encouragement during the progress of my work. He was, to me, a perpetual source of spirited enthusiasm and constructive suggestion. I owe a deep debt of gratitude to those scholars of Gothicism: Professor Mario Praz of the University of Rome, and Professor A. E. Longueil of California, who gave me much needed encouragement and inspiration to shape this book.

My thanks are due to the Superintendent and Staff of The British Museum Library, London, for making available necessary journals and newspapers; to Harvard University, U.S.A., for lending microfilm copies of works not obtainable in England; to Leeds Reference Library and Leeds University Library for procuring some important works through their splendid system of inter-loan. I am obliged to Professor Robert D. Mayo of Illinois, U.S.A., for sending me reprints of his valuable and scholarly articles on Gothic literature.

I have been greatly aided by the practical assistance of Mr. Harry Fairhurst who spared no pains in tracing some obscure publications. I am thankful to Mr. Cox for placing at my disposal some minor works of the late eighteenth century; and specially to Mr. F. Beckwith, whose antiquarian interests and wise suggestions were always an inspiration, and who helped me to trace some obscure novels and even more obscure reviews. I am obliged to Mr. Caton for giving me valuable information about the unpublished works, and the lost papers of Montague Summers. To Miss Audrey C. Stead and Miss Helen White, I owe more than I can express. Thanks are due to Mr. H. van Thal, the bibliophile and learned Director of Arthur Barker Ltd., who inspired this publication; and to my friend Mr. Julian

Franklyn who saw this work through the press on my behalf.

I cannot forget the generosities of Sir Charles Morris, Vice-Chancellor, Leeds University, whose constant care and patronage sweetened my three-year stay in England; and I close with my grateful thanks to Sir Herbert Read and Dr. J. M. S. Tompkins who have inspired my further investigations and advanced researches on Gothic 'fragments' and 'tales.'

DEVENDRA P. VARMA.

" A sad tale's best for winter ; I have one of sprites and goblins."
WILLIAM SHAKESPEARE (*The Winter's Tale*).

"Je vous avoue . . . que de tous mes ouvrages c'est l'unique ou je me sois plu."—HORACE WALPOLE (Letter to Mme du Deffand).

FOREWORD

At the beginning of his book Dr. Varma quotes me as suggesting (not ' asserting ' !) that it is possible that ' Monk ' Lewis, Maturin, and Mrs. Radcliffe should, relatively to Scott, Dickens, and Hardy, occupy a much higher rank among English novelists. This opinion was expressed about twenty years ago, in the heyday of Surrealism, but now, after reading Dr. Varma's revealing account of the origins and development of the Gothic novel, I feel more convinced than ever that our neglect of this phase of English literature is unjust. I know exactly what will be said in defence of this neglect : that the plots of the novels are fictitious, that the characters are unreal, that the sentiments they excite are morbid, and the style in which they are written artificial. All these judgements merely reflect our present prejudices. It is proper for a work of the imagination to be fictitious, and for characters to be typical rather than realistic. Realism is a bourgeois prejudice—what is there of realism in the characters of Sophocles or Racine, Dostoevsky or Sartre ? As characters Schedoni or Melmoth are just as typical as Iago or Faust. As for morbidity, our modern tales of violence and horror constitute a *Schauer-romantik* that exceeds anything conceived by Mrs. Radcliffe or Maturin. In defence of all such literature it can be said that we express such sentiments to be purged of them.

We are left with the obstacle of an outmoded style, but this is a question of degree. *Vathek* and *The Castle of Otranto* survive as ' classics ' because, no doubt, they are stylistically more restrained than the master-pieces of Ann Radcliffe, Lewis, and Maturin : their authors had a more instinctive literary taste. But Lewis and Maturin had intensity of vision (read, for example, the description of Moncada's dream which Dr. Varma quotes on page 168), and their images are frequently as vivid as one could wish ("the kiss of childhood that felt like velvet "). Mrs. Radcliffe was given to poetic ' effusions ', but she could be powerfully evocative, and there are many minor virtues in all these writers. It is a pity that most of their works should have become so inaccessible, and if he had done nothing else, Dr. Varma has made out a case for the re-publication of a selection of these novels. But he has done more. By his industrious research and the clear presentation of his material, he has rescued a dream literature from oblivion, and shown that our aesthetic prejudices deprive us of an experience that is always pleasurable and may be profound. Burke himself, preoccupied with the sublime at the time these novels were being written, would have held that the Gothic flame is capable of tempering the soul to a purity beyond the range of our dingy realism.

HERBERT READ

CONTENTS

ix

INTRODUCTION

THE change in the attitude of critics to the Gothic Romance during the last generation is indicated by Professor D. P. Varma when he writes that it was " not a cul-de-sac but an important arterial development of the novel ". Perhaps a more exact image would be " not a field-path " ; for before the business acumen of Mr. Elkin Mathews, as Professor Varma informs us, started the Gothic industry of theses and special studies by the purchase and judicious advertisement of these old best-sellers, students knew that the disused tracks had somewhere joined the high-road, though they did not think that the traffic they carried had been very important. The great coach of the English Novel of Manners and Character, supported, as Saintsbury used to say, on the four wheels of Richardson, Fielding, Smollet, and Sterne, had not travelled on them, or had made only a brief détour. None the less, Scott's generous appreciation of Mrs. Radcliffe and De Quincey's preference of her to Dickens were well known and led some of us to *The Romance of the Forest*, which we found better than we had expected. *Northanger Abbey*, carefully read, yielded evidence of a more subtle attitude than lay behind the corrective burlesque of E. S. Barrett's *Heroine*. Both the Tilneys, admirable young people, have enjoyed *The Mysteries of Udolpho*, and Henry's response, at least, has been perfectly adequate, for his hair stood on end the whole time. But certainly neither he nor his sister nor Jane Austen herself could have thought of these romances as a vehicle of truth. They were a pastime, belonging to the permissive, not the obsessive, aspect of the imagination, to be enjoyed with a clear perception of their limitations and discarded, perhaps, as the taste matured, since the main business of life, they would hold, is always in the daylight. The absence of sour, contemptuous or angry notes in the gentle chiding of Catherine Morland, however, was always noticeable. This amused tolerance was very much the attitude of the literary historians who assessed the Gothic fashion. The qualities they usually distinguished in it were the sentiment of the past (highly anachronistic in detail), the development of the intricate plot of suspense, and the conflict of imagination and rationalism in the explained supernatural ; and there was always the baffling aesthetic question of ideal terror to lead us on, and the perception that something, submerged since the Jacobean Drama, had reappeared at a lower literary level.

When, however, we turned to Mrs. Radcliffe, the most accessible and attractive example of the Gothic romance-writer, we found that her charm had not entirely waned. These absurd stories (as they are to the daylight mind) could still exert the essentially romantic power of making the reader into a co-creator. One wandered farther in her landscapes, tried new variations on her materials, rewrote sections of her dialogue more acceptably. When I was working on the Gothic section of my book, *The Popular Novel, 1770–1800,* I found that this could still happen to me, and I tried to be on my guard against it. I reminded myself, for instance, that it was Stephen Cullen's work that I had to consider, not my own fancies on his themes. Yet I find that I allowed myself to write of *The Haunted Priory* : " It has passages of incomplete poetry that induce the reader to piece out its imperfections." I now see this process as more significant than I then supposed. No doubt it took place in the first readers of Gothic writings on a grand scale and at a deeper level. What De Quincey calls the " dreaming organ ", the inlet of the " dark sublime ", " the magnificent apparatus which forces the infinite into the chambers of the human brain ", was activated (and it does not need first-class literary achievements to bring that about) and the access to the reader's emotional, imaginative and subconscious life opened. It is along these lines that the revaluation of the Gothic Romance is proceeding ; and it is when the critical guard is temporarily lowered that the modern reader can best understand the enthusiasm of contemporaries and feel the vivifying force of the irregular stream of power that runs through these books, with all its grotesque flotsam and jetsam. Professor Varma writes his best when he thinks of the " dark underground river beneath the surface of human life ", of the " intrinsically healthy . . . magic Dionysian spring " and of the " quest for the numinous ", and sees the Gothic romance-writers as contributing to the recovery of the vision of a spiritual world behind material appearances.

A far cry from Lewis's *Monk,* one thinks, recovering one's critical stance. It seems to me that Professor Varma also has the experience of coming back to the page itself and of perceiving anew its frequent crudity, but he is not disturbed by this shifting of planes. He is able to accept the effect of the Gothic mode on his own imagination as an inherent virtue in the mode. He does not suspect himself of contributing too much. If Lewis's drastic contrasts between amorous and corrupting flesh, between passionate heat and the chill of the spectral visitant, kindle in him thoughts of love and death and an immaterial reality beyond the life of the senses, then that is what they do ; that is a genuine effect of Lewis's queer, immature, violent talent which, powerful still, must have been still more powerful when it came bursting through the restrictive decorum of respectable literature at the end of the eighteenth century. This is a fruitful attitude and opens the way to deeper explorations.

For what has altered our attitude to Gothic writings is, of course, the application of Freudian psychology to literature and literary periods, together with the Surrealist dependence on dreams and the unconscious. What came to light in the Gothic Romances, on this theory, were the suppressed neurotic and erotic impulses of educated society. Their scenes of horror, Professor Varma suggests, may have been " the harmless release of that innate spring of cruelty which is present in each of us, an impulse mysterious and inextricably connected with the very forces of life and death ". The Gothic castle itself, that formidable place, ruinous yet an effective prison, phantasmagorically shifting its outline as ever new vaults extend their labyrinths, scene of solitary wanderings, cut off from light and human contact, of unformulated menace and the terror of the living dead—this hold, with all its hundred names, now looms to investigators as the symbol of a neurosis ; they see in it the gigantic symbol of anxiety, the dread of oppression and of the abyss, the response to the political and religious insecurity of disturbed times. No doubt we must distinguish here between individual writers : to some of these castle builders the pleasure of the dream is avowedly enhanced by the knowledge that it is a dream, that at any moment they can run up the flag of rational freedom over the keep ; and they are, in fact, as chirpy about their feudal remnants as a French tourist spitting into the dungeon at Mont-St. Michel. But these, we agree, are not Gothic spirits of the true dye.

Such stimulating theories have given a new dimension to the study of Gothic writing. They have related it to the psychological condition of literate Western Europe at the end of the eighteenth century, and to the psychological condition of other periods when men experienced similar pressures, and thus, ultimately, to the permanent nature of man. This, indeed, is to see Otranto and Udolpho not as mirages on distant hills but as structures standing beside Professor Varma's arterial way. In his book is to be found a mass of material bearing on such interpretations, drawn from a wide field of reading. At the same time, he has considered his subject chronologically ; he has tracked the ' footprints ' and watched where the ' shadows ' pointed, and sought to establish the facts of origin, efflorescence, disintegration and residuary influence more fully than has ever been done before. The term ' Gothic ', meanwhile, rather like the term ' Metaphysical ' during the last quarter-century, enlarged by a rich complex of meanings and associations, ceases to be of much use to the literary historian in the same measure as it becomes valuable to the critic. We can no longer distinguish briefly between the energetic independence of Scott's imagination in the scene where in *Old Mortality*, Henry Morton expects death at the hands of the Covenanters, and the relaxed following of models already out of date in the illusory haunting in *The Betrothed*, by calling the latter ' Gothic '. Both are ' Gothic ' in modern terminology since both are drawn from the same submerged layer of experience.

The modern approach throws into new perspective the means by which the more self-aware of these writers tried to control their inspira-tion and keep their balance. They may not have recognized all the fellows in the cellarage that now pressed forward into light—modest Mrs. Radcliffe certainly cannot have done so—but they had some sense of danger as well as the strong joy of release. The Gothic flame, in fact, was often carried in a safety-lamp ; and this convenience could be constructed in various proportions of humour, nationalism and moral propriety. Walpole carried the flame in such a lamp, and Mrs. Radcliffe ; but not Lewis. Professor Varma rejects the notion that *The Castle of Otranto* was a joke ; but it is not derogatory to consider it as a serious pastime, like the play of children, all-absorbing for an hour. Or at least, that is the shape he forced upon it. The image is his own, when he wrote, as an ageing man, of his beloved Strawberry Hill : " The old child's box is quite full of toys." Certainly the compulsive element in his tale was exceptionally strong, and he let himself be carried on it ; but not too far. Small dry phrases, slight touches of irony are the tell-tale defensive manoeuvres by which he keeps intact his links with the daylight world. Nor does Beckford wholly deliver himself to the dark sublime until he reaches the Hall of Eblis ; it is not till then that his sophistication and grotesque buffoonery fall away. As to dear Ann Radcliffe who, as Talfourd tells us, smilingly handed to her husband pages that he shuddered to read, she too clung to her safety-lamp. What else is her explained supernatural, her unremitting propriety, but her effort, conscious or instinctive, to control the influx of the dark sublime ?

The very inadequacy of the explanations gives her away. Like other English Romantics, she exemplifies the instinct for compromise and the demands of self-respect. But the Gothic flame was not quenched ; it burnt brightly in its container. As her biographer wrote, what matters is not the objective truth of the apparition, but the tremblings of the human spirit in its supposed presence, since these are the " secret witnesses of our alliance with power which is not of this world ".

Such defences and adjustments have, naturally enough, small part in Professor Varma's learned and enthusiastic book. His object is to explore the nature and assert the importance of the Gothic impulse, and to trace its growth, decline and dispersal in our literature. He has cast his net widely and dredged up much interesting material. But it is the conviction in his study that challenges interest. He sees the Gothic writers as restoring the sense of the numinous to a literature cramped by rationalism and bleached by exposure to unvarying daylight. He sees them renewing its contact with the fertile depths of mystery and primitive emotion. And, against this, what are all the little gestures with which they gainsaid their essential self-committal ?

J. M. S. Tompkins

Royal Holloway College

CHAPTER I

FOOTPRINTS AND SHADOWS : THE 'GOTHIC' SPIRIT

A STUDY devoted to the analysis and investigation of a body of fiction that is usually left to moulder in the libraries of the curious, perhaps stands in need of justification. Professor Phelps, writing in *The Times Literary Supplement* (21 July 1927), observed that the Gothic novels " except by students of origins and curios . . . have long ceased to be read ", and he doubted if even " the laborious book " of criticism, *The Haunted Castle*, would " cause their pages to be turned again ". *The Times Literary Supplement*, on 24 December 1938, under the title *Gothic and Later Thrillers*, echoed the scoffing and formidable voice of Professor Saintsbury :

> There is hardly a more unprofitable, as well as undelightful, department of literature than that which harrowed and fascinated Catherine Morland and Isabella Thorpe.

Yet perhaps both the Goth and the Thriller have their rights. It is significant that aspects of Gothic and Terror literature have long been a favourite topic of thesis writers, and monographs from England, America, France, Germany, Scandinavia and elsewhere are surprisingly numerous.

On the other hand, some critics are prepared to agree with Mrs. Barbauld who, in *On the Origin and Progress of Novel Writing* (British Novelists, Vol. I, 1810) says, " books of this description are condemned by the grave, and despised by the fastidious ; but their leaves are seldom found unopened, and they occupy the parlour and the dressing-room while productions of higher name are often gathering dust upon the shelf. It might not perhaps be difficult to show that this species of composition is entitled to a higher rank than has been generally assigned it." The Gothic novel is definitely of intrinsic merit. As Sir Walter Scott says, in his memoir of Mrs. Radcliffe, " a thousand different kinds of shrubs and flowers, not only have beauties independent of each other, but are more delightful from that very circumstance . . . so the fields of literature admit the same variety ". He has, too, justly observed : " The infinite variety of human tastes require different styles of composition for their gratification. . . . There are many men too mercurial to be delighted by Richardson's beautiful, but protracted, display of passions ; and there are some too dull to comprehend the wit of Le Sage, or too saturnine to relish the nature and spirit of Fielding. And yet these very individuals will with difficulty be divorced from *The Romance of the Forest*, or *The Mysteries of Udolpho* ; for curiosity and lurking love of mystery, together with a germ of superstition, are more general ingredients in the human mind, and more widely diffused through the mass of humanity, than either taste or feeling."

Herbert Read, in *Surrealism*, makes a strong plea for a thorough revision of the whole field of English fiction, and asserts, " It is possible that ' Monk ' Lewis, Maturin, and Mrs. Radcliffe should relatively to Scott, Dickens, and Hardy, occupy a much higher rank ".

The critical assessment of literature has been a continual series of corrections of earlier impressions by those who have the opportunity to examine the question in hand more thoroughly and with a more accurate background of knowledge as an aid to their considerations. Thus the field of Gothic fiction, long viewed as uninteresting and barren, has gradually come to be recognized as of distinct artistic and literary importance, and is undergoing a new and more favourable critical survey.

Hitherto the study of the Gothic novel has been confined almost entirely to certain attitudes and themes regardless of the specific ways in which it developed and disintegrated. The problem of its ultimate origin has never been seriously examined : how from the surface of life it pointed towards the darker latent powers of creation and fertilized life from the newness of death, ghastliness and the mysterious unknown. Even the latest monumental work of criticism in this field, *The Gothic Quest*, stops short at ' Monk ' Lewis, and omits completely the genius of Charles Robert Maturin, the creator of immortal Melmoth. The story of ' Gothic ' disintegration has never been narrated, nor have scholars traced the residuary influences. The tale of its death and rebirth has yet to be told : how at the time of its death it bloomed once more, with such colours as it had never before displayed, with a fragrance that awakened a longing anticipation of a metaphysical world ; how finally the exotic rose was blown, and its withering leaves and discoloured and faded petals scattered by the remorseless wind. The object of this study is to outline its origins, efflorescence, disintegration and residuary influences : to examine what the Gothic novel actually was, in what direction it began to exercise an influence ; to trace its first manifestations and its gradual rise, when and why it ceased to be an active force ; to estimate its real significance, and evaluate its structure and characteristics ; to investigate whether or not the Gothic novel was a living, vital force, or merely a string of tales born out of notorious eccentricities ; in short, to discover if it may be justified as something fundamental and authentic in fiction. The study of literature as an organic progress gives added significance to periods of transition and enables us to place the various works in their relative perspectives. An attempt to blaze a trail through the rank wilderness of English novels from 1762 to 1820 is a difficult task, and this study purports to be nothing more than a wide investigation of the major trends of Gothic fiction.

The Gothic epoch falls in a neglected and dim period : the interval between the four great eighteenth-century novelists, Richardson, Fielding, Smollett, and Sterne, and the nineteenth century with its Scott and Jane Austen. Although this interim contains probably no names which the history of the novel has acknowledged great, its large body of fiction enjoyed a prodigious success with its readers, reflected and shaped their imaginations, and often broke out into fanciful and creative adventure. It influenced the main course of English literature in a surprising number of ways, and in order to follow the wayward current of literature through the early years of the nineteenth century, one must be familiar with the notable exemplars of Gothic romance. Many honest craftsmen, unknown to fame, light up its pages, men and women who took pleasure in their craft and gave pleasure by it. Moreover, a book is valuable in literary history not so much intrinsically as for the influence it exercises upon greater and more significant works. Even the smaller names and lesser currents in literature have their value, their direction, their proportionate and material worth. " No branch of literature which has once, for any considerable time and in any considerable degree, occupied the attention of the reader, ought to be despised by the student," writes Saintsbury, in *Tales of Mystery*. This body of fiction may well have established the popularity of the novel-form. The Gothic novel is also well worth studying, if not for its particular literary form, at least as an expression of the general taste of the period and because of its function as " the leaf-mould " in which more exquisite and stronger plants were rooted. And yet the ultimate end of all study of literature is an effort to place an assaying finger on that mystery which for lack of a better name we call genius.

In the Bath Pump Room, a century and a half ago, a Miss Andrews, "one of the sweetest creatures in the world", recommended Isabella Thorpe some seven novels which, " having read every one of them ", she vouched for as " horrid ". The excessive rarity of these novels today has encouraged the idea that they never existed except in the imagination of Jane Austen. Professor Saintsbury thought they had been selected for their colourful titles :

> I have not read a single one of the list which was " all horrid "—*Castle of Wolfenbach, Clermont, Mysterious Warnings, Necromancer of the Black Forest, Midnight Bell, Orphan of the Rhine,* and *Horrid Mysteries.* I should indeed like some better authority than Miss Isabella Thorpe's to assure me of their existence.

Montague Summers was the first person to feel assured of their existence, and to state as much. Michael Sadleir, in *The Northanger Novels,* pronounced that these works will survive " as tiny stitches in the immense tapestry of English literature ". Soon afterwards Montague Summers began editing the " Jane Austen Horrid Novels " for Robert Holden, but only two came out, and complete republication awaits the boldness of a modern Gothic enthusiast.

One may assert that Jane Austen deliberately selected those particular seven ' horrid ' titles, for, according to Montague Summers, they reveal three or four distinct traits of Gothic fiction. Despite her satire, Miss Austen was not oblivious to the merits of the ' Gothic ' from which her genius had profited. Had it been her intention to mock or startle, she could have chosen from : *The Animated Skeleton, The Mysterious Hand : or Subterranean Horrours* (sic), *The Sicilian Pirate : or Pool of Blood.* Michael Sadleir has stated that the Northanger Novels fall into three divisions : *Clermont,* a sample of the rhapsodical romance ; secondly, *The Castle of Wolfenbach, Orphan of the Rhine, The Mysterious Warning, Midnight Bell,* all aping German fashions, together with *Necromancer,* a manipulation of genuine German material ; and lastly, *Horrid Mysteries,* a lurid translation from the German.

Of course, one cannot find represented here every feature of the Gothic school, but for me this list shows the broad lines of development from one phase to another. Does not the list begin with ' Castle ' (cf. *The Castle of Otranto*) and end in ' Horrid ' (cf. the Schauer-Romantik or School of Horror) ? Between these *The Mysterious Warning* parallels *The Mysteries of Udolpho* ; *Orphan of the Rhine* recalls *Children of the*

Abbey ; while *Necromancer of the Black Forest* strongly savours of *Melmoth the Wanderer.*

The Castle of Wolfenbach is by Mrs. Eliza Parsons, also the author of *The Mysterious Warning,* which has all the sadism of the terror novel. *Clermont,* from the pen of Regina Maria Roche (whose *Children of the Abbey* reached an eleventh edition by 1832), contained the distilled essence of Radcliffian fiction, mingling domestic felicity with dramatic horror. Written by an ingenious bookseller or antiquary of Freiburg *The Necromancer of the Black Forest* initiates the supernatural-expliqué : the Necromancer is a charlatan and a cheat, and the spectres a band of robbers. The tale is a series of violent episodes loosely connected. *Midnight Bell,* by Francis Lathom, is a Gothic masterpiece whose very title suggests atmosphere. Lathom was skilled in dialogue and dramatic incident, in which this novel abounds. Belonging to the Radcliffian school of sensational landscape fiction, *The Orphan of the Rhine* also resembles the writings of Mrs. Roche in its lurid sentimentality. *Horrid Mysteries,* a translation of *Der Genius,* and more horrid in translation, progresses in a series of apocalyptic visions, and tells of a hero who finds himself embroiled in murder and bloodshed beneath the pretext of liberty and education. This work is very potent Schauer-Romantik, and resembles Lewis's *The Monk* in its " enraptured fleshiness ". It is mentioned in Peacock's *Nightmare Abbey* that Scythrop " slept with *Horrid Mysteries* under his pillow and dreamed of . . . ghastly confederates holding midnight conventions in subterranean caves ". Scythrop's interest in *Horrid Mysteries* was especially awakened by the Illuminati (a German sect, openly professing Satanism, that had existed in the fifteenth century) who play so large a part in that romance.

Thus the list of seven horrid novels provided by Jane Austen in her *Northanger Abbey,* far from being haphazard, is by itself a chronicle of the origin, efflorescence, and disintegration of Gothic Romance, revealing not only the various types of Gothic fiction but also the consequential phases of its development from one shade to another.

" The scarcity of the Gothic novel and its successors constitutes a very real difficulty, and is a practical stumbling-block in the way of research," says Montague Summers. The Gothic romances are indeed extraordinarily elusive. Michael Sadleir has rightly emphasized that " there are probably no items in the lumber rooms of forgotten literature more difficult to trace than the minor novels of the late eighteenth century ". Only a few of the hoard of romances which issued from the cheap presses are now remembered. Their names are widely sprinkled throughout the pages of *Bibliotheca Britannica* and other bibliophile compilations, where books that become extinct get a Christian burial and a little headstone reserved for them.

A craze for fiction was a fashionable amusement during the last quarter of the eighteenth century, the circulating library catered for the taste of " the leisured fair ", although the reading of the novels was despised as a waste of time by serious-minded persons. Actual purchase of these novels was exceptional : confidential maids got them from Lane's or other circulating libraries, and regular borrowing and library circulation soon reduced the few copies to scraps. And as they were more or less a transient entertainment no one cared about their survival. Even if a solitary copy or two survived by some chance, they were thrown out contemptuously as unworthy of the bookshelf, and the children who played with them for their pretty pictures accomplished their destruction. Many of them lacking the vital protection of good binding perished without trace. Any surviving copies were cast out from lumber-rooms and remote country libraries to suffer death by fire, or the ignominy of cheap auction. Thus these works are of an excessive rarity today, and good clean copies sometimes fetch as many pounds as they were once sold for pence.

The revival of interest in Gothic literature during the present century we owe perhaps to the commercial ingenuity of one man. At the end of the First World War, when country halls and old mansions set to clearing out their lumber, piles of old books were indiscriminately sent for auction. Elkin Mathews, an enthusiastic London bookseller, purchased all such books at a cheap rate, and by printing a tempting catalogue of these late eighteenth- and early nineteenth-century works, began an aristocratic fashion among book collectors.

John Carter, in *Taste and Technique in Book-Collecting* (1947), says this catalogue " was the considered manifesto of a new movement in bibliophilic taste ", and " a milestone in the history of bookselling, for in it appeared books . . . which had never appeared in any West End catalogue before ". The Gothic novels were now discovered to be valuable and fetched several pounds apiece. Many volumes travelled to America, the material upholder of antique values, and England lost many of her eighteenth-century treasures. Mr. F. Beckwith, of Leeds Library, told me that, with the fortune they had earned him, Elkin Mathews accompanied his books across the Atlantic. But at least he had aroused a new interest in Gothic fiction, which, like so much else in the 'thirties, became another literary candidate for revaluation. During the last few decades these novels have aroused an intense new interest. In particular, the Freudian psychologists and the Surrealists seem to have rediscovered the Gothic novel. They reveal interesting attitudes towards the Gothic romance, but do not contribute much towards interpreting it. Montague Summers, in *Essays in Petto* (1928), has stated that " the Gothic romances . . . have been studied in at least half a dozen academic thesis ; none of these, however, proving . . . altogether satisfactory or authoritative ". But I must acknowledge my indebtedness to the work of predecessors in the same field. It would be worth while therefore to record the amount and nature of work already accomplished on Gothic romance : some are immature investigations, others revealing interesting attitudes.

With the turn of the century in 1902 Hans Mobius submitted a dissertation at the University of Leipzig. His work covers the field only up to and including Mrs. Radcliffe and omits the later School of Horror. In 1913 Miss Elizabeth Church wrote a thesis at Harvard, which comprises merely a series of plot summaries and lists of names useful but not conducive to sustained interest or argument. Two years later Miss Alice M. Killen treated the subject with a patronizing flippancy, doing little justice to the sociological or psychological significance of the Gothic romance. She deals rather more fully with the fashion in France than in England.

Miss Clara F. McIntyre's work (1920) is a monograph written in eulogistic tone. Not much light is thrown on the entire genre of fiction. A similar work is Miss Wieten's monograph on Radcliffe. Professor Longueil, in his doctoral dissertation, touched upon the influence of Gothic romance. Commencing with a plan for " a thesis of two parts : a discussion, first, of the origin, development, and literary success of Gothic fiction ", he eventually stated in his preface " like many a more experienced builder . . . I have gathered appreciably more timber than the practical design can embody. . . . The former half of this design must await a later opportunity for their publication." The first part never saw print.

Miss Birkhead's *The Tale of Terror* was reviewed by Professor Edith J. Morley, who deplored that it did not examine " the motive of terror in art and literature with a view to determining the aesthetic effect and value of the thrill ". The next work is Eino Railo's exhaustive study of Gothic literature from the point of view of emergent romanticism in the later decades of eighteenth-century literature. Railo assembles various definite mental images which he resolves into a synthesis of materials that gave to English Romantic literature its particular tone and individuality. He groups his materials round certain themes : ' The Haunted Castle ', ' the Criminal Monk ', ' The Wandering Jew ', ' The Byronic Hero ', to instance only four out of his eleven chapter headings. Professor Edith J. Morley pointed out that " this method of treatment necessitates a certain amount of repetition . . . doubling back on tracks already traversed. Nor does the author make any attempt in his final chapter to sum up and to clarify the conclusions to which his wanderings have led him. More serious defects in the book are the absence of both index and bibliography."

Professor W. L. Phelps added that Railo does not answer what was the nature of the need that ' horror-romanticism ' attempted to supply. Ernest Bernbaum also remarks that " in the search for the origins and causes of the ' horror-romantic ' novel—he (Railo) fails utterly " : but Railo's materials have proved definitely useful to later students. " What is now needed is a philosophical history of the way in which the narrow domestic sentimentalism of Richardson developed into the broader and more adventurous sentimentalism of Prévost, and so onwards, almost by logical steps, to the complex and extravagant sentimentalism of the Gothic novelists."

On 11 August 1932 The Times Literary Supplement reviewed Dr. Tompkins' book, The Popular Novel in England, which it described as " a serious and original work of criticism ". Within the large range of her study Dr. Tompkins records the rise and fall of ' sensibility ', of didacticism in fiction. She gathers up many contributary causes of the literary fashion which preceded the French Revolution, and places Gothic romance in relation to the tastes and conditions of its period. The book is one of permanent value.

In the following year appeared The Romantic Agony, by Professor Mario Praz, which is more in the nature of a study of algolagnia and masochism in literature, and incidentally of such fatal myths as have emanated from the domain of Gothic fiction. His approach is purely psychological, an attempt to fit the Gothic romance into the pattern of a general theme.

1934 saw the publication of an enthusiastic monograph, Horace Walpole and the English Novel . . ., by K. K. Mehrotra. This Oxford dissertation narrates the story of revolt against the realistic fiction of the years 1740–60, culminating in the victory of 'romance'. Carried away by devotion to his subject Mehrotra is inclined to under-estimate the importance and proportionate worth of other Gothic novelists. His work does not pretend to be a history of literary movement and concentrates attention on "the influence directly and indirectly exercised over half a century of novel writing by a single book—Horace Walpole's famous story *The Castle of Otranto.*" Mr. Mehrotra overstresses the importance of material to his hand, and belittles books and tendencies which do not fit into his preconceived scheme.

Baker's monumental *History of the English Novel* contains a chapter on the Gothic romance. Although methodical and painstaking in exposition he makes it simple and plausible for the reader by the omission of critical controversies and the absence of any new theories on the genesis or influence of the Gothic novel. It remains only a work of reference and a testimony of the author's learning. "The later eighteenth century has proved a difficult period", he tells us.

The latest work on the subject is *The Gothic Quest* by Montague Summers, a keen collector and voracious reader of Gothic novels, who spent forty years poring over tales of Terror and Love, of ruined castles, dungeons, skeletons and ghosts. His book undoubtedly contains data about novels and novelists never before studied in detail, and Montague Summers has been in a position really to know the books about which he wished to write. This publication is as imposing as its bulk, a monument to its author's scholarship and indefatigable zest for his subject. But as "a work of criticism and literary history . . . it suffers from a want of selective discipline, from a tendency to extremism in praise and blame, and from a certain turgidity of style. Its main argument is coherent and logical enough, but not always easy to disentangle from the digressions, hostilities and interpolations of irrelevant learning which Montague Summers too often allows himself." He deals sharply with the Surrealists who in recent years have intruded on his domain, annexing the ruins where love and death and vengeance and retribution dwell, and adjures them to remove their heretical fingers from the sacred relics.

Yet any literary genre is surely entitled to a revised interpretation with each succeeding period of history if it is to remain a vital force and not merely an adored and useless relic. The Surrealists, as a legitimate branch of modern thought, are as justified as Montague Summers himself in approaching from their own particular angle the fantastic, inexhaustibly fecund Gothic novel. Gothic fiction may be " an aristocrat of literature " as Montague Summers deems it, none the less it is not thereby sanctified by an unassilable Divine Right.

Whereas his tirade against the surrealistic interpretation of Gothic novels is more personal than intelligible, the interesting papers of three exponents of Surrealism, namely, Sir Herbert Read, Monsieur André Breton, and Mr. Hugh Sykes Davies hint at the initial possibilities of a surrealistic line of approach.

In the introduction to *The Gothic Quest* Montague Summers had stated that :

> In a second volume, then, I propose to treat in detail the work of Mrs. Radcliffe, Mrs. Charlotte Smith, Mrs. Parsons, Mrs. Roche, Mrs. Meeke, Mrs. Helme, Mrs. Bennett, Godwin, Charlotte Dacre, Jane and Anne Maria Porter, Mrs. Shelley, Maturin, Robert Huish, Charles Lucas, Mrs. Yorke, Catherine Ward, and very many more, the central place being, of course, held by " the mighty magician of *The Mysteries of Udolpho* ".

Again, on 31 December 1938, in a letter to the editor of *The Times Literary Supplement* thanking him for the review of *The Gothic Quest* and stating why he neglected Shelley's two Gothic experiments, *Zastrozzi* and *St. Irvyne*, he noted that :

> I have reserved a consideration of these two fascinating pieces for a second volume, provisionally called *The Gothic Achievement*.

These two promises he did not live to fulfil, and they still remain a daring task for any subsequent Gothic enthusiast.

Walpole described *The Castle of Otranto* as " a *Gothic* story ", and by doing so unconsciously gave a name to a body of fiction that was destined to please the fancies of an age. Doubtless he characterized it thus only for definite reasons, and so it is necessary to examine the significance ' Gothic ' held for the late eighteenth-century mind.

The term ' Gothic ' is usually associated with the frost-cramped strength, the shaggy covering, and the dusky plumage of the northern tribes ; and the ' Gothic ' ideal wrought in gloomy castles and sombre cathedrals appeared dark and barbarous to the Renaissance mind. At the close of the so-called Dark Ages, the word ' Gothic ' had degenerated into a term of unmitigated contempt ; it masked a sneer, and was intended to imply reproach. Wm. C. Holbrook, in *Modern Language*

Notes (November 1941), said " the word gothique had come to mean ' archaic, uncouth, ugly, barbarous ' ", expressive of the barbaric character of the nations with their rude and wild architecture. But with the emergence of the democratic-romantic side of the Renaissance, when the ' medieval ' rose to favour again, ' Gothic ' acquired a flavour of respectability as an adjective. Even during the eighteenth century the term continued to be a synonym for the barbarous, and stood for ignorance, cruelty, and savageness, which were part of the inherited Renaissance view of the Middle Ages. " If in the history of British art ", says Eastlake, " there is one period more distinguished than another for its neglect of Gothic, it was certainly the middle of the eighteenth century." But at no time since the Reformation had the Gothic tradition been wholly dormant, and as the eighteenth century sensibility broadened and deepened, there was a shift of emphasis in literature from ' decorum ' to ' imagination ', and ' Gothic ' ceased to have entirely a derisive implication. " One of the most obvious traits of the period is its changing attitude toward the Middle Ages, and no one word better reflects that change than does the critical adjective *gothique*." And before the century was very old, lesser men had begun to re-adapt Gothic ideas, and from the dormant seeds of Gothic tradition strange and unlovely flowers had begun to spring. There came a change in the overtones of ' medieval ' and words associated with it. " There was one literary connection, however, in which *gothique* was used without a sneer : coupled with the word tragedie it meant merely ' medieval ', or as we might say, ' pre-classical ' ; so that *tragedie gothique* was a mystère."

Robert B. Heilman has pointed out, in *Modern Language Notes* (1942), that Fielding's description of the Palace of Death in *A Journey from this World to the Next*, written in 1741–42, lays stress on " the structure of the Gothic order " which was " vast beyond imagination ". By ' Gothic order ' Fielding meant the Gothic architecture producing those impressions of venerableness, vastness, and gloominess, which are often loosely designated by ' Gothic '. While writing *Tom Jones* (1746–48) Fielding's disposition towards Gothic is apparent in the description of Allworthy's house :

> The Gothic style of building could produce nothing nobler. . . . There was an air of grandeur in it that struck you with awe, and rivalled the beauties of the best Grecian architecture.

He continues with a description of the surroundings, by telling us of hill, grove, cascade, lake, river, on the right of which appeared "one of the towers of an old ruined abbey, grown over with ivy ".

Richard Hurd, in his *Letters on Chivalry and Romance* (1762), not only claims recognition for Gothic art, but actually suggests that Gothic manners were superior. He fairly strews his pages with expressions like ' Gothic ages ', ' gothic warriors ', ' gothic manners ', ' gothic enchantments ', ' gothic tales ', ' gothic poems ', and ' gothic romances '. The word ' Gothic ', with all that it implies, ceased to be a synonym for ' barbarous ' and ' violent ' and became associated with the poetry and chivalry of the Middle Ages : thus ' Gothic ' assumed a second meaning, ' the medieval '. " The same term (Gothic) was used with both eulogistic and disparaging connotations." In English the real history of ' Gothic ' begins with the eighteenth century, when " the word seems to have three meanings, all closely allied—barbarous, medieval, supernatural ". A growing taste for Gothic was but one symptom of a great change of ideas, which evolved into the Romantic movement.

It was left for Walpole to launch ' Gothic ' on its way as a critical term in prose fiction. " This literary impulse, if anything, can be called the true starting-point of the Gothic Revival." His archaeological studies fostered his medieval interests. " It is impossible to peruse either the letters or the romances of this remarkable man without being struck by the unmistakable evidence which they contain of his Mediaeval predilections. His *Castle of Otranto* was perhaps the first modern work of fiction which depended for its interest on the incidents of a chivalrous age, and it thus became the prototype of that class of novel which was afterwards imitated by Mrs. Ratcliffe (*sic*) and perfected by Sir Walter Scott. The feudal tyrant, the venerable ecclesiastic, the forlorn but virtuous damsel, the castle itself, with its moats and drawbridge, its gloomy dungeons and solemn corridors, are all derived from a mine of interest which has since been worked more efficiently and to better profit. But to Walpole must be awarded the credit of its discovery and first employment," says Eastlake. The thought of ' Gothic ' brought to his mind not only " the dark ages " of superstition and church domination, but also the days of chivalry and the Crusades. And he transplanted these ideas in *The Castle of Otranto*. " The castle was gothic ; terror and superstition were gothic—chivalry and the Middle Ages were gothic ; . . . and at the head of everything Gothic, with his ghost story, and the house at Strawberry, stood Horace Walpole."

To Walpole belongs the credit for having reversed the popular conception of the word 'Gothic'. He changed it from an adjective of opprobrium into an epithet of praise. "The epithet 'Gothic' became not only a . . . trope for the 'free', but also in religious discussion a trope for all those spiritual, moral, and cultural values contained for the eighteenth century in the single word 'enlightenment'."

Otranto opened the flood-gate of 'Gothic' tales. Barbauld's *Sir Bertrand* (1775) is a 'gothic' story, and the author spoke of the 'old Gothic (medieval) romance' in contrast to oriental tales. Miss Clara Reeve's *The Old English Baron* (1777) is 'a gothic story, being a picture of Gothic times and manners'. These gothic novels aimed at a medieval atmosphere by the use of medieval background—haunted castles, dungeons and lonely towers, knights in armour and magic—but to an average reader the outstanding feature of these tales was not the Gothic setting but supernatural incidents. Imitators and followers of Walpole gradually accentuated the spectral side of the genre, and the original medieval tone and setting of the romances faded away in Lewis's *The Monk* (1796) and Godwin's *Caleb Williams* (1794). But the name 'Gothic' remained stamped indelibly upon the type even when the original occasion for its use had vanished. The term lost all connotation of 'medieval', and became a synonym for the grotesque, ghastly, and violently supernatural or superhuman in fiction. Gothic romance became the romance of the supernatural, and 'Gothic' identified itself with ghastly. And thus the third meaning 'supernatural' grew out of 'gothic' as a by-product of 'barbarous' and 'medieval'.

In 1798 Nathan Drake wrote in a miscellany *Literary Hours* : "The most enlightened mind, involuntarily acknowledges the power of Gothic agency", a phrase in which 'Gothic' unequivocally is 'supernatural'. Six years later Drake again employs the term 'Gothic' imagination for "wild or ghastly imagination". In this way, a subject considered not worthy of attention, and disposed of contemptuously as 'barbarous', as "abounding with false provocation of enchantment and prodigies", suited to gratify only a vitiated and uncultivated taste, gradually regained through the efforts of scholars, editors, antiquaries, some of its lost prestige, and the stigma of inferiority was taken away. "The term 'Gothic' emerged not as a synonym for barbarism but enshrining the highest moral and spiritual values." It evolved "from a race-term to a sneering word, from a sneering word to a cool adjective, from a cool adjective to a cliché in criticism ".

Professor Ker pointed out that the first appeal of the Romantic

Revival was primarily architectural. " The Middle Ages have influenced
. . . literature more strongly through their architecture than through their
poems. Gothic churches and old castles have exerted a medieval literary
influence on many authors. . . . The thrill of mystery and wonder came
much more from Gothic buildings than from *Morte d'Arthur*." It is
not surprising that the more cultured and prosperous persons diverted
themselves by reconstructing Gothic romance in bricks and mortar.
Horace Walpole built his castle and formed his collections at Strawberry
Hill long before he wrote *Otranto*. But, as Ruskin says in *The Stones of
Venice*, " pointed arches do not constitute Gothic, nor vaulted roofs,
nor flying buttresses, nor grotesque sculptures ; but all or some of these
things with them, when they come together so as to have life ". And
it is interesting to trace out the characteristics of this grey, shadowy,
many-pinnacled image of the Gothic spirit, whose characteristics mani-
fested themselves in one form or other in the novels of the late eighteenth
century, and justify the title ' Gothic novel '.

The Savageness of Gothic stands for wildness of thought and roughness of work, and impresses upon us the image of a race full of wolfish
life, and an imagination as wild and wayward as the northern seas. The
darkened air, the pile of buttresses and rugged walls uncouthly hewn out
of rocks over wild moors, speak of the savageness of their massy architecture, which was rude, ponderous, stiff, sombre and depressing. " Un-
fortunately it is impossible to show a smooth interaction, or even a
close parallel between eighteenth-century Gothic novels and buildings.
The Gothicness, so to speak, of the romances consisted in gloom, wildness,
and fear." The Gothic architecture, its pinnacles and fretted surfaces,
the intricacy of its broken shadows, appealed to the rebel minds of the
mid-eighteenth century, who saw in the Gothic art the grandeur of
wildness and the novelty of extravagance which were originally the
inspiration of Gothic artists. Even in the century of its origin, the
pointed arch, according to John Harvey, " stood for . . . reawakened,
quickened life, . . . the eager acceptance of new ideas, and for the establishment of a new conception of humanity, a new ideal ". In the eighteenth
century it stimulated imagination ; its bulk and variety made the pious
wonder at an age which could propitiate God so lavishly. " The ruin,
the bristling silhouette, the flowing untidy lines of piled masonry or
creeper-clad rocks became, in terms of emotion, ' sensibility ' and an
elegant disequilibrium of the spirit," says Michael Sadleir.

Critics have commented upon the intimate and pregnant connection between the Gothic architecture and Gothic romance, but have not yet attempted any analysis of this closer and deeper relationship. Perhaps an intuitive perception of Gothic art, and a knowledge of the general aspirations of Gothic man is necessary to explain this relationship.

Professor Worringer, in *Form in Gothic* (1927), precisely establishes a connection between Gothic proper and the Gothic spirit at large. The external world had pressed upon primitive man with obscure breathings of mystery, its very atmosphere had tingled with apprehension of the unknown. From this uncertain, phenomenal universe he was impelled to seek the spiritual assurance which lies in absolute values. He felt that surely some awful power controlled all things to him unpredictable, and in his metaphysical anxiety made clumsy approaches towards religion, which was for him a propitiation for his own safety. Life became secure for the Classical man ; beautiful and joyful, but lacking the energy of fear ; well devised but shallow, having no splendour nor depth of mystery. "For him the world is no longer something strange, inaccessible, and mystically great, but a living completion of his own ego." The veil of Maya, before which primeval man trembled, and which Augustan man forgot, was drawn aside by the inquisitive spirit of the Gothic novelists.

A work of Renaissance or Classical art often excites a feeling of elevated beauty, and an exalted notion of the human self; but the Gothic architecture makes the beholder abashed with awe. By making us aware of our nullity, it exalts us by suggesting that life maintains its greatness thereby. "The Greek art is beautiful," says Coleridge in *General Character of the Gothic Literature and Art*, " when I enter a Greek church, my eye is charmed, and my mind elated ; I feel exalted and proud that I am a man. But the Gothic art is sublime. On entering a cathedral, I am filled with devotion and with awe ; I am lost to the actualities that surround me, and my whole being expands into the infinite ; earth and air, nature and art, all swell up into eternity, and the only sensible impression left is ' that I am nothing ! ' " A Gothic cathedral seems filled with the pervading immanence of some great spiritual power. Herbert Read expressed it, in *Contemporary British Art*, thus, " you are in the presence of a unity which is spiritual and your feelings are roused by a sense of beauty ".

In an ecstasy of communion the Gothic spirit makes humble obeisance before the great Unknown : fear becomes acceptance, and senseless existence fraught with a dark, unfathomable, sacred purpose. The

Gothic attitude relates the individual with the infinite Universe, as do great religions and mystic philosophy. Such a mind grasps the infinite and the finite, the abstract and the concrete, the whole and the nothingness as one : and from the tension between the human and divine is kindled the votive glow that ever contemplates the world of Gothic mystery.

The great religious painters and sculptors and architects of massive and intricate cathedrals express the subtle interrelations of this attitude. It is much like the concern of the saint who tries to touch the still centre of intersection of the timeless with time. And when the Gothic novelist attempts the same he remembers the grand design of the cathedrals, and tries to blend into his novel the same volatile ingredients of fear and sorrow, wonder and joy, the nothingness and infinitude of man. The reader is terror-stricken and lost ; carried away and redeemed ; found and made whole in the same manner. The Gothic novel is a conception as vast and complex as a Gothic cathedral. One finds in them the same sinister overtones and the same solemn grandeur.

Edmund Burke wrote in his *Sublime and Beautiful* : " Hardly anything can strike the mind with its greatness which does not make some sort of approach towards infinity." Classical architecture stresses static beauty, the Gothic voices energetic strength : a Gothic cathedral arouses the same sublime sensations as horrid rocks and savage prospects, and inspires romantic devotion and reverential awe. " One must have taste to be sensible of the beauties of Grecian architecture, one only wants passions to feel Gothic," says Walpole in *Anecdotes of Painting*. " A Gothic cathedral expresses aspiration, and a Greek temple satisfied completeness," comments H. A. Beers in *A History of English Romanticism in the Eighteenth Century*. Sir Herbert Read has rightly called the Gothic cathedral " transcendentalism in stone ". " If we cast a glance at the Gothic cathedral ", he says, " we see only a kind of petrified, vertical movement from which every law of gravity seems to be eliminated . . . an enormously strong upward movement of energies in opposition to the natural downward weight of the stone. . . . Weight does not appear to exist ; we see only free and uncontrolled energies striving heavenward. It is evident that stone is here entirely released from its material weight, that it is only the vehicle of a non-sensuous, incorporeal expression."

Moreover, Gothic architecture combined in itself the greatest variety of appeals : it had about it " a gloomy grandeur ", and an atmosphere and colour which evoked " terror and suspense and gloom ". " Gothic gloom was one of the conventional descriptive phrases for characterizing its effect upon the mind." The gloom and " a dim religious light " touched the imagination with impressiveness and solemnity ; it evoked sensations of awe, and played upon that ingrained primitive element of natural and superstitious fear. The ingredient of fear creeps in only as a by-product of the union of Gothic with gloom, giving Terror a close association with Gothic architecture, which in its turn became the characteristic atmosphere of the Gothic novel which contains elements directly associated with Gothic architecture : castles, convents, subterranean vaults, grated dungeons and ruined piles. Inspired by this Gothic world of art, it found sinister properties in the natural world.

Later Gothic machinery developed logically as an intensification of the earlier variety. For the whole paraphernalia of a terror novel is designed to continually quicken the imagination with weird apprehensions. Soon the castle and the convent were joined by the cavern ; the Gothic tyrant by banditti ; the vaults and galleries by dark forests at midnight ; and the scene of languorous amours became the haunt of howling spectres. Gothic villains pursued heroines outside the walls of the castle into the surrounding forest, whose gloom was deepened by the shades of night, and where lurked the banditti. Thunder and lightning hurled their terrors against the affrighted heroine's soul. The banditti frequented gloomy caverns with dank walls, secret exits and entrances. To all this were added devils and black magic, evil monks, the tribunal of the Inquisition, secret societies, enchanted wands, magic mirrors, and phosphorescent glow. Thus with the Schauer-Romantiks terrors became more dynamic, animated with the one purpose of giving a succession of nervous shocks. They specialized in the ghastly effects of horrid crimes and death embraces.

Imagination inspires the Gothic mind to carry itself back to the past and observe the artistic effect of the truly mysterious. The cathedrals or castles look like spectres of ancient times, and permit indulgence in a melancholic nostalgia. According to Kenneth Clark, " Gothic was exotic ; if not remote in space, like *chinoiserie*, it was remote in time." Besides the ' gloom ' and ' delightful horrors ' of a castle, there are a number of pleasing elements linked with a Gothic mansion. Castles are traditionally associated with childhood stories of magic, and the Gothic romances are themselves in the nature of adult fairy-tales. Moreover, an antique edifice satisfied the craving for something strange, emotional, and mysterious. Antiquity inspires us with veneration, almost with a

religious awe, and the Gothic mind loves to brood over the hallowed glory
of the past.

The element of terror is inseparably associated with the Gothic
castle, which is an image of power, dark, isolated, and impenetrable. No
light penetrating its impermeable walls, high and strengthened by
bastions, it stands silent, lonely and sublime, frowning defiance on all
who dare to invade its solitary reign. Through its dim corridors now
prowl armed bandits ; its halls ring with hideous revelry or anon are
silent as the grave. Even when presented in decay, the castle is majestic
and threatening : a spot where we encounter the mysterious and demoniac
beings of romance.

The grandeur of these relics recall the scenes of ancient chivalry and
whispers a moral of departed greatness, inspiring us with a feeling of
melancholy awe and sacred enthusiasm. It awakens musings on those
who lived there in former times : if those walls could speak, they could
tell strange things, for they have looked upon sad doings. It is an emblem
of life and death, and the ruinous walls seem still to echo tremors of life.
One feels that in the halls but late the banquet revelled, or the spectre
of justice threatened, where the hurrying foot passed by and the hum of
voices rose upon the now silent air. This ruined edifice is the symbol of
joy and mourning and human passions, of hopes and fears, triumphs and
villainy, of the extremes of princely grandeur and domestic misery, of
supernatural power and mortal weakness, the embodiment of all emotions
and themes displayed in the Gothic novels.

Thus the castle itself is the focal point of Gothic romance. ' Udolpho '
is situated in the Appenines ; the incidents of *The Romance of the Forest*
take place in a deserted abbey buried in the depths of the woods ; the
mysteries of *The Italian* are set in the background of the cloister of the
Black Penitents. A number of Gothic novels set their scenes in convents
among the hills, governed by the Draconian rule of some proud abbess,
where the terraces overhang vast precipices shagged with larch and
darkened with gigantic pine ; whose silences are disturbed only by the
deep bell that knolls to midnight office and prayer. These authors were
drawn by the mystery of monastic dwellings, by their remoteness and
inscrutability. The enveloping monastic garb of the swart black cowl or
pallid Carmelite habiliments, insinuated perfervid imaginings. Its
glamour was mixed with a delicious fear and entrancing dread which
remains an essential ingredient of the Gothic novel.

From the castle, the Gothic novel derives its usual accessories :

massive doors swaying ponderously on rusty hinges, invariably closing with a resounding crash ; dark eerie galleries ; crumbling staircases, decaying chambers and mouldering roofs, tolling bells or stalking phantoms. Curious heroines or rightful heirs explore the deserted wings where they are able to solve the mystery of a murder perpetrated by the ancestors of the current usurper. The deserted wings may also typify some of the unexplored impulses of the nascent Romantic Movement, where the castle stands as a central image of the lonely personality.

While the passive agent of terror is the castle, the active agent of terror is the Gothic villain. He was born as adjunct to the ruinous castle, and his nature is dictated by his origin. His function is to frighten the heroines, to pursue them through the vaults and labyrinths of the castle, to harass them at every turn.

The Gothic novels present no restful human shades of grey : the characters are mostly either endowed with sombre, diabolical villainy or pure, angelic virtue. Interfering fathers, brutal in threats, oppress the hero or heroine into a loathed marriage ; officials of the Inquisition or the characters of abbots and abbess are imbued with fiendish cruelty, often gloating in Gothic diabolism over their tortures. The pages of these works are crimsoned with gore and turn with a ghostly flutter.

Besides the tyrant who inherited it, the primary source of terror was the ruin itself. Round the nucleus of a ruin, the Gothic novelists built up such elaborate machinery as accorded with their mood and furthered the purposes of mystery, gloom, and terror. This convention of ‘ruin’ was not a new thing, for the preceding Classical enthusiasts had imbibed from Italy and Greece a keen appreciation of antique survivals. By adorning their parks with artificial ruins, says Michael Sadleir, “they wanted to perpetuate in English meadows the glories of a vanished civilization”.

The year 1764 saw three symbols in an architectural ruin. Hurd interpreted it through the pages of Spenser, as a golden age of chivalry, of splendour, and noble manners ; the antiquaries valued it as the remnant of an historical epoch, providing wide scope for research ; but the large audience of the Gothic novel saw in it the symbol of a dark, barbarous, and superstitious age. Finally the appeal of the ruin like a towering crag contributed to the conception of the ‘picturesque’, which was an essential of the Gothic spirit. Ruins were eminently picturesque for the Gothic writer, surpassingly lovely in decay, as the dark ivy clambered over the crumbling architecture, shutting out the light, and adding to the general gloom, weeds and wild flowers waving along the roofless aisles.

Meditations upon such scenes fed the delicious sensibility of the Gothic enthusiast. The Schauer-Romantik was implicit even in these inclinations, for ivy is as much an accessory of inorganic decay as worms are of organic.

To these authors a ruin is not only a thing of loveliness but also an expression of Nature's power over the creations of man : the minds " which dwelt gladly on the impermanence of human life and effort, . . . sought on every hand symbols of a pantheist philosophy ". Ruins are proud effigies of sinking greatness, the visual and static representations of tragic mystery, " a sacred relic, a memorial, a symbol of infinite sadness, of tenderest sensibility and regret ". They express the fundamental, simple truth stated by Mrs. Radcliffe in *Gaston de Blondeville* :

> Generations have beheld us and passed away, as you now behold us, and shall pass away. They have thought of the generations before their time, as you now think of *them*, and as future ones shall think of you. The voices, that revelled beneath us, the pomp of power, the magnificence of wealth, the grace of beauty, the joy of hope, the interests of high passion and of low pursuits have passed from this scene for ever ; yet we remain, the spectres of departed years, and shall remain, feeble as we are, when you, who now gaze upon us, shall have ceased to be in this world.

Such scenes evoke a sensation of sublimity rising into terror, a suspension of mingled astonishment and awe. In *The Romance of the Forest*, she writes :

> These walls where once superstition lurked, and austerity anticipated an earthly purgatory, now tremble over the mortal remains of the beings who reared them.

The love of natural objects combined with a depth of religious feeling constitutes a part of the Gothic spirit. It stresses scenic effect rather than detail, and establishes a concord in literature between man's mood and the predominant aspect of nature. These novelists present both scenery and weather subjectively : the Gothic villains plan dark, unholy murders against a background of black clouds, hellish thunder, and lurid lightning. Such a method is on a par with the melodramatic treatment of character. The agitation of the elements is made to accord with the agitated life of man ; never did a blast roar or a gleam of lightning flash that was not connected in the imagination of someone with a calamity to be dreaded, with the fate of the living, or the destination of the dead. The tints of an autumnal sky or the shade of the autumnal woods—every dim and hallowed glory is indefinably combined with recollections.

There are scenes in Gothic novels that stand out benevolent, and great—powerful, yet silent in their power—progressive and certain in their end, steadfast and full of a noble repose. D. C. Tovey expresses it in *Gray and his Friends*. . . . " Not a precipice, not a torrent, not a cliff, but is pregnant with religion and poetry." " The sounding cataract" haunts them like a passion, "the tall rock, the mountain, and the deep and gloomy woods, their colour and their forms " are to them " an appetite ". The view of these objects lifts the soul to their great Author, and we contemplate with a feeling almost too vast for humanity—the awfulness of His nature in the grandeur of His works. The horrid rocks and roaring torrents, " raise the imagination to sublime enthusiasm ". But one does not get only a religious exultation, one feels also the deep regenerating power of nature.

The Gothic mind is rarely content to perceive merely the features of the landscape ; it sees them affected by atmospheric conditions. Its spirit revels in the fierce howling winds, portentous stormy clouds, and the dark wild imagery of nature, so that it finds rest in that which presents no end, and derives satisfaction from that which is indistinct. Most of the scenes are wrapped in profound darkness, occasionally pierced by a glint of moonlight or by the faint glimmer of some taper. The effect of light and darkness is contrasted in the following way : approaching night plunges the wide arches in gloom until the moonbeams darting through the emblazoned casements tinge the fretted roofs and massy pillars with a thousand various shades of light and colour. Sometimes one part of the hall is plunged in pitch-black darkness, while the other is lit up in festive light. Different sounds are heard in the encircling gloom : they may be unearthly yells or half-stifled groans.

A supernatural effect is built up by the accumulation of successive details : desolate scenery, tempests, screeching owls, hovering bats, exciting events in burial vaults or on dark, windswept moors ; melancholy birds circle portentously over dilapidated battlements. The ' gothic ' scenes are set in sober twilight or under the soft radiance of the moon in some ruined abbey, or half-demolished tomb, or a vaulted arch wreathed with ivy ; we listen to the uncanny murmur of trees in some lonely romantic glen, while a broken streamlet dashes down in the distance.

The effective romantic setting, the continuous spell of horror, the colour of melancholy, awe, and superstition : all these impulses of the

Gothic spirit first converged in Walpole, who gave them form, coherence, and the language of the " Gothic Novel ". He had lived entirely in a world of ' Gothic ' fantasy. All over England stood ruined monasteries and castles, neglected and crumbling. Traces of paint were still visible on their carvings, while broken figures of saints and portraits of antique knights and damsels still adorned their broken windows. Their arrogant colours had not yet faded, and they still glowed with something of their original fire. In cathedrals and castles and ancient folios lay unexplored treasures of Gothic ready to be plundered. Walpole's antiquarian interest in this " Gothic world " became a passion which influenced the taste of a century : the new route he struck out paved a road for men of brighter talents. " Other and far greater hands than Walpole's sowed the furrows he had driven ; yet to his credit be it recorded that it was he who broke the first clod," says Dorothy M. Stuart in her book *Horace Walpole* (1927).

The spirit of nascent Romanticism first shone faintly in his whims and fancies. His genealogical and antiquarian studies led his fancy into ' Gothic ' paths ; and his deeply implanted ' Gothic ' instincts flowered in *The Castle of Otranto* (1764), the parent of all goblin tales. Strawberry Hill, which gave the vital spark to the first Gothic novel, was neither affectation nor triviality, but the ruling passion of his life. " It was built to please my own taste, and in some degree to realize my own visions." It fast assumed the splendours of *The Castle of Otranto*. At times his house would lose for him its air of studied artificiality. In hours of reverie, on long summer afternoons while the sun glittered on the Thames and splashed the colours of his painted glass windows ; or in his solitary musings late at night, when the moonlit dew lay heavy on the daisies on Strawberry meadow—the flimsy materials that surrounded him : the fretted wood, the fine traceries, the painted windows, assumed new dimensions and propensities. The narrow staircases and intricate chambers of Strawberry swelled into the echoing vaults and sombre galleries of Otranto. " These *Gothic* charms are in truth more striking to the imagination than the classical. The magicians of Ariosto, Tasso, and Spenser have more powerful spells than those of Apollonius, Seneca, and Lucan. . . . Who that sees the sable plumes waving on the prodigious helmet in the castle of Otranto, and the gigantic arm on the top of the great staircase, is not more affected than with the paintings of Ovid and Apuleius ? "

These wild and wondrous tales were a distinct manifestation of the Gothic mind and spirit.

CHAPTER II

THE BACKGROUND : ORIGINS AND CROSS-CURRENTS

THE Gothic novel derives its inspiration from a turbulent confluence of many sources. The classical mode was being rejected for the ebullience and more adventurous questing of a new romanticism, and by the mid-eighteenth century ' gothicism ' recommended itself to public esteem. Since the second quarter of the eighteenth century, men of talent in England had been revising their attitude towards ' nature ' and ' feeling '. In literature, however, the change was gradual : first, poetry assumed a deepening colour of melancholy and frequented dark cemeteries haunted by the shades of the departed. Whereas the Augustans had dared not step outside the sparkling life of their trim and brilliant salons, death, loneliness, and ruinous profusion were a familiar and fascinating abode for the Gothic mind.

Robert Arnold Aubin, in a small article in *Harvard Studies and Notes in Philology and Literature* (1935), has finely summed up the different facets of the Gothic Revival. " The chief influence leading to the revival . . . were the picturesque, *chinoiserie*, antiquarianism, ruin and graveyard sentiment." Gothic was found acceptable by a literary analogy, and by the feeling that the barbarous mode was actually more natural than the Palladian. Dr. Reinhard Haferkorn has analysed the effect of Gothic architecture and ruins upon the poets ; Dr. Elizabeth Manwaring has traced the influence of Claude Lorrain and Salvator Rosa on the general taste of the period ; and Dr. Amy Reed has sought out the earliest manifestations of romantic melancholy among the elegists who anticipated Gray.

The Gothic Revival was a literary movement besides being a move-ment in plastic arts. It derived inspiration not merely from medieval romantic literature but—fostered by scholarly interest in archaeology and sentimental delight in decay—also from the more conspicuous image of the architectural ruin. Although Englishmen of the late seventeenth and early eighteenth centuries deprecated Gothic architecture, they unwittingly constructed buildings in that mode, while medieval cathedrals drew an occasional vague appreciation. Funeral elegies continued to admit traditional Gothic structures to the mortuary setting.

There was a renewal of antiquarian interest in the Middle Ages and ancient poetry, and in objects imprinted with the marks of time, such as collections of old coins, suits of armour, illuminated missals, manuscript romances, black letter ballads, old tapestries, and wood carvings. Thus the despised Dark Ages began to assume the sentimental glow of adventurous, Utopian centuries. It was not until about 1760 that writers began to gravitate decidedly towards the Middle Ages. The fifty years following the year 1760 are characterized by a renewed interest in things written between 1100 and 1650.

This revival is closely related to the growing taste for landscape painters like Claude Lorrain, Salvator Rosa, and Nicolas Poussin. Fantastic melancholy remains of old buildings adorn their landscapes, and " ruins and the Gothic are absorbed in the sentimental tendencies of the day. It is in this time that the pseudo-gothic style of Walpole, Beckford, and others commences." Earlier, Locke had drawn attention to the importance of sense experience, and Berkeley emphasized the value of perception especially in his *Essay towards a New Theory of Vision*. Addison, in a series of essays *On the Pleasures of the Imagination*, popularized the belief that visual images are a powerful force in literature. These theories jointly stimulated new interest in the ' picturesque '.

A. O. Lovejoy, in *The First Gothic Revival and Return to Nature*, says : " The earliest Gothic Revival . . . had for its herald and precursor the new fashion in the designing of artificial landscapes and the new liking for wildness, boldness, broken contours, and boundless prospects in natural landscape." Rousseau introduced his new conception of Nature in the later eighteenth century and it soon became an elaborate cult, a self-conscious worship. His admiration for Nature in her more disordered and cataclysmic forms demanded those wild and dynamic contours that suggest the Titanic frenzy of primal energy. The early eighteenth century had conceived Nature in terms of marble fountains, trim hedges, and gravelled paths. To Rousseau Nature was not a pattern but a presence : a vague and vast identity dimly astir with life, and in some dark fashion able to participate in the moods of man. English gardens about this time began to take on the appearance of wildness, whose freedom, variety, and irregularity was a fresh stimulus to explore the Gothic ages.

The Gothic novel draws its plots, its motifs, its ghostly effects from various sources : the supernatural realm of the ballad, and all that was mysterious and eerie in epic and the drama. The traditional lore of old,

heathen Europe, the richness and splendour of its mythology and superstitions, its usages, rites, and songs, in short everything wild and extravagant,
was rediscovered by scholars about the middle of the eighteenth century
and was immediately recognized as a source of powerful material
by contemporary writers.   Consequently the late eighteenth-century
generation readily imbibed the atmosphere of *Ossian* and Rousseau,
enjoyed Percy's *Reliques,* shuddered at Mrs. Radcliffe's romances, and
relished *The Sorrows of Werther.*

The transition in taste was gradual and the following works helped
to bring about the change.   The brothers Joseph and Thomas Warton
were both impassioned supporters of medievalism : Joseph Warton
(1722–1800) delighted in portraying solitude, thick woods, ruined
castles, and twilight landscapes ; Thomas Warton (1728–90), in his
Observations on the Faerie Queene (1754), pleaded for the acceptance of
the imagination and a new appreciation of Spenser.

An article in *The Adventurer* of 1752 compares old romances to epic
poems with equal appreciation.   But Hurd's *Letters on Chivalry and
Romance* (1762) was the first conscious and sustained defence of the
Gothic : " May there not be something in the Gothic Romance peculiarly
suited to the views of a genius and to the ends of poetry ?   And may not
the philosophic moderns have gone too far in their perpetual ridicule and
contempt of it ? "

The primitive mystical past was resurrected primarily by Macpherson's
Ossian (1760–63), replete with all its spectres and shades.   He assembled
genuine legendary material, and believed " more stories of giants,
enchanted castles, dwarfs, and palfreys in the Highlands, than in any
country in Europe ".   Ossianic poetry contributed a barbaric richness of
colour, misty melancholy, and an air of dim and sweeping vastness :

> Autumn is dark on the mountains ; grey mist rests on the hills.   The
> whirlwind is heard on the heath.   Dark rolls the river through the narrow
> plain.   A tree stands lone on the hill and marks the grave of Connal.   The
> leaves whirl round with the wind, and strew the graves of the dead.   At
> times are seen here the ghosts of the deceased, when the musing hunter alone
> stalks slowly over the heath.

All this powerful strength of description induces a sublimity of
sentiment such as may have inspired Mrs. Radcliffe.   And indeed the
later writers of Gothic romance showed the influence of Ossian in their
ornate language and moonlit scenery.   Ossian's note is in harmony with
Rousseau's dictum of back to Nature in France and with the Sturm und

Drang in Germany. Goethe's appreciation of its significance is evident in Werther's fondness for this wild poetry.

Besides Macpherson, Percy appealed widely to a growing love of the strange and marvellous. His *Reliques of Ancient English Poetry* (1765) has prefixed to it an *Essay on the Ancient Minstrels* which embodied original research into ancient customs, folk lore, and the Middle Ages. Percy recommended his little volume by saying that " the poetry of the Scalds chiefly displays itself in images of terror ". His ballad world abounds in supernatural wonders : the spirit of a forsaken beloved visits her false lover at midnight ; there are witches, fairies, omens, dreams, spells, enchantments. Here tragic passions of pity and fear find expression : love is strong as death, and jealousy cruel as the grave. There are in-cidents of primitive savagery, treachery, violence, cruelty, and revenge, balanced against incidents of honour, courage, fidelity, suffering, and devotion. The increasing love of chivalry and Gothic architecture, and the tremendous impetus which Percy gave to ballad literature, were two formidable streams that gathered speed and size to flow into the Gothic epoch.

The literature of the Middle Ages was deeply imbued with the macabre and its scenes were full of sinister and terrible import. Those were the days of the Sabbat and the witch ; old chronicles narrate deeds more horrible and facts more grim than any writer of fiction could weave. The supernatural of the legends which passed from one genera-tion to another had not lost its power to thrill and alarm, and slowly worked its way into literature. A widespread belief in witches and spirits lived on into the eighteenth century, and there was also a steadily intensifying interest in questions of life, death, and immortality ; angels, demons, vampires ; the occult, magic, astrology ; dreams, omens, and oracles.

Ghosts were believed in as proofs of immortality, and books such as Glanville's and More's were favourite reading, even in the late eighteenth century. Joseph Glanville's *Sadducismus Triumphatus, or a Full and plain evidence concerning Witches and Apparitions* (1681) was a popular work running into five editions before 1726, and was a favourite book of 'Monk' Lewis's mother. An earlier work by John Dee, *A True and Faithful Relation of what passed for many years, etc.* (1659), which is based on the author's supposed communication with the spirits, graced the bookshelf of Horace Walpole at Strawberry Hill. Stray remarks by Browne and Burton, and even Addison's *Spectator* No. 110, credit the supernatural, as also did Defoe's preface to *Essay on the History and Reality of Apparitions* (1727).

Obviously people believed in the supernatural more then than now and were given to telling of ghost stories and folk-tales. Leisure combined with great open fires was conducive to the romances of shudders, which again encouraged the creation of Gothic romance.

Some of the crude scientific speculations which occupied the eighteenth-century mind are also reflected in the substance of Gothic romances. Novels of Godwin, Shelley, and Maturin hinge upon the theme of the elixir of life. *Vathek* contains alchemy, sorcery, and other supernatural sciences, while Mrs. Dacre's *Zofloya, the Diabolical Moor*, performs experiments in hypnotism, telepathy, and satanic chemistry.

It was Milton's early poem, *Il Penseroso,* that with its love of "twilight groves", cathedral architecture, and contemplative melancholy, penetrated deep into the spirit of ' graveyard ' and ' night ' poets. Even the opening lines of Pope's *Eloisa to Abelard* contain such nuances of Gothic as might be paralleled in Mrs. Radcliffe. This poem tells of the hopeless and guilty love of a nun fast dying of melancholy in her cell among desolate crags and pines. The impressive setting of the story is purely romantic and gothic in character.

" Within the decade from 1742–51 there flourished that particular kind of contemplative and melancholy verse known as ' graveyard poetry '," says Calvin Daniel Yost, Jr., in an article entitled *The Poetry of the Gentleman's Magazine* (Philadelphia. 1936). The Graveyard School was a blend of the earlier funeral elegy and the eighteenth-century contemplative verse. It combined the general philosophic and religious conceptions of the latter with the details of the charnel house and physical dissolution common to the former in the seventeenth and early eighteenth century. Thus it was a synthesis of elements already familiar to readers. The terror of the tomb had been vividly depicted by Donne and Francis Quarles in the early seventeenth century, and in the mid-century by Thomas Jordan and Henry Vaughan. The broadside elegy witnessed to a popular taste for this type of literature where gruesome corruption was made to preach that " All is Vanity ".

Kenneth Clark, in *The Gothic Revival* (first published 1950), says :

" The Gothic novelists were the natural successors to the graveyard poets, and nearly all the paraphernalia of graveyard poetry . . . reappear in the novels." Common elements of this poetry are melancholy, subjective tone, vague longings, together with ghosts, chains, tombs, veils, that fill the reader with terror and sound a note of mystery and other-worldliness. The usual settings comprise: "ivy-mantled towers", "long-drawn aisles", "fretted vaults", cypress and yew, owl and midnight bell, nettle-fringed gravestones, and dim sepulchral lamps. The tones of despair, the odour of the charnel house, meditations on the shadow of the grave and the mystery of the future, contained the seeds of the Gothic epoch. " Mutability and decay compelled the deepest tremor in their emotions. . . . They did feel a metaphysical shudder at decay passing from the microcosm to the macrocosm." Such was the fear of death, which found expression in poetry when Young, in the years 1742–45, published his *Night Thoughts*; and Blair, *The Grave*, in 1743.

Graveyard poetry begins with Parnell's *Night Piece on Death* (1722), and was continued in Young's *The Complaint, or Night Thoughts on Life, Death and Immortality* (1742), Blair's *The Grave* (1743), and Gray's *Elegy* (1751). Parnell's melancholic *Night Piece on Death* has echoes of medievalism and is expressive of gloom and darkness suggesting the ugly horrors of death. The works of Young and Blair are distinguished by a sensational touch of supernatural horror, which sets the imagination vibrating like the murky air of night at the hootings of a moping owl. All these poets exploited the " luxury of woe " and the " joy of gloom ", but the *Elegy* of Gray " is the masterpiece of this whole Il Penseroso school, and has summed up for all English readers for all time, the poetry of the tomb ". To Gray the landscape was not a mere setting ; it was infused with sentiment and character, it had a meaning and personality. His *Elegy* with its pensive mood and love of twilight is in line with *Il Penseroso*, but its meditation on death and the grave belongs more properly to the school of Blair and Young.

Collins, in *Ode to Evening*, introduces twilight and bat, solitude and shade, mossy hermitage, ruined abbey mouldering in moonlit glade, ivied corners and curfew bell. Stevenson's *On Seeing a Scull* (1749) strikes a ghoulish note characteristic of the Graveyard school. The Rev. Mr. Moore of Cornwall, in *A Soliloquy written in a Country Church-yard* (1763) is " struck with religious awe and solemn dread " when he " views the gloomy mansions of the dead ". He meditates on a skull and the hollow sockets, which once " two bright orbs contained ". J. Cunnigham's *Elegy on a Pile of Ruins* (1770) retains elements of solitude and melancholy ; its setting is a ruined abbey displaying gothic grandeur, and some rude remains of a castle, inhabited by ravens and rooks.

Even earlier, Mallet's *Excursion* (1728) contained horrors of the grave in the shape of sightless skulls and crumbling bones, the fatal plant ivy, and a general setting of decay. In the seventeenth century Burton had suggested in his *Cure of Love-Melancholy* (III—240) : " suppose thou saw'st her sick, pale, in consumption, on her death-bed, skin and bones, or now dead, etc." And in 1729, James Ralph, in *Night, a poem* in four books, had summoned mournful thoughts and dreadful horrors amid the black, melancholy gloom of night. In a hard world " the silent dead are only kind ; so in the dreary vault, in heaps of mouldering bones, they seek repose ". The living await the " horrid call of Death ".

The emergence of Gothic fiction coincides roughly with a revival of interest in Elizabethan drama. Between 1709 and 1765 appeared eight editions of Shakespeare ; Massinger's work, re-edited 1761 ; Dodsley published twelve volumes of Old Plays, 1744 ; Beaumont and Fletcher's work, reprinted 1778 ; Middleton's *The Witch*, first published 1778 ; Tourneur's *The Atheist's Tragedy*, reprinted 1792. Ashley H. Thorndike in *Tragedy* (1908), p. 322, gives a list of thirteen plays revived during 1778–88 ; fifteen of Shakespeare's plays were acted on the London stages in 1773 alone. One may also see the evidence of Shakespeare's popularity in D. Nichol Smith's *Shakespeare in the Eighteenth Century*, 1928, pp. 25–26. Miss McIntyre finds many Gothic trappings in the horrors and monstrosities of Elizabethan drama, and concludes that " the novels of Mrs. Radcliffe and her followers . . . are not an expression of the life and spirit of the Middle Ages. . . . They are, rather, an expression of the life and spirit of the Renaissance, as Elizabethan England had interpreted the Renaissance." Be that as it may, the Gothic novelists certainly share with the later Elizabethans a tendency to dwell upon morbid thoughts of death and its sepulchral accompaniments. The cruder presentation of the macabre, physically horrible and revolting, was a characteristic of Webster, Ford, Marston, and Tourneur, the melancholy fantasies, the Nocturnals and Obsequies of Donne, and the startling convolutions of the Metaphysical school. Reprints of the works of later Elizabethans, displaying lurid violence and scenes of crime, may well have provided models in theme and structure for Gothic romance. Certainly there are striking resemblances in characters, situations, and even in narration.

Some Elizabethan and Jacobean dramatists had devised almost Gothic motifs to feed a taste for terror. Webster's *The White Devil* introduces a Monk-villain in the character of Cardinal Monticelso. Brachiano's ghost " in his leather cassock and breeches, boots, and cowl ", and " a pot of lily-flowers, with skull in't " throws earth on Flamineo, and shows him the skull. A dead hand, corpse-like images, and a masque of mad men in *The Duchess of Malfi* have intense dramatic potentialities of terror.

The incest-theme and use of banditti occur in Ford's *'Tis Pity she's a Whore*. Tourneur's world is " vibrant with imaginative horror ", and the luxurious D'Amville in *The Atheist's Tragedy* is a typical selfish villain. In *The Revenger's Tragedy* Tourneur presents a gruesome scene where the Duke kisses the poisoned lips of the skull presented to him in the dark to cheat his passion. The plays of Beaumont and Fletcher unfold adventures of heroes and heroines through disasters and trials finally meeting a happy end. Roderigo, the outlaw-captain of *The Pilgrim*, is very much a Gothic character, and *The Knight of Malta* has a tendency to dwell upon thoughts of death. Massinger's *The Duke of Milan* is a blend of Revenge Tragedy and Tragedy of Blood. Marlowe's *Dr. Faustus*, with its theme of a pact between man and the devil, may have inspired Lewis's *The Monk* or Maturin's *Melmoth the Wanderer*.

Shakespeare's plays provide good examples of the supernatural and weird atmosphere : *Hamlet, Macbeth, Julius Caesar,* and *Richard III* have ghosts ; *Macbeth* and *Julius Caesar* use prophecies and supernatural portents ; *King Lear* has a desolate heath and nature at her wildest in thunder, lightning, and rain ; *Romeo and Juliet* has a whole gamut of horrors : tombs, vaults, sepulchres, bones, and fumes ; *Hamlet* has stark battlements in the dead of night ; several other plays set their scenes in old castles ; *Macbeth* has a variety of apparitions, a signal bell, a forest, thunder and lightning, a cavern, a castle, and a midnight murder done to the accompaniment of supernatural sounds. Banquo's spectre " with twenty trench'd gashes on his head ", is a distant precursor of the Schauer-Romantik method.

Inevitably the Gothic novelists sought to shelter themselves under Shakespeare's authority. According to their professed theory, they were copying Shakespeare's magic. Jess M. Stein has argued that " Walpole was not centrally influenced by him [Shakespeare] in his own writing. . . . The influence was . . . mainly incidental and marginal." Yet Walpole called Milton and Shakespeare " the only two mortals I am acquainted with who ventured beyond the visible diurnal sphere, and preserved their intellects ". On many occasions he referred to Shakespeare as " that first genius of the world ", " that most sublime genius ", " our first of men ". Towards Shakespeare there was a " steady rise of idolatory . . .

throughout the eighteenth century ". Walpole, in his preface to the second edition of *Otranto*, apologized for the coarse pleasantries of his domestic servants by claiming Shakespeare as his model.

The early eighteenth century brought about a revival of Spenser and Milton, who were perhaps the earliest poets to exploit the Gothic mood. Dr. Johnson, in *The Rambler* for 14 May 1751, wrote : " The imitation of Spenser . . . by the influence of some men of learning and genius seems likely to gain upon the age." Hurd, in *Letter VIII*, while analysing the structure and design of *The Faerie Queene*, stresses its Gothic " unity of design ", and calls it " an epic with Gothic materials ". " By its subject-matter . . . *The Faerie Queene* is Gothic and Spenser therefore rightly based his design on Gothic customs, the feast and the quest." Rescued from oblivious contempt by Hurd, the influence of Spenser, which had been dormant through the Classical period, after having inspired Milton, once more asserted itself as a powerful quickening force. Colour, music, and fragrance stole back into English poetry, and " golden-tongued romance with serene lute stood at the door of the new Age, waiting for it to open ". Yet, as in Radcliffe's Arcadian landscapes, the shadow of terror lurks in Spenser's beautiful fairyland : in the winding forests, dark caves, mysterious castles, with creatures like Despair or giant Orgoglio, wicked witches or the ghostly Maleger who crowned himself with a skull and rode upon a tiger swifter than the wind. King Arthur's Excalibur and the correspondingly large helmet, may have given the hint for the Brobdingnagian sword and the monstrous helmet in *Otranto*.

The Gothic novel had innumerable branching roots nourished by the whole of European literature and tradition. It " drew much of its vitality from obscure and even sub-literary sources, though it did not own to them ". The spell of Italy, her poets and story-tellers, her dark romantic history exerted a singular fascination on individual novelists. Frequent translations of French and German works undoubtedly stimulated the development of the Gothic novel in England. " Exaggerated sensibility came from France, horrors and Werther-like sorrows from Germany ; and these stirrings and changings of spirit acted on a tradition older than Otranto." Indeed, the overlapping of these two parallel influences on English gothicism forms an interesting but intricate study.

From Germany writers of *Sturm und Drang*, themselves imitators of Horace Walpole, had filtered into England and thus whetted the public appetite for the Middle Ages, bloody scenes, secret tribunals, feudal tyrants, mystical jargon, and necromantic imagery. Germany has always been a land of superstitions and fairy legends : even in earlier German literature there is a fascination " for superstitions, dreadful events, awful spectacles ". Rhine is the haunted river of the world ; its banks are studded with castles as romantic as any in a fairy-tale ; in its dark forests one may encounter Demon-Huntsmen, witches, and were-wolves ; its haunted sacred wells and ancient magic date back to the dim twilight days of medieval times. Mrs. Barbauld, in *On the Origin and Progress of Novel-Writing*, expressed her opinion that " the Germans abound in materials for works of the imagination ; for they are rich in tales and legends of an impressive kind, which have perhaps amused generation after generation as nursery stories, and lain like ore in the mine, ready for the hand of taste to separate the dross and polish the material. . . . It is calculated that 20,000 authors of that nation live by the exercise of the pen ; and in the article of novels it is computed that 7,000, either original or translated, have been printed by them within the last five-and-twenty years."

Montague Summers is incorrect when he asserts that " French and German writers . . . directly influenced the development of the Gothic novel in England ". Within the main stream of the Gothic Movement there flowed a dangerously complicated assembly of cross-currents. Coleridge asserts that *The Robbers* and its progeny were due to the popularity in Germany of the translations of Young's *Night Thoughts*, Hervey's *Meditations*, and Richardson's *Clarissa* : " Add the ruined castles, the dungeons, the trap-doors, the skeleton, the flesh-and-blood ghosts, and the perpetual moonshine of a modern author (cf. Mrs. Radcliffe), and, as the compound of these ingredients duly mixed, you will recognize the so-called *German* drama, which is English in its origin, English in its materials, and English by re-adoption."

Agnes Murphy, in *Banditry and Chivalry in German Fiction* (1935), says that Walpole's *Otranto* " served as a model for many similar works in England and was ultimately the inspiration of the German genre ". His sensational ' gothic ' story was assimilated into three genres in Germany, each with its distinguishing characteristics but with many common elements that had been supplied by the English gothicists.

The progenitors of these genres—the *Ritter-*, *Räuber-*, and *Schauer-romane*—were Goethe and Schiller. Goethe's *Götz von Berlichingen*, or " Götz with the Iron Hand " (1773), introduced the vogue of chivalric romance, medievalism, and tyrannical barons, yet the later German writers accumulated elements and motives of terror which were absent in Walpole, Clara Reeve or Ann Radcliffe. The second German type, the robber-novel, was initiated by *Die Räuber* (1781) which demanded justice for the oppressed, freedom from any established social order, and in which character was destiny. The third German genre, *Schauer-romane*, is a later development which absorbed the characteristics of the other two kinds in its violent machinery, motives, characters, and atmosphere. It is interesting to note the two developments of Walpole's Gothic nucleus in Germany and in England. The English Gothic machinery combined with the materials of the movement initiated by Goethe and Schiller to produce a third German genre. When English Gothic fiction reached its efflorescence by 1789, the German Gothic was still lagging a decade behind England in its maturity. It is a factor worthy of note that the supernatural came to be explained in Germany only after 1800, whereas Mrs. Radcliffe's supernatural expliqué was introduced in England in 1789. Bertrand Evans, in *Gothic Drama from Walpole to Shelley* (1947), observes : " Up to 1798 the stream of influence flowed from England to Germany rather than from Germany to England. When the flood then turned, it brought both the substance originally lent and several additions from a foreign heritage. It arrived in England with a rush of dramatic adaptations, translations and borrowings." The debt was repaid with interest : bandits, monks, feudal barons, poisonings, dungeons, tortures, and shrieking spectres flooded the country.

Schiller's *Die Räuber* (1781) contains violent sensationalism and a formidable set of dramatic personae : banditti, monks, inquisitors, tortures and poison, haunted towers and yelling ghosts, dungeons and confessionals. The *Dublin Chronicle* noted : " For many years past the Germans have been making gigantic strides towards perfection in literature. . . . The first tragedy of Schiller, entitled *The Robbers*, had unexampled success in the theatres. . . . Schiller is a youth born to astonish the age by the vigour of his genius."

Schiller's *Ghost-Seer* (1795) was widely read in translation about this time. Like Mrs. Radcliffe, he piles up a succession of mysterious occur-rences and then explains them away as the result of natural probable events. Contemporary readers relished the spasms of terror they got from this stupendous story of the Armenian who, possessing superhuman attributes, performs unheard-of miracles. Perhaps the art of thrilling could go no further. This Armenian disappears and reappears in in-explicable ways (cf. Schemoli of Maturin). The entire tale veers round the adventures of a foreign prince who sojourns in Venice and becomes the object of a secret conspiracy. This work of Schiller perhaps influenced Maturin's *Montorio*.

Until the end of the eighteenth century German literature found hardly any appreciation in England, being eclipsed by the influence of French literature. But, says V. Stockley in the *Times Literary Supplement* (13 March 1930), " the tide really began to flow in 1796, the year of the translation of Bürger's *Lenore*, and three years later reached a high-water mark with translations of Goethe, Schiller, Kotebue ". The title pages of books coming from the Minerva Press display sub-titles like : " translated from the German ", " a tale adapted from the German ". Whereas in many instances the originals may be traced, in not a few the German ascription was labelled solely to enhance the popularity by giving a fashionable air to the work. Popular pamphlets, chapbooks, and translations from the German *Volksbücher* brought about the renaissance of the Wandering Jew in the eighteenth century. This legend had prospered in popular tradition since the Middle Ages and " was also nourished . . . by the picture of the Jew drawn in the early German *Volksbücher* of the seventeenth century ". As early as 1787 an unknown writer in *The Critical Review* expressed a feeling of "congenial warmth for everything of German origin ". Later it speaks of " the daily extension of the German language amongst us ". It is significant of the trend of the times that the books which were first translated were works dealing with the supernatural and the terrible, works which supplied a demand for mystery and excitement. The following were of importance : *The Necromancer* (1794), *Herman of Unna* (1794), *The Ghost-Seer* (1795), *The Sorcerer* (1795), *The Victim of Magical Delusion* (1795), *Horrid Mysteries* (1797). These translations as a whole gave impetus to the English Schauer-Romantiks.

Yet the influence of French or German writers was based on a principle of beneficial exchange. Germany rivalled the output of English native writers and provided Matthew Lewis, Peter Will, Lathom, Edward Montague, and others, with a vast quantity of material which they adapted and freely utilized to enrich and elaborate the sensationalism of English Gothic fiction. Meanwhile, Mrs. Radcliffe, Lewis, and Maturin, were inexhaustible springs from which France and Germany continued to draw. Walter Moss writes in *English Studies*, No. XXXIV, that " Lewis should . . . be one of the leading names in the history of German literature. Miss McIntyre has pointed out that although *The Robbers* influenced Mrs. Radcliffe's villain-heroes, especially Montoni and Schedoni, Schiller himself was originally strongly influenced by English Elizabethan literature.

Counter to the usual opinion that French influence on the English novel (1750–1800) is negligible, Professor Foster suggests that the Gothic novel was a product of sensibility originating in Richardson and Prévost. The delicious shudder evoked by Gothic mystery began in tears of sensibility : the Gothic heroine does remind us of Clarissa and Pamela in tragic suffering, and the Gothic villain recalls Richardson's Lovelace. " The novels of Richardson were rendered into French by L'Abbé Prévost, the author of Manon Lescaut. . . . The wave of sensibility which swept over England, France and Germany resulted in an interchange of influence." The many imitations of Mmes De la Fayette, D'Aulnoy, De Tencin, Riccoboni and De Genlis, Marivaux and Abbé Prévost could not outnumber those of native inspiration, yet perhaps determined the form of the English novel during the last two decades of the eighteenth century.

Victor H. Hamm has pointed out that even Hurd, an early Gothic enthusiast, may have been indebted to Chapelain's De la Lecture des Vieux Romans for his inspiration and appreciation of ' Gothic '. Moreover, " adaptation of French drama on the English stage at the end of the eighteenth century and the beginning of the nineteenth century has been curiously overlooked by students of English drama ". Miss Wary appends a list of such plays, and further states that " French plays echoed the current Rousseauistic philosophy, such as we find in Mme Genlis's Zélie, adapted by Mrs. Inchbald as The Child of Nature. Finally, many of the French plays afforded spectacular, melodramatic material, popularized by Pixerécourt."

Translations from the French were very popular in the first half of the eighteenth century : Madame de la Fayette's Princess de Clèves was translated early in 1688, and read in her youth by the grandmother of Miss Harriet Byron in Sir Charles Grandison. " Towards the middle of the eighteenth century the romances of Marivaux and of Crébillon fils began to be fashionable in England." Marivaux's Vie de Marianne had appeared in 1736–42, and Horace Walpole was delighted by the translation of Crébillon's Sopha, an Arabian story, which was by 1801 in its eighteenth edition.

Monsieur Maurice Heine attempts to establish a connection between De Sade and the Gothic novel. De Sade's work was certainly known to M. G. Lewis, Francis Lathom, and other Gothic novelists. The literary influence of De Sade has been treated in detail by Signor Mario Praz. Baculard D'Arnaud (1716–1805) whetted the reader's sombre appetite with a panorama of dungeons and flickering flames, horror-haunted castles, dark-souled Inquisitors, and rotting skeletons in his *Euphémie* (1768), and together with Schiller influenced Mrs. Radcliffe's *The Italian*.

Dr. B. M. Woodbridge's article upon the Abbé Prévost, published in 1911, and Étienne Servais's *Le Genre Romanesque en France*, published 1922, provide clues to the historical causes and link them with the Gothic novel. Professor J. R. Foster, in *Publications of the Modern Language Association* (XLII—1927), throws light upon the origins of the Gothic novel and states that the immediate causes of the movement lie precisely in the French prose fiction of the eighteenth century : " Prévost had a hand in its development in England just as here in France." Of his first three novels *Cleveland* was the most popular in England. John Colin Dunlop remarks, in *History of Prose Fiction* (1911), that Prévost's novels " indeed had a prodigious currency : they were spuriously imitated on all sides, sometimes, as in the case of *Cleveland*, continuations were published under his name : the demand of the book-trade was for more of Prévost ". Another reputable critic, Ernest Bernbaum, has maintained, in *Modern Language Notes* (XLIII—1928), that " Prévost, or his French imitators, were well known to writers like Sophia Lee, Clara Reeve, and Mrs. Radcliffe ". But the chief disseminator of Prévost and French sensibility was Mrs. Charlotte Smith.

When English fiction reacted from adventure towards realism, Prévost supplied just the right material and spirit for the romanesque and sentimental novel. " He was the first who carried the terrors of tragedy into romance. . . . He is chiefly anxious to appal the minds of his readers by the most terrifying and dismal representations," says Dunlop. Prévost's painting of lugubrious and melancholic settings had an immediate appeal for the audience of Young and Blair. Although his predecessors had employed the " ghost haunted chateau ", Prévost developed a synthesis of horror-romantic material. His stories abound in moving adventures, the supernatural, portentous dreams, ruins, dungeons, and types of character such as ominous priests or Byronic heroes. An atmosphere of shuddering dread, suspense, and gloom broods over his castles and impenetrable forests. Prévost was also the precursor of another Gothic motif : the rebellious assertion of the rights of love against the tyranny of social convention.

While enumerating influences from abroad one must not minimize the importance and contribution of the East. The Oriental allegory or moral apologue as practised by Addison in *The Vision of Mirza* (1711) and by Johnson in *Rasselas* (1759) at least gave some colour to Gothic romance. An interest in Oriental literature had been stimulated early in the eighteenth century by Galland's translation of *The Arabian Nights* (1704–17), the *Turkish Tales* (1708), and the *Persian Tales* (1714). The glittering splendour and colour of the East provided the settings for such works as Ridley's *Tales of the Genii* (1764) and Mrs. Sheridan's *History of Nourjahad* (1767). The tendency towards such popular Anglo-Oriental tales culminated in the wild fantasy of Beckford's *Vathek* (1786). But according to Wallace Cable Brown, in *Publications of the Modern Language Association* (LIII—1938), " it was not until the last quarter of the century that new developments brought the Orient much nearer to England than ever before ", and inspired works such as Isaac D'Israeli's *Mejnoun and Leila* (1800), James Morier's *Adventures of Hajji Baba of Ispahan* (1824), and Thomas Hope's *Anastatius, or Memoirs of a Greek* (1819). Morier's novels mark the culmination of English prose fiction about the Near East between 1775 and 1825.

At least two dozen Oriental tales appeared in the *Spectator* and *Guardian* in their short period of existence. Chinese tales, Mogul tales, Tartarean tales, Peruvian tales, appeared in rapid succession. Of the Turkish tales translated in English (1708), the best is the story of *Santon Barsisa*, told by Addison in *The Guardian*, No. 148, which was drawn on by Lewis for *The Monk* (1796). Persian tales, or *Thousand and One Days* (translated 1714), relates stories narrated by an old nurse to her sceptical and obdurate princess to convert her to marriage, and may have given *Vathek* a name for a similar character (cf. Sutlememe, the nurse of Nouronihar). Dr. Johnson contributed not less than sixteen Oriental tales in *The Idler* and *The Rambler* (1750–60). *The Tales of Terror and Wonder* (1808) by ' Monk ' Lewis includes three Oriental tales.

By their extravagant language, thrilling incidents and poetic justice, the Oriental tales furnish an interesting parallel to Gothic romance. Although their supernatural is of the fairy kind and never makes one afraid, their exotic use of the marvellous and magic left definite traces on quite a number of Gothic novels.

Nevertheless the previous account of outside influences should not lead one to suppose that every thought and image in the Gothic novel is traditional, and that all their invention was but a new combination. As Coleridge observed, in his preface to *Christabel*, " there are such things as fountains in the world, small as well as great ", and one must not " charitably derive every rill [as] flowing from a perforation made in some other man's tank ". There is no disputing that the Gothic romance drew its inspiration from a tangle of many external sources, yet its originating impulse sprang from the creative personal dreams and repressed ' unconscious ' of its sensitive authors.

The writers who rediscovered the nebulous world of the supernatural described it as grotesque and nightmarish because that is how, unconsciously, they reacted to unfamiliar passions. Encouraged by their classical education to put aside barbaric emotion and ultra-diurnal contemplation, now that upsurging currents of new thought revealed unfamiliar spheres, they were compelled to approach the speculations surreptitiously in dreams, for that was the only way they could achieve super-reality.

It has long been realized that dreams are intimately related to an apprehension of the supernatural world and the emergence of subversive impulses. Dreams were a subject of contemporary investigation and *A Philosophical Discourse on the Nature of Dreams* was translated in 1764 from the German of the Rev. Mr. Saalfeld. In many instances the Gothic writers were subsequently influenced in their choice of material by dreams. *The Castle of Otranto* is the outcome of a dream of Walpole's thinking about medieval structures :

> " It was so far from being sketched out with any design at all, that it was actually commenced one evening, from the very imperfect recollection of a dream with which I waked in the morning," he says in a letter, dated 17 April 1763, to the Rev. Mason.

Mary Shelley's *Frankenstein*, likewise, is the product of a romantic biological dream.

Charles Robert Maturin, writing in *The British Review* (1818), said that " the transition from the vapid sentimentality of the novel of 50 years ago to the goblin horrors of the last 20 is so strong and sudden that it almost puzzles us to find a connecting link ". But Smollett's *Ferdinand Count Fathom* (1753) and Leland's *Longsword, Earl of Salisbury* (1762) provide a literary link between the realistic novel and the future novels of terror. While poetry was heralding the dawn of Romanticism, fiction, which had revealed signs of a tendency to become more rational, began itself to react. Despite the great success of the novels of Richardson and Fielding, the novels of Smollett marked a return towards the older idea of fiction : the novel of adventure.

Smollett had already anticipated the Gothic romance by special devices and moods. *Ferdinand Count Fathom* foreshadows *Otranto* and the tale of terror ; the prefatory address by the author of the former vindicates the use of terror :

> The impulses of fear, which is the most violent and interesting of all the passions, remain longer than any other upon the memory.

The gloomy scenes in deserted forests, and the tremors of fear to which Ferdinand is subjected, as well as the depiction of skilful and imaginary terrors evoked by darkness and solitude, have quite a Gothic tone :

> The darkness of the night, the silence and solitude of the place, the in-distinct images of the trees that appeared on every side, stretching their extravagant arms athwart the gloom, conspired, with the dejection of spirits occasioned by his loss, to disturb his fancy, and raise strange phantoms in his imagination.

Smollett depicts natural terrors with, as Nathan Drake says in *Literary Hours*, " such vigour of imagination indeed, and minuteness of detail, that the blood runs cold, and the hair stands erect from the impression ".

When Count Fathom takes refuge in a robber's hut in the storm-swept forest, the lightning begins to flash, the thunder to roll as the clouds break in a deluge of rain. To his horror he discovers " the dead body of a man, still warm, who had been lately stabbed, and concealed beneath several bundles of straw ".

Another scene in this novel, where Renaldo stumbles over deserted vaults in a night of uncommon darkness and thinks he sees the ghost of Monimia, is enveloped in circumstances of gloom and mystery char-acteristic of the Gothic romance. As he is walking up the " dreary aisle ", " the clock struck twelve, the owl screeched from the ruined battlement ". His ear is suddenly

> invaded with the sound of some few solemn notes issuing from the organ, which seemed to feel the impulse of an invisible hand. . . . Reason shrunk before the thronging ideas of his fancy, which represented this music as the prelude to something strange and supernatural. . . . The place was suddenly illuminated. . . . In a few minutes appeared the figure of a woman arrayed in white, with a veil that covered her face. . . . His hair stood upright, and a cold vapour seemed to thrill through every nerve.

Other incidents and characters, too, have ' gothic ' qualities : the mother of Renaldo is treated with barbarity by her husband and immured in a " west tower " and his sister also is shut up in a convent.

Although Smollett's work precedes *The Castle of Otranto*, his treatment of terror and mystery is more suggestive of Mrs. Radcliffe than the clumsy magic of Walpole's tale. Smollett's machinery is incidental, and later accounted for, although he occasionally touches a reader's nerves with forebodings. Since the adventures narrated in *Ferdinand Count Fathom* are too picaresque, and entirely lack the idealism and ' romance ' of chivalry, something else was necessary to create the first authentic Gothic novel. *Count Fathom* was an incidental incursion into the realms of terror, while *The Castle of Otranto* gave the ' gothic ' tale a form and a fashion by combining historical background with supernatural machinery. All the same, Smollett's attempt remains an interesting precursor of Walpole's achievement.

Nine years after *Ferdinand Count Fathom* appeared another work which announces the immediate birth of Gothicism. *Longsword, Earl of Salisbury, an Historical Romance* in two volumes (1762) by the Rev. Thomas Leland, D.D., has all the ingredients of Gothic-Historical Romance except supernatural machinery. This work is the heir of old Romance, and was described by Clara Reeve in *The Progress of Romance* (1930), as " a story like those of the Middle Ages, composed of Chivalry, Love and Religion . . . [which] . . . seems to be formed on an intimate acquaintance with the romances of the 15th to 16th centuries ". It is a novel different from Walpole's genre, and did in no way undermine Walpole's influence and position.

In point of structure *Longsword* is weak and lacking in mystery : two people meet each other at the beginning and relate their histories ; the progress of the story is delayed by other interpolated narratives ; the dialogue is a series of epic harangues. Yet, as *The Monthly Review* for March 1762 put it : " the characters of the persons, the manners of the times, and the style of narration, agreeable to the ages of chivalry, the valour of knighthood, and the chaste pride of female honour, are all well supported. The truth of history is artfully interwoven with agreeable fictions and interesting episodes."

This work may have given Walpole impulse to write *The Castle of Otranto*, but it certainly influenced Clara Reeve's *The Old English Baron*. Miss Reeve substituted private for public history and added the ghost, otherwise her romance is a close parallel to *Longsword* ; her plot is too much the same to have been accidental. The diction of *Longsword* is unlike any early Gothic romance, but resembles that which was invented and popularized by Scott :

> " By my halidame ! " exclaimed the king, " it rejoiceth us that Lord William hath found his suspicions false ; not the unexpected deliverance and happy arrival of our noble cousin give us greater joy.—But let us forget all jealousies, and despise all false rumours.—Embrace and forgive Lord Hubert, command our power, and enjoy the reward of thy gallant toils."

The Gothic heroine, or " beauty in distress ", had long been a familiar sentimental comedy heroine. She first appears in *Longsword* as the wife persecuted by a detested lover.

Thus the Gothic romance did not spring fully grown and armed, like Minerva, from *The Castle of Otranto*. Walpole merely outstripped a gradual accumulation of influences which would all have eventually brought about the birth of something resembling Gothic literature. He provided a tradition, a legacy.

CHAPTER III

THE FIRST GOTHIC TALE : ITS POTENTIALITIES

THE *Schauer-romantik*, or "horror-romanticism", of the eighteenth century may be said to have originated one midsummer night, when Horace Walpole, sleeping beneath his stucco pinnacles at Strawberry Hill, dreamt he saw a giant hand in armour on the balustrade of the staircase. In this dream was born the first Gothic story, *The Castle of Otranto* : a bold and amazingly successful experiment in an absolutely untried medium. This immensely popular wild tale stands as a land-mark in literary development and literary fashion. Although it has been alleged that this work is crude in attempt, incongruous and grotesque in its use of the supernatural, unrefined, distorted, and inartistic as a story form, yet it is not to be denied that this tale had far-reaching potentialities that were consciously developed by authors of succeeding generations. It is the parent of all goblin tales, the prelude to a long line of novels as unending as the spectral show of Banquo's progeny. It anticipates the genteel shudderings of Clara Reeve and Ann Radcliffe, and sets the scene for the crazy phantasmagoria of *Vathek* and the prurient nightmares of 'Monk' Lewis, while its properties were to receive artistic touches of genius at the hands of Scott and Byron, Coleridge and Poe.

    Otranto opened the floodgates for a whole torrent of horror-novels. Since Walpole's time, for a stretch of about forty years, readers " supped full with horrors ", but none of those compositions had a livelier play of fancy than *The Castle of Otranto*. " It is the sportive effusion of a man of genius, who throws the reins loose upon the neck of his imagination. The large limbs of the gigantic figure which inhabits the castle, and which are visible at intervals ; the plumes of the helmet, which rise and wave with ominous meaning ; and the various enchantments of the palace, are imagined with the richness and wildness of poetic fancy," we read in Mrs. Barbauld.

    Walpole's Gothic story, like Bishop Percy's *Reliques of Ancient English Poetry* (1765), was at once a symptom and a cause of that change in sensibility which has been styled by Watts-Dunton " The Renascence of Wonder ". Indeed, as W. P. Ker says in his essay on Horace Walpole,

Walpole " in so many things touches . . . slightly on a region that was to be explored and exploited after him by a great host of followers ". Walpole records in a letter to Richard West one of the first vivid appreciations in English of romantic and savage landscape ; an experience on his journey to Italy with Gray, of " precipices, mountains, torrents, wolves, rumblings, Salvator Rosa " :

> But the road, West, the road ! winding round a prodigious mountain, and surrounded with others, all shagged with hanging woods, obscured with pines, or lost in clouds ! Below, a torrent breaking through cliffs, and tumbling through fragments of rocks ! Sheets of cascades forcing their silver speed down channelled precipices, and hasting into the roughened river at the bottom ! Now and then an old foot-bridge, with a broken rail, a leaning cross, a cottage, or the ruin of an hermitage !

Horace Walpole stands as one of the most interesting literary figures of the eighteenth century. By training, literary tastes, and antiquarian propensities, he was the one man in England most likely to foster Gothic romance. A monumental edition of his letters has been published revealing the various facets of his personality and recording anecdotes of a long life of eighty years. These vivid, detailed, and quotable memoirs and letters, chronicle the social and political history of his age, and behind them lurks an elaborate panorama of his own experiences. Biographers have brought to light incidents of his school and college days, his relation to his father and to politics, his travels and books, his Whiggism and virtuoso tastes, his ' castle ' at Strawberry Hill and its famous printing press, his detestation of war, whist, and Italian opera, his love of gossip and scandal, his intimate acquaintance with so many famous people. The personality of this writer has now emerged from the clouds of critical disapproval which hung round him during the nineteenth century. Macaulay's famous essay in the *Edinburgh Review* for October 1833, was a brilliant distortion of Walpole's mind, but it was accepted by an unsympathetic age. Walpole's serious achievement was dismissed as insignificant and his character much maligned. The twentieth century looks upon him with a more friendly eye, although traces of old prejudice linger on. But through the efforts of reasonable critics, the age has now tried to give full value to the extent and variety of Walpole's achievement.

His sensitive and dreaming mind absorbed the growing romantic influences of the early eighteenth century. His delicate and sensitive imagination shaped them into visions of a lost medieval world. His love of the Gothic, of old castles and abbeys, his romantic dreams of a pseudo-medieval world, inspired the creation of his ' castle ' at Strawberry Hill, which reflected the curious, nightmarish nature of the romantic imaginings hidden in his unconscious mind : and how extraordinarily powerful was his imagination ! At times, in his retirement, he imagined his castle a monastery and himself a monk !

The year 1764 reveals to us a Walpole disillusioned and exhausted by political and personal tension. We imagine him worried and depressed, wandering about his little mock castle of brick and wood and plaster. His secret hopes of political preferment were dying at last, and he began to stay away from the House of Commons. He had seen politics at close quarters as a sport for fools and knaves. Additions to Strawberry had ceased for some time and he was bored. The outer world was slow to perceive his finer qualities. He found those on whom he lavished his affections comparatively heedless or openly indifferent, and he was hurt and sad. Already Montagu failed to respond with sufficient ardour to his warmth of affection. Conway was to disappoint him bitterly and long afterwards Mann also was to wound him by what he deemed neglect. Thus many circumstances in the earlier months of 1764 drove Walpole into sombre retreat at Strawberry, and there he experienced, as never before, his increasing disgust with reality. This mental and spiritual detachment and physical isolation liberated his romantic imagination. Gradually the repressed dream world of his youth was re-created about him, enriched by the antiquarianism of his later years. Oswald Doughty describes him thus : " the tall, thin, unhealthy, pale eighteenth-century gentleman with eyes strangely bright, sitting alone in his brick and cement castle, wielding his goose-quill so persistently, was to himself one of that rough, rude world of chivalry and piety, the middle ages ".

Professor Dobrée has called Walpole " an uneasy romantic " who, like Hamlet, felt that the time was out of joint. Failure in politics, his father's downfall, the influence of Gray and Cole, his own natural impulses—all made him shrink from the Downing Street world, and as Oswald Doughty in his (above quoted) admirable essay on Walpole expresses it, he was " a spiritual exile in his native land ". He longed to escape from " the haven of bright, calm, and serene civilization "—its politics, wars and follies, its drabness and dullness to the superior and mystic realm of the Middle Ages. He observed the hard, coruscating brilliance of eighteenth-century society with the detachment of a visionary dreamer, and all the while became more engrossed in his medieval interests. Paul Yvon, in *Horace Walpole as a Poet* (1924), says, " How often did he tell Madame du Deffand, that in order to forget the unpleasant realities of life, he not seldom took refuge in visions, the outcome of which were *The Castle of Otranto* and *The Hieroglyphic Tales* ". Not completely stifled by his man-of-the-world character, his love of solitude is constantly hinted at in his letters, and it was his true artistic nature that elaborated his fantasies. Gray wrote to him from Cambridge : " You are in a confusion of wine and roaring, and bawdy, and tobacco. . . . I imagine however you rather choose to converse with the living dead, that adorn the walls of your apartments . . . and prefer a picture of still-life to the realities of a noisy one." And Walpole remained, to the last, an inveterate dreamer of dreams.

The Castle of Otranto is an expression of Walpole's repressed, romantic, visionary nature. From a thousand circumstances of his environment, from antiquarian interests and the abundant impressions of the past which they invoked, from Gothic castles and abbeys, from pictures by Claude, Poussin, and Salvator Rosa, from landscape gardens modelled upon their works, and from the poetry of Shakespeare and Spenser and Milton, he fashioned dreams of a world in which the beauty of antiquity, of wonder and terror and awe were supreme.

These influences were bodied forth in dreams, and Otranto rose in gloom and terror upon the slender foundations of Strawberry. The winding wooden staircase, " the most particular and chief beauty of the castle " took a grim, bare, and enormous shape. Elegant bedrooms transformed themselves into forbidding chambers, hung with tapestry and carpeted with matting or rushes of more ancient days. The walls of Strawberry decorated with antelopes holding shields became the echoing cloister of an ancient castle. And even earlier impressions, the subconscious memories of Cambridge, helped to form his dream castle. The structure of Trinity Great Court, another Gothic building, was lying dormant in Walpole's mind. Walpole had visited Cambridge in 1763, and when five years afterwards he went there again, on entering one of the colleges, " he suddenly found himself in the courtyard of Otranto", as he expresses his impression in a letter to Madame du Deffand. This College, which was later identified with Trinity, supplied Otranto with a courtyard, great Hall and other features which were absent in Strawberry Hill.

From dreaming at Strawberry, through a long summer moonlight, of knights in armour, clanking swords, and menacing portents, Walpole awoke with a head filled with materials for a Gothic tale. His letter to Cole, in which he narrates the details of his dream, has often been quoted. He dreamt of " the gigantic hand in armour " on " the uppermost banister of a great staircase "—" a very natural dream for a head like mine filled with Gothic story "—and he experienced an immediate reaction in his impulse towards romance writing. " The scene is undoubtedly laid in some real castle " he says in his preface to the first edition, and the staircase at Strawberry Hill which was " the most particular and chief beauty of the castle ", as he had mentioned earlier in 1753, was indelibly associated with his romance. The fact is well illustrated by his letter to Countess of Upper Ossory, when he made a triumphant purchase in Paris of the complete armour of Francis the First. " The armour ", he writes in December 1771, seven years after the publication of Otranto, " is actually here, and in its niche, which I have had made for it on the staircase ; and a very little stretch of imagination will give it all the visionary dignity of the gigantic hand in armour that I dreamt of seeing on the balustrade of the staircase of Otranto. If this is not realising one's dreams, I don't know what is."

Mario Praz, in The Times Literary Supplement of 13 August 1925, says of him, " In Horace Walpole the romantic impulses of the eighteenth century converge to a fine point ". He embodies in himself the particular antiquarian phases of early English romanticism. He, indeed, largely initiated all three sides of it : the collection of things having old world associations, the revival of Gothic architecture, and the taste for the chivalric tales of long ago. The one followed naturally out of the other. The enthusiasm for old collected things deepened into an appreciation of Gothic architecture which later gave impetus to the creation of the first Gothic novel.

Walpole did not love Gothic for its virile or aspiring qualities, but for its suggestiveness to a truant fantasy. What appealed to him in Gothic art and in romance generally was its quaintness. As Lytton Strachey states : " He liked Gothic architecture, not because he thought it beautiful but because he found it queer." For Walpole, at least in the beginning, to Gothicize was a game. The Gothic was, to begin with, a decorative motif as is evident from his letter to Mann, 27 April 1753 :

> I thank you a thousand times for thinking of procuring me some Gothic
> remains from Rome ; but I believe there is no such thing there ; I scarce
> remember any morsel in the true taste of it in Italy. Indeed, my dear Sir,

kind as you are about it, I perceive you have no idea what Gothic is ; you have lived too long amidst true taste, to understand venerable barbarism. You say you suppose my garden to be Gothic too. That can't be ; Gothic is merely architecture ; and as one has a satisfaction in imprinting the gloomth of abbeys and cathedrals on one's house, so one's garden, on the contrary, is to be nothing but *riant*, and the gaiety of nature.

But this should not lead us to suppose that he was at bottom a dilettante, as it has been suggested in certain quarters. A man who took great pains over his prodigious and prolific literary output like the *Anecdotes of Painting in England, Historic Doubts on the reign of Richard III, Description of Strawberry, History of Tastes in Gardens,* the essays in *The World,* the amazing number of short satirical pieces, and over the monu-mental *Letters,* was no dilettante. His printing press, which worked for some forty years, certainly did something to improve typography and it involved considerable personal labour on his part. For it, Walpole did a fair amount of editing, including the first edition of the delightful *Memoirs of Lord Herbert of Cherbury.* Then there was his astonishing collection of things of no intrinsic or artistic worth, but of great associative interest.

Walpole took pains to pretend that his work was not work but a pastime, for he feared being thought erudite. He was abnormally self-conscious but he was not trivial. Professor Ker pointed out that " Horace Walpole was a man of taste and sensibility, interested in all trifles if only they had anything of singularity, tolerant of everything except what was commonplace ". Cole once wrote that it was a misfortune to have so much sensibility in one's nature as Walpole was endued with. It is true that Walpole's mind was easily pleased by oddities rather than by things of more solid worth ; and accordingly his Gothic castles which he himself constructed, whether of Otranto or at Strawberry, were more remarkable for their queerness than for their beauty. Macaulay as well wrote : " . . . with the Sublime and the Beautiful Walpole had nothing to do, but the third province, the Odd, was his peculiar domain."

Strawberry Hill started as a toy—straight out of Mr. Chevenix's toy-shop, as he declared ; and then early in 1750 he tells Mann : " I am going to build a little Gothic structure at Strawberry Hill." A new chapter in the life of Walpole now begins. It all started as a fanciful game : but it soon became serious. From now onwards, for full fourteen years, before he wrote the first Gothic novel, Walpole was deep in architectural activities, full of enthusiasm about his miniature castle : decorating a grotesque house with pie-crust battlements ; procuring rare engravings and antique chimney-boards ; matching odd gauntlets ; and laying out a maze of walks within five acres of ground. The villa at Strawberry Hill " gradually swelled into a feudal castle, by the addition of turrets, towers, galleries . . . garnished with appropriate furniture of scutcheons, armorial bearings, shields, tilting-lances, and all the panoply of chivalry ". *The Edinburgh Review* writes : " The motto which he pre-fixed to his ' *Catalogue of Royal and Noble Authors* ', might have been inscribed with perfect propriety over the door of every room in his house, and on the title page of every one of his books. ' *Dove diavolo, Messer Ludovico, avete pigliate tante coglionerie ? * ' In his villa every apartment is a museum, every piece of furniture is a curiosity ; there is something strange in the form of the shovel ; there is a long story belonging to the bell-rope. We wander among a profusion of rarities, of trifling intrinsic value, but so quaint in fashion, or connected with such remarkable names and events, that they may well detain our attention for a moment. A moment is enough. Some new relic, some new curio, some new carved work, some new enamel, is forthcoming in an instant. One cabinet of trinkets is no sooner closed than another is opened. It is the same with Walpole's writings. It is not in their utility, it is not in their beauty, that their attraction lies. . . . Walpole is constantly showing us things—not of great value indeed—yet things which we are pleased to see, and which we can see nowhere else. They are baubles ; but they are made curiosities either by his grotesque workmanship, or by some association belonging to them."

Walpole had a purse long enough to give visible and tangible expression—in prints, in gates, in Gothic temples, in bowers, in old manuscripts, in a thousand gimcracks, to the smouldering and inarticulate passion for the darkness of the Past. William Lyon Phelps judges that, " As a collector of curiosities he was probably influenced more by a love of old world associations than any sound appreciation of artistic design ". The deckings and trappings of the chivalric age infused into him a boyish delight, while the glitter and colour of the Middle Ages offered unto him an escape from the prosaic dullness of his own times. Oliver Elton thinks that " his house and Museum, along with his letters, may be regarded as his chief work of art and as the mirror of his mind and taste ". The romantic ideals of his literary mind were realized in actual life at Strawberry. His letters to Montagu during the period of architectural activities reveal a mind full of buried manuscripts and valuable documents concealed behind Gothic panelling.

His interest in things medieval may not have been that of an antiquary, but it was surely that of an artist who loves things old because of their age and beauty. Virginia Woolf in an article stated that " Walpole had imagination, taste, style, in addition to a passion for the romantic past ". On the contrary Professor Saintsbury holds : " Of real poetry, real romance, and real passion of any kind, he had no share, no inkling even ". We beg leave not to agree with this remark. " I have got an immense cargo of painted glass from Flanders," Walpole wrote in 1750, " indeed several of the pieces are Flemish arms, but I call them the achievements of the old Count of Strawberry."

Visiting Stratford, he is disgusted with the " wretched old town ", which he expected " for Shakespeare's sake to find smug and pretty, and *antique*, not *old* ". This extract illustrates the quality of Walpole's medievalism ; things smug and pretty and *antique*, not *old*, were what he loved ; things approaching the imaginative reconstruction of the past were never foreign to his thought. As Scott said : " A Horace Walpole, or a Thomas Warton, is not a mere collector of dry and minute facts, which the general historian passes over with disdain. He brings with him the torch of genius, to illuminate the ruins through which he loves to wander." Indeed, the ointment is rare and rich, of a subtle and delicious perfume. The aroma of a wonderful age comes wafting out from the hundred pages of *The Castle of Otranto*, and enchants our senses : who else could have written the first Gothic novel but this amiable virtuoso, who dreamed of ghosts, went about collecting armour and tombstones in a Gothic castle, and read Dr. Dee on spirits ?

Although *The Monthly Review*, commenting upon *The Castle of Otranto*, said, " To present an analysis of the story would merely introduce the reader to ' a company of skeletons ', but to refer him to the book would be to recommend him an assemblage of beautiful pictures ", it is worth while to recount the major incidents of the story.

Manfred, the usurping prince of Otranto, haunted by a mysterious prophecy, hastens to secure Isabella, the only daughter of the real heir of Otranto, as bride for his only son Conrad. On the very eve of marriage, Conrad is crushed to death by the mysterious fall of an enormous helmet shaded with black plumes. Theodore, a peasant boy, who discovers that the miraculous helmet is identical with the one now missing from the black marble statue of Alfonso the Good, is imprisoned as a sorcerer under the helmet itself. Frantic with rage and fear, Manfred declares his intention of himself marrying Isabella, on which some prodigies appear : the sable plumes of the helmet wave backward and forward in a tempestuous manner ; the portrait of his grandfather utters a deep sigh, quits its panel, descends on the floor and vanishes into a chamber.

Isabella meanwhile escapes through a subterraneous passage to the church of St. Nicholas. On her way she encounters Theodore who has been accidentally released, and sympathy very soon ripens into love. As Manfred, in his hot pursuit of Isabella, enters the vaults of the castle, the affrighted servants bring news of a ghost or giant whose foot was seen in the upper chamber. Nevertheless, Manfred pursues his designs, and orders Father Jerome to deliver Isabella from the sanctuary. He also orders Theodore to be beheaded, but the execution is set aside as Father Jerome, by means of a birth-mark, discovers in Theodore his long-lost child.

Frederic, Marquis of Vicenza, father of Isabella and the real claimant of Otranto, arrives, and his arrival is followed by further prodigies : a brazen trumpet miraculously salutes him at the gate of the castle ; the plumes of the enchanted helmet nod vigorously. He is accompanied by a hundred knights who bear an enormous sword which, bursting from their hands, falls on the ground opposite the helmet and remains im- movable. Manfred tries to quell animosities by a matrimonial alliance by which each is to marry the daughter of the other. Frederic agrees. On the mere proposal three drops of blood fall from the nose of Alfonso's statue. The apparition of the holy hermit of Joppa discloses to Frederic " the fleshless jaws and empty sockets of a skeleton wrapt in a hermit's cowl " and adjures him to forget Matilda. The story ends with the tragic death, by mistake, of Matilda at the hands of her father.

As she expires, a clap of thunder shakes the castle to its foundations, and the form of Alfonso, dilated to an immense magnitude, appears in the centre of the ruins, exclaiming " Behold in Theodore the true heir of Alfonso ! "

Besides the atmosphere and background of chivalry and enchantment typical of " old romances ", there are three other literary forms shedding influences on The Castle of Otranto : the heroic romance, the fairy-story, and the tale of Oriental Magic ; and these blend and fuse with three other elements from contemporary prose fiction : excessive sensibility, exemplary piety, and an explicit moral. Walpole's historical and antiquarian knowledge is well illustrated in his collection of books at Strawberry Hill. Over two hundred of the volumes were works on ancient chivalry and historical themes. These were sufficient to bestow a consistent atmosphere of chivalry on his romance, by means of stories of knights in armour and crusades, through descriptions of feudal tyrants and dungeons, and by recorded incidents of challenge and chivalric procession. Details, such as a lady arming her knight, his vow of eternal fealty to her, and knightly oaths as " by my halidame " (cf. Longsword), though this is oddly put into the mouth of a chattering domestic, does create an old-world chivalric atmosphere. We note the influence of heroic romance and drama in the struggle of generosity between the " sentimental, self-sacrificing heroines " and in the melting forgiveness of the pious hero for the barbarous treatment of the tyrant—the supernatural magnanimity of the heroic prince type (cf. for example Dryden's *Aurengzebe*). The temporary emergence of the " tender-hearted villain " in the scene where Manfred is ' touched ' and weeps, seems to be influenced by *Longsword*.

The supernatural element in the book is probably its greatest innovation, and is a curious blend of fairy-tale and magic, with one genuine spectre episode, the appearance of the skeleton hermit in the oratory, of which Scott said that it " was long accounted a masterpiece of the horrible ". The appearance of this spectre as an instrument of fate, with its sepulchral warning, influenced the later Romanticism of Horror. But no one apparently ever attempted to imitate the much more elaborate but fantastic creation of the dismembered giant distributing himself piecemeal about the castle and at last shaking it to its foundations. This is quite different from the conventional ghosts, spirits, and spectres that stalk rampant through the pages of the later Gothic novels. In *The Castle of Otranto*, curiously, the word ' ghost ' does not occur, but instead we find occasional references to ' sorcerer ', ' talisman ', and ' enchantment '. Certain episodes, too, such as the apparition of the giant seen by Bianca, when she was rubbing her ring, definitely suggest the fairy-tales of the East that Walpole was so fond of reading. The episode reminds us of the appearance of the genii in *Aladdin and the Wonderful Lamp*, one of the stories in *Arabian Nights Entertainments*.

Walpole raised the apparition of Alfonso to gigantic proportions. In this particular device Walpole seems to have imitated Eastern tales, in which enormous size not only suggests embodiment of power, but also strikes and evokes a feeling of terror. Various forms of Oriental fiction had become popular in England during the first twenty years of the eighteenth century. Most of these works reached England through

France.   Antoine Galland's French version of the *Arabian Nights Entertainment* was translated into English between 1708 and 1715.   In the following few years Turkish, Persian, Arabic, Chinese, and Mogul tales were translated from the French of François Pétis de la Croix, Jean Terrason, Jean Paul Bignom, and Simon Gueullette.   It is likely that these may have attracted Johnson to seek in Abyssinia the scene of Rasselas, and they give clues to the extravagant incidents and luxuriant descriptions in Beckford's *Vathek* (1786), " the most famous Oriental tale in the English language ".

There had also been during the period a growing interest in voyage, travel, and discovery, and a heightening of curiosity concerning the mystic charms of the East.   Also, the opening of the first Gothic novel : " Manfred, Prince of Otranto, had one son and one daughter . . ." reads almost like a fairy-tale, with its irrational parent, one lovely and one unlovely child.   The tragic ending, however, is typical neither of fairy-stories nor of later Gothic romances, which ring incessant changes on the conventional fairy-tale endings like : " And they were married and lived happily ever after."

There is a definite resemblance between the supernatural machinery of *The Castle of Otranto* and that treated in Dr. Dee's book on imps and spirits.   We get here a profusion of gigantic dismembered limbs, such as the " mighty arm and hand ", the arm " with a broad-axe " " a right hand (and no body appearing), the hand being very big ", " a great huge man, with a great sword in his hand ", " a head cut off from a body ", and, more than once, a figure ascending heavenward, like Alfonso the Good at the climax of *The Castle of Otranto*.   Taken all together, these suggestions of resemblances are too numerous and too striking to be overlooked as even a minor influence that went to the making of Walpole's Gothic story.   Nor did these stray suggestions exist only in Dr. Dee's book.   Ideas of this kind may be traced in the folk-lore of different nations ever since the fairy-tale of *Jack and the Bean Stalk*.

One of Madame D'Aulnoy's fairy-tales, *The White Cat*, mentioned by Walpole, has examples of dissected beings, and in it the prince is served by *bodiless hands*, in the palace of the white cat.   Also, Becquer's legend of *The Devil's Cross* records an extraordinary story of dismembered armour that at the touch of a ray of light could always gather itself together, no matter how hewed and separated, and continue the devilish raids.   Also there is a reference to a gigantic hand grasping a gigantic key on the keystone of the Alhambra's portal. W. B. Yeats's collection of old *Irish Fairy and Folk Tales* includes the story of *A Queen's Country Witch* who takes the form of a man's legs walking without head or body. So, besides Dee's work, other literary models may have played their part in the formation of the first Gothic tale. Pope's description of the Paraclete in *Eloisa to Abelard*, and Swift's Brobdingnag in *Gulliver's Travels*, had appealed to Walpole, and they did leave some impress on *The Castle of Otranto*. And so the readers who eagerly explored Walpole's Gothic castle had previously enjoyed the thrill of chimney-corner legends by a winter fireside.

There is a tale by Count Anthony Hamilton, *The Four Facardins* (1646), with which Walpole was perhaps quite familiar. The 'giant' and 'his leg' and 'armour' occur there. Facardin of Mount Atlas, during the course of his adventures, has a fight with 'an enormous giant' who had a very long nail on the toe of his right foot. Facardin is injured by this nail, and being infuriated lops off the right leg of the giant. The fall of the giant " was like that of a tower and the earth trembled as he touched it ". Facardin, to his great surprise, finds that the giant has disappeared and carried his leg away with him ! While Walpole enlarged the suggestion of his dream of " a big hand in armour " in *The Castle of Otranto*, he might have had the subconscious memories of Hamilton's supernatural as well. There is a great similarity in the handling of the material by Walpole and Hamilton in their characteristic naive simplicity in the use of the supernatural where atmosphere or suggestion does not play any part. The crude machinery of their tales belongs to an ideal world of fancy and fairy-tale, where there is neither probability nor a necessary correspondence between effect and cause.

Walpole looked to ancient romances as well for inspiration. He knew the *Arcadia* of Sidney, and had a tender regard for the works of Scudéry and the Heroic school. These may have partly been the source of the supernatural in *The Castle of Otranto*. In the *Arcadia* the oracle predicts strange events ; the plot of *Otranto*, too, veers round a similar mysterious prophecy. In *Arcadia*, as the story slowly unfolds itself, we find the predictions of the oracle unrelentingly fulfilled, although King Basilius endeavours to prevent their materialization. Manfred too, in *The Castle of Otranto*, fruitlessly attempts to ward off the realization of the prophecy.

These minor points go to establish that Walpole cannot be said to have invented anything absolutely new as far as mere machinery goes.

His originality lay in combining such machinery with historical romance, and in assigning to his unearthly beings a definite role in enforcing retributive justice—just such a part as common belief assigned to departed spirits. The old properties of folk-lore and fairy-tales were ill-balanced and ill-conceived. Walpole welds these ingredients together with the fire of his innovating genius.

In the Preface to the second edition, the title of which was merely *The Castle of Otranto, a Gothic story*, the still generally unknown author explained his purpose in writing it by the oft-quoted statement that " it was an attempt to blend two kinds of romance, the ancient and the modern ", a remark sufficiently illuminated in a letter to Dr. Warton. The book reveals these dual characteristics. The ' modern ' element is evident in the method of characterization and dialogue. The characters happen to be mostly stock-figures, while the domestics of the story stand as contrast to the figures of high life. The minor characters, and specially the loquacious maid, Bianca, have their clay from Shakespeare, as Walpole said. Referring in his preface to the second edition of these domestic minor figures, he writes : " That great master of nature Shakespeare was the model I copied." Then follows a spirited defence of the Shakespearean trick of relieving tragic scenes with flashes of farce. The actions of the actors are within bounds of reason, and here " the natural of modern novel " comes to an end. The union of real life with the wonders of romance was a reconciliation between nature and imagination, giving a new lease of life to Romance in England. The type made strides towards development and consequently entered the borders of fine art.

Walpole's manifesto in this second preface that his object in this tale was to make the supernatural appear natural, by the portrayal of characters placed in unusual circumstances, was identical with the aim which Coleridge set before himself in the *Lyrical Ballads* some thirty-five years after. Walter Scott, remarking upon " the wild interest of the story ", pointed out that it was " the first modern attempt to found a tale of amusing fiction upon the basis of the ancient romances of chivalry ". He goes on to say : " As, in his model of a Gothic modern mansion, our author had studiously endeavoured to fit to the purposes of modern convenience or luxury, the rich, varied, and complicated tracery and carving of the ancient cathedral, so, in *The Castle of Otranto*, it was his object to unite the marvellous turn of incident, and imposing tone of chivalry, exhibited in the ancient romance, with that accurate exhibition of human character, and contrast of feelings and passions, which is or ought to be, delineated in the modern novel."

It has been alleged that Walpole could not fully achieve his aim of blending ancient romance and the contemporary novel ; that the characters in *The Castle of Otranto* speak the language of eighteenth-century fiction and exhibit corresponding emotions. Although Walpole could not bestow upon his heroine those delicate shades of character which we get in Richardson and Fielding, Matilda and Isabella talk and behave, amid a welter of phantoms and supernatural portents, as Clarissa Harlowe or Sophia Western could have done. " Certainly the blending of supernatural events and Gothic savagery with the *beaux sentiments* of his own day was the least successful feature of Walpole's novel," says R. W. Ketton-Cremer ; but Walpole employed the old supernatural agencies of Scudéry and La Calprenède as the background to the adventures of personages modelled as closely upon ordinary life as the personages of *Tom Jones*. According to Austin Dobson " the actions, sentiments, conversation, of the heroes and heroines of ancient days were as unnatural as the machines employed to put them in motion ". Walpole did model his characters on a contemporary pattern, but borrowed from the old romances some fancy and imagination and art of invention which, in the literal reproduction of life, he found neglected and forgotten.

It has been assumed in some quarters that Walpole's story was a literary ' joke '. This appears to be a wild surmise, and this conjecture has no sound foundation. Walpole meant it as seriously as he ever meant anything, and was quite sincere about it. He told Élie de Beaumont that when he published his " little story " it was because he " was so diffident of its merit " that he gave it as a translation from an Italian manuscript. Walpole seriously repeated and amplified in this letter what he had already conveyed to Dr. Warton : " To tell you the truth, it was not so much my intention to recall the exploded marvels of ancient romance as to blend the wonderful of old stories with the natural of modern novels." The latter kind of writing, Walpole added, Richardson had made ' insupportable ' to him : " I thought the *nodus* was become *dignus vindice*, and that a god, or at least a ghost, was absolutely necessary to frighten us out of too much sense." In another letter, written a few days later to the Earl of Hertford, he says, the success of the romance has at least brought him to own it, though the wildness of it made him terribly afraid.

Probably this conception of a literary joke arose out of some casual statements made in the past. Scott has called it " one of the standard works of our lighter literature ". Miss Dorothy M. Stuart remarked that " Otranto . . . was a pastime, the sequel to a Gothic dream, the *tour de force* of a brilliant amateur ". Walpole himself had ridiculed the ghosts and omens of Clarendon's stories in his *Catalogue of Royal and Noble Authors* and his dictum was " there is no medium between believing and laughing at them ". These need not, however, lead us to assume that this romance was necessarily a literary joke.

Horace Walpole, in his letters to the Rev. William Mason, the Rev. William Cole, and Robert Jephson, frequently discussed the revival of the Gothic romance as initiated by himself and carried on by Clara Reeve. He felt that during the 'eighties the reaction against neo-classicism had gone too far from reason and common sense. In the 'sixties people needed to be impressed with the charms of the fanciful. While writing to Miss Hannah More, he ventured to tell the truth : " It was fit for nothing but the age in which it was written ; . . . that required only to be amused . . . and rather wanted to be brought back to imagination, than to be led astray by it." Besides, it was of all his writings, the one Walpole himself most liked. " I confess, my dear," he wrote to Madame du Deffand, " that of all my works this is the only one I enjoyed writing." And the subsequent rendering may follow thus : ". . . I have given reins to my imagination till I became on fire with the visions and feelings which it excited. I have composed it in defiance of rules, of critics, and of philosophers ; and it seems to me just so much the better for that very reason. I am even persuaded, that sometime hereafter, when taste shall resume the place which philosophy now occupies, my poor Castle will find admirers ! "

Walpole was a genius of no ordinary kind. C. S. Fearnside, in his introduction to *Classic Tales*, says : " *The Castle of Otranto* deserves the praise of being the outcome of a vision of a world beyond and above that in which the author himself moved and which he described in his letters with a vivacity that would never be expected by those who knew him solely in his ' Gothic Story '." Even though it has been abused, criticized, praised, and even laughed at, " *The Castle of Otranto*, despite its tinselled gloss, is historically important because of its influence ". A. T. Hazen of Yale says that " In the total number of editions the book has displayed a rather astonishing vitality ". It is not a great work— Walpole was not a poet, not a creator, but it was, indeed, a fruitful work. It would be, therefore, worth while to look into the potentialities of this first Gothic tale.

There is hardly a feature of Gothic romance that was not employed by Walpole in *The Castle of Otranto*. Walpole bequeathed to his successors a remarkable collection of useful ' properties ', and his ' machinery ' and ' motifs ' quickly accumulated as conventions of the Gothic school. *The Castle of Otranto* possessed potentialities in three directions, of which the ingenious innovator was Horace Walpole : the Gothic machinery, the atmosphere of gloom and terror, and stock romantic characters. Countless Gothic novels have in their titles ' castle ', ' abbey ', ' priory ', ' convent ' or ' church '. A glance at *A Gothic Bibliography* by Montague Summers would satisfy anyone. The buildings seem to acquire a personality and an empery of their own, ever since the Gothic tale of *Otranto*. The shilling shockers of the Gothic school that flooded the market during the nineteenth century exploited many of the devices employed in the first Gothic tale. Walpole had called his novel *The Castle of Otranto : a Gothic Story*. The shockers imitated Walpole's method of using a secondary title. Eventually the crude materials in the novel were transformed to finer qualities in romantic poetry. What in Walpole's compact book are merely hints were expanded in the later novels to a greater breadth and variety.

The background of Walpole's story is a Gothic castle, singularly unenchanted, but capable of being invested with mysterious grandeur as later in the novels of Ann Radcliffe. The Castle has been called the true hero of the book, the hub around which all action gravitates. The remote castle, with its antique courts and ruined turrets, deserted and haunted chambers where hang age-old tapestries ; its grated windows that exclude the light ; its dark, eerie galleries amid whose mouldering gloom is heard the rustle of an unseen robe, a sigh, a hurried footfall where no mortal step should tread ; its dark, machicolated and sullen towers set high upon some precipice of the Apennines frowning upon the valleys below—it is the Castle itself which is the focal point of Walpole's romance. The haunted castle forms the stage-setting ; while its accessory properties powerfully seize the imagination. If we eliminate it, the whole fabric of the romance would be bereft of its foundation and its predominant atmosphere would fade away.

The Castle brought in its train other architectural associations evoking an atmosphere of Gothic gloom. The bewildering vaults and secret panels, the subterranean passages, the broken winding spiral staircases, the trap-door creaking on rusty hinges, the decayed apartments and mouldering floors—objects trivial and insignificant in Walpole's hands, were fraught with terrible possibilities. The convent and the cavern, and the deepest dungeon of the darkest tower, all were the accessories of this Gothic castle of romance, and are hinted in the story of Otranto. "Horace Walpole's experiments in Gothic architecture and the machinery of medieval romance are easily ridiculed", says W. P. Ker, "but the meaning of these diversions can hardly be mistaken : the quickness of his nature required more vivid fancies, more exciting pictures for the mind, than were commonly provided by contemporary taste."

Walpole successfully creates an atmosphere of mystery, gloom, and terror, through his specialized settings, machinery, character-types, theme, plot, or technique. They are so selected and combined as to throw out dark suggestions and intensify the mystery. A heavy pall hangs over the Gothic scene, and "the gloomth of abbeys and cathedrals" spreads over the atmosphere. The tolling of the midnight bell, and the clank of chains break the silence of the night. Walpole's "subterranean passage" connecting the castle with the church of St. Nicholas, became very popular with the later romance writers of the Gothic school. The palpitating heroine Isabella escapes through these very awfully silent subterranean regions. Her flight is an episode of eerie atmosphere :

> The lower part of the castle was hollowed into several intricate cloisters. . . . An awful silence reigned throughout those subterraneous regions ; except now and then, some blasts of wind, that shook the doors she had passed, and which grating on the rusty hinges, were re-echoed through that long labyrinth of darkness. Every murmur struck her with new terror. . . . In one of those moments she thought she heard a sigh. She shuddered and recoiled a few paces. In a moment she thought she heard the step of some person. Her blood curdled. . . . Every suggestion that horror could inspire rushed into her mind.

A sudden gust of wind extinguishes her lamp, leaving her in total darkness, and then a "clouded ray of moonshine" comes to her aid. "Words cannot paint the horror of the princess's situation." The succeeding generation of authors attempted to paint the horror of just such situations after Walpole wrote that most fruitful and creative description. That paragraph, well adapted to heighten curiosity, bristles with appropriate atmospheric conditions. The blasts of wind, which at the critical moment extinguished Isabella's lamp, were for more than half a century to be

heard whistling through the pages of Clara Reeve, Mrs. Radcliffe,
' Monk' Lewis, Scott, and others.   And there is the pale gleam of the
moon as

> gliding softly between the aisles, and guided by an imperfect gleam of moon-
> shine that shone faintly, Manfred steals forward.

In later Gothic novels, at the very moment when the tyrant is engaged
in blackest night on some deed of darkness, the same moon emerges
from behind a patch of cloud, revealing a ghastly scene that alarms him
and prevents the crime from being committed.   It shines through the
Gothic windows of ruined abbeys, dim and mysterious, illuminating
to the tyrant's view the glassy eyes of his dead heir, a witness to the
violent and tragic end of his line.   The moon is intended to awaken a
nocturnal atmosphere fraught with mystery and tinged with fantasy,
fear, and sadness.   It lends an indistinct and weird shape to each feature.
As Eino Railo observes, in *The Haunted Castle* (1927), the moon " is a
theatrical searchlight cast from the wings at suitable moments to reveal
to the terror-stricken audience visions and scenes of fear ".

The wind that caused the doors to creak on their rusty hinges, the
draught that wandered through the subterranean passages, had a special
duty assigned to it by Walpole.   It sweeps fast through the vaults in
sudden gusts, to extinguish the fluttering candle flame borne by the
persecuted heroine just at the time when her flight is at its climax, launch-
ing her into awful, pitch-black darkness.   In later novels, when it whines
in the night outside the despairing and trembling maiden's window, the
loquacious chamber-maid takes it for a sighing ghost.   The lamp of
Isabella in the later works, develops the virtue of " burning blue " to
warn its possessor of an approaching ghost, or reveals the emaciated
' unknown' locked in the dank dungeon ; its one defect being that it
has to go out when most needed by an intrepid explorer or palpitating
heroine.   Lightning is the mighty ally of wind and storm ; at a critical
moment there comes a sudden burst of thunder shaking the foundations
of the haunted castle, hinting at the existence of avenging eternal powers.
Thunder and lightning recur again in the later work of the Schauer-
Romantiks.

While enumerating Walpole's innovation of Gothic machinery, one
cannot afford to omit " the Ancestral Portrait " and " the time-yellowed
scroll ".   The mysterious manuscript is usually discovered in some
secret drawer or dusty corridor of the deserted wing and contains the

detailed confession of some foul murder committed in the past, or perhaps uselessly warns the inquisitive heroine or hero to "look no further". In later works, these scrolls are tied with faded ribbon, and around them hovers a breath of past happiness or of sorrows now ended. Walpole endowed "the ancestral portrait" with life, and the power of stepping down from its frame. In the hands of Mrs. Radcliffe it turns into a miniature invested with tender memories, and in the later Gothic novels there is displayed on every castle wall the feature of some glorious ancestor. Finally it was to prove effectual in transmitting a sombre impression of that mysterious Melmoth the Wanderer, where this property is endowed with a demonic power, awakening an indefinite suspicion of some hidden dreadful crime, as the portrait instils a magnetic terror with its mysterious blazing eyes.

Besides these Gothic settings, Walpole had anticipated the character-types. The gloomy tyrant or Byronic hero is foreshadowed in Walpole's Manfred, imitated in Radcliffe's Montoni. Walpole gave the first sketch of the dark, handsome, melancholy, passionate, and mysterious hero of Byronic poems. Bianca describes to her mistress her ideal love "with large black eyes, a smooth white forehead and manly curling locks like jet". Theodore, at the end of the story, carried with him "a melancholy that had taken possession of his soul". Here is the progenitor of melancholy Lara, or the wild Corsair, or the handsome Giaour. The Gothic heroine or damsel in distress had always been a beautiful shadow, ever since Walpole pictured Isabella. Her beauties and virtues attain perfection in later works as the realism in her character tends to melt away.

With Theodore the noble peasant hero with his birth-mark, the theme of the long-lost relative emerges. The chief characters of Walpole's romance, the usurping tyrant, the persecuted heroine, the "noble peasant" hero, the hermit, the monk, and the comic element supplied by garrulous, ghost-scared domestic servants—all became stock properties of later Gothic novels ; as did the general plan of Walpole's plot : the restoration to hereditary rights of an unknown and defrauded heir by means of supernatural agents acting on behalf of divine justice. Jerome is the prototype of many a count disguised as father confessor, Bianca the model of many a chattering servant. The imprisoned wife reappears in countless romances, including Mrs. Radcliffe's *Sicilian Romance* (1790), and Mrs. Roche's *Children of the Abbey* (1798). Along with all this, Walpole's importation of "old romance" material bequeathed to the later novels the pirates, prophecies, dreams, and birth-marks, which recur again and again.

In order that the passions and characters could develop new dimensions, Walpole placed the setting of his tale in Italy, and horror-romanticism long retained this love for a southern setting. This longing for the South, for an alien and distant setting, is typical of the romantic attitude, and reflects the effort of the Gothic mind to break away from the fetters of homely experience. The southern setting made possible truly romantic effects ; it was associated with monasteries and mysterious monastic life, and there the reign of the Inquisition was no very distant matter, and could supply a series of pleasing and torturing visions to Protestant readers. *The Castle of Otranto* is in Italy, whither also Mrs. Radcliffe places her *Udolpho* and *The Italian* and her *Sicilian Romance*. The action of *The Romance of the Forest* takes place in France, and that of *The Monk* in Spain. St. Leon is a Frenchman, Schemoli an Italian.

Thus the hints vaguely thrown out by Walpole, his stray suggestions and use of crude Gothic properties—castle, picture, vaults, galleries, subterranean passages, monasteries, convents, statues, ruins, music, moon, and wind—everything was developed by later novelists and made to yield maximum results.

The defects of the machinery are glaring to a modern eye, but they matter as little as the fallen tree-trunks, the strewn rocky pebbles or the snowdrifts which retard for a while, but do not stem, the Alpine torrent in its tumultuous course down the mountain-side. Austin Dobson, in his memoirs of Horace Walpole, says : " A generation like the present for whom fiction has unravelled so many intricate combinations . . . no longer feels its soul harrowed up in the same way as did his hushed and awe-struck readers of the days of the third George. . . . We doubt if that many-plumed and monstrous helmet, which crashes through stone walls and cellars, could now give a single shiver." To Miss Birkhead " His (Walpole's) supernatural machinery is as undignified as the panto-mime properties of Jack the Giant Killer. The huge body scattered piecemeal about the castle, the unwieldy sabre, borne by a hundred men, the helmet ' tempestuously agitated ', and even the ' skeleton in hermit's cowl ' are not alarming but mildly ridiculous." It is true that the supernatural machinery, its actions and interference, is rather too frequent and palls constantly on the reader's mind ; while supernatural occurrences are brought forward sometimes in strong daylight. But Walpole's task was stupendous ; his object was to wind up the feelings of his reader till they became for a moment identified with those of a ruder age, and to harmonize the phantoms and apparitions with the manners of feudal times. This was a task which required no little learning, no ordinary degree of fancy, and no common portion of genius to execute. And he very nearly succeeded !

The potentialities of the book can never be questioned. When we look at the careless profusion of cyclamen petals, we are amazed that such a rich exotic sprinkle of colours should have sprung from a mere grain of seed. And so it was with the productive seed *The Castle of Otranto* that gave rise to an immortal school in fiction.

Considering what Walpole contributed to the novel as an art-form, it would be worth while examining his technique, and analysing his art of characterization, atmosphere and description, his method of plot construction, and use of dialogue, suspense, and climax.

Fiction in the first three-quarters of the eighteenth century had concentrated on reason, common sense, and satirical wit. The birth of *The Castle of Otranto* satisfied the requirements of the new age which was groping after new sources of pleasure. There was from now onwards a longing for imagination, mystery, and gloom. From a stress on photographic representation of life, there was an increased interest in action and adventure. Walpole furnished writers with the materials to work on. Under his influence, the attraction towards chivalry paved the way for historical tales. But Walpole's goblin tale also gratified the love of mystery by its castle, its technique of suspense, and its element of terror. It diffused a new spirit, and became a finger-post to mark the art of fiction undergoing a romantic revival. The novel was to make great strides towards maturity. The theory of truthful characterization was constantly emphasized during the eighteenth century, but Walpole injected variety into the plot and setting of the story by bringing in medieval marvels. From now onwards fiction would gradually tend to favour the romantic rather than the realistic type.

In more than one way *The Castle of Otranto* was a challenge to the methods and subject-matter of contemporary novelists. It substituted invention for observation, a picture of the past for that of the present, the supernatural and the marvellous for ordinary everyday experiences. The conception was original, and the attempt was abundantly rich in results. *Otranto* was a revolt against the moral lessons, sentiment, domestic familiarities, and boisterous rowdyism of middle-class fiction.

Walpole's crude manifesto of the novel of the future hints at the confession of poetic faith put forward forty years later in *Lyrical Ballads*.
Transferred to the realm of poetry and generalized into philosophy,
these were the respective spheres of Wordsworth and Coleridge. We
miss in *Otranto* the delicate representation of the follies and foibles of
eighteenth-century life, as well as that healthy animalism that characterized
the school of Fielding ; we are now bordering on regions of romance,
of secluded cottages and Rousseauistic sentiment, of hills and barren
moors.

Walpole endows his characters with distinct individuality, in tune
with the age and nature of the story. Manfred is presented as an embodiment of feudal tyranny, whose courage, art, and duplicity are true
ingredients of the barbarous chieftain of dark ages. He can excite fear
and pity when his pride is quelled and his race extinguished. The touches
of remorse and natural feeling in his character make him human and
draw our sympathies. As a contrast to this selfish and tyrannical prince
stand the pious monk and the patient Hippolita. Theodore is the
juvenile hero, who seems to have walked out of the pages of old fairy-
tales, and Matilda has all the necessary interesting sweetness to match
him as the heroine. Walpole deliberately keeps the character of Isabella
subdued, in order to relieve that of Manfred's daughter. But the magic
spell of romance is broken when Isabella becomes the bride of Theodore.

The Critical Review, making allowances for the " monstrosities of
this story ", said that " the characters are well marked, and the narrative
kept up with surprising spirit and propriety ". The *Monthly Review*
praised Walpole's language as " accurate and elegant " and the characters
as " highly finished ". It concluded : " The disquisition into human
manners, passions, and pursuits, indicate the keenest penetration and the
most perfect knowledge of mankind." It was " a work of genius
evincing great dramatic powers ".

Indeed, *The Castle of Otranto* is a deftly constructed piece of work
preserving all the dramatic unities, moving straight towards the climax,
and emphasizing the structural technique to excite the reader's curiosity.
The five chapters of the story resemble five acts of a tragedy, and the
complications of the plot are resolved only in the end. The various
portents succeed one another in a most striking manner and gradually
prepare us for the grand catastrophe. They bear each upon the other
towards the accomplishment of the ancient prophecy, announcing the
ruin of the house of Manfred. Despite the extraordinary incidents of a

dark and barbarous age, the story within the compass of natural events is happily detailed ; its progress is uniform, its events interesting and well combined, and the conclusion grand, tragical, and affecting. Warburton, writing in his notes to Pope's *Imitations of Horace*, said : " . . . We have been lately entertained with what I venture to call, a Masterpiece, in the Fable ; . . . The piece I mean, is, *The Castle of Otranto* . . . where a beautiful imagination, supported by strength of judgment, has enabled the author to go beyond his subject, and effect the full purpose of the Ancient Tragedy ; that is, to purge the passions by pity and terror, in colouring as great and harmonious as in any of the best dramatic writers."

While this dramatic conception was, in the hands of Walpole, an innovation in technique, the desire to arouse curiosity and suspense was another new feature of this novel. The basic principle of construction in *The Castle of Otranto* is ' suspense ', and Walpole creates suspense even in minor incidents and scenes, and employs various tricks to excite curiosity and heighten the tension of nerves :

> " What noise is that ? "
> " It is the wind ", said Matilda, " whistling through the battlements in the tower above. You have heard it a thousand times."

Matilda and Theodore are both startled by " a deep and hollow groan ". " They listened ; but perceived no further noise : they both concluded it the effect of pent-up vapours." This very technique was to become a fine art in the hands of Mrs. Radcliffe. Half-finished sentences are another device used by Walpole. When Frederic seeks the holy hermit in the Holy Land, he finds him dying ; but the actual death does not take place till the hermit has excited curiosity by the revelation of half a secret.

Written with a vigour, violent and abrupt in methods of treatment, the story moves briskly, with dialogue and action ; and it is for the dialogue that Walpole reserves his strength. He mentions in his preface to the first edition of the novel : " There is no bombast, no similes, flowers, digressions, or unnecessary descriptions. Everything tends directly to the catastrophe." The dramatic power of the story holds our attention from the opening sentences. Even the prejudiced Macaulay said : " The story . . . never flags for a single moment. . . . There are no digressions, or unseasonable descriptions, or long speeches. Every sentence carries the action forward. . . . The excitement is constantly renewed. . . . No reader probably ever thought the book dull." He goes on to add : " He keeps the mind of the reader constantly attentive, and constantly entertained. He had strange ingenuity peculiarly his own." The language is simple, nervous, and appropriate to the several characters. George Hardinge, writing to John Nichols on 22 June 1813, said " *The Castle of Otranto* is a model of its kind ; and there is a wonderful grace in the language, which is neither too familiar nor too elevated. It seems inseparable from the characters, the scenery, and the incidents."

Although there are none of the luxuriant, florid, and highly varnished landscape paintings with which Mrs. Radcliffe often adorned her romances, yet there are in *Otranto* certain astonishing pictorial effects that were exclusive to Walpole. One brief and sublime description is of the moonlight vision of Alfonso dilated to immense magnitude, with the astonished group of spectators in the front, and behind them shattered ruins of the castle. Miss Dorothy Scarborough has asserted that " the genealogical founder of the family of Gothic ghosts is the giant apparition in *The Castle of Otranto* ". Walpole's canvas resembles the manner of El Greco where in a sombre, arid landscape, hung with thunderclouds, emaciated figures flicker with unearthly emotion while a streak of pallid lightning adds a mysterious terror to the scene.

Walpole reflects the passions and the sins and miseries of human souls in the magic glass of *Otranto*, and sets out to offer a combination of the supernatural agency with human interest. He makes use of the supernatural not merely as an instrument of terror, but also as a means to create a medieval atmosphere. The novel is set in Italy, at some vague period between 1095 and 1243 during the period of the crusades. Walpole used the Castle of Otranto as Victor Hugo used Notre Dame. Giving a medieval flavour to the whole, it was more than a setting for his story. Walpole attempted to paint a picture of domestic life and manners such as might actually have existed during feudal times, and by bringing in the supernatural machinery he hinted at the superstitions of the olden times. Therefore the natural parts of the narrative are blended with marvellous occurrences. Surprise and fear founded on supernatural events are harmoniously adjusted to the main spring of interest in the central plot. The bold assertion of the actual existence of phantoms and apparitions seems to harmonize naturally with manners of the Middle Ages, and casts a powerful spell upon the reader's mind.

The desire to be true to medieval costume contributes in part to the atmosphere of the period which Walpole very successfully creates in the description of Lord Frederic, his Knights, and their train entering the castle. This picture evokes a realistic impression of those olden times : the bell tolls at the postern gate ; the brazen trumpet sounds when the Cavalcade arrives at the castle ; a herald conveys to Manfred the wishes of his lord, and in failure of compliance delivers his master's challenge to a single combat by throwing down his warder ; there are references to the laws of arms, of hospitality, and chivalry ; Matilda waits on her mother on the ramparts of the castle in the cool of the evening. All these and other details are a true reflection of bygone ages.

One need not be surprised when the Surrealists claim *The Castle of Otranto* as an example of their school, for it is a claim they can justifiably make. Professor Dobrée has pointed out that " Horace Walpole was a sensitive, and perhaps the first surrealist, writer ". It is a pity that the bibliophile genius of Montague Summers, a keen admirer and collector of Gothic novels, failed to perceive the surrealistic element in the first Gothic tale. In the beautifully written last chapter of his monumental work, *The Gothic Quest*, he remarks : " The connexion which the Surrealists are anxious to trace between their own paths and principles and the ideals and inspiration of the Gothic novelists . . . to me appears to have no existence. . . . Such arguments as are adduced . . . seem to be based upon misapprehensions . . . are far-fetched and fantastical." But when we consider the romantic principles of surrealist art, as evident in *The Castle of Otranto*, the part played by ' unconscious ' and ' automatic writing ' in this goblin tale, and the methods employed by Walpole, the claim of the surrealists is finally established. It is interesting and fruitful therefore to compare the effect of this novel with some of the paintings of the Surrealistic School, and attempt an analysis of the impulses that led Walpole to such a fantastic creation.

Let us first determine what exactly is implied by Surrealism, what are its methods and aims, and where lie hidden the qualities, values and inspiration of this " conscious and deliberate artistic principle ". Herbert Read has defined Surrealism as " a reaffirmation of the romantic principle —a process like that of life, of creation, of liberation ". To use a grandi-loquent phrase to describe the general aim of Surrealism, we may call it " The Renascence of Wonder ". A surrealist painter " turns all his perceptive faculties inwards, to the realm of his subjective fancies, his day dreams, his pre-conscious images. He replaces observation by intuition, analysis by synthesis, reality by super-reality." The dream and the reality resolve therefore into a reality absolute, a surreality. Arnold

Hauser describes it thus : " The dream becomes the paradigm of the whole-world picture, in which reality and unreality, logic and fantasy, banality and sublimation of existence, form an indissoluble and inexplicable unity."

The ' surréaliste ' finds his best inspiration in " psychic automatism " and in " the mystery of the subconscious ". The first of these is directed towards expressing the true processes of thought, and the latter translates objects into strange, horrible, or sentimental forms. So the main doctrine of this school expresses a belief in the higher reality of certain forms of association : in the omnipotence of dreams, and in the detached play of thought. It believes that these hidden springs of the ' unconscious ' can be tapped if imagination is given free rein, and if thought is allowed to be automatic ; and a new truth, and a new art, will arise from the chaos of the ' unconscious ' and the irrational. And thereby, plunging into the unconscious, what Breton calls " a vertiginous descent into ourselves " into the whole force of the mental personality, the Surrealists take over the psycho-analytical method of free-association, that is, the automatic development of ideas and their reproduction without any rational, moral, or aesthetic censorship. The repressed content of the ' unconscious ' mingles freely with the more conscious images and a new art form results.

There was a constant conflict between the ' personality ' and ' character ' of Walpole, and if we begin to psychoanalyse Walpole's personality we may suspect that he had suppressed his impulses in the process of building up character. But his repressed self broke loose that fateful night in 1764 when he had a dream that gave birth to *The Castle of Otranto*. The part played by ' unconscious ' and the " automatism of creative activity," which André Breton has always made the criterion of a surrealist attitude in art, is apparent in the formation of the first Gothic novel. The story sprang from a dream. The writing was guided by impulse into which the subconscious partly intruded. " The production of such a work (*The Castle of Otranto*) . . . approaches, indeed, nothing less than the surrealist method . . . highly significant in their cumulative effect, must be put to the credit of *dreams* and of the employment of *automatic writing*."

We have already noted that the Castle is a picture of Trinity College, Cambridge. Walpole had paid a visit to Cambridge in 1763 (a year before he wrote *The Castle of Otranto*) and saw Trinity, St. John's, and Queen's. He had probably forgotten how closely this short visit preceded the writing of his romance. Walpole probably found his courtyard at Trinity College, since Trinity's main court was the only one to possess towers and gates, as well as chapel and hall. " Otranto's hall corresponds more closely to a Cambridge hall than to any room at Strawberry."

So during those hours of feverish creation Walpole unconsciously utilized a number of experiences, incidents, and impressions, buried in his unconscious memory. Pacing the silent and deserted chambers at Strawberry, and walking along its lonely galleries in summer dusks or winter eves with a candle in hand, he probably yielded to strange imaginings ; ghosts, " magic shapes and visions airy ", haunted him, and the eyes in the portrait of Lord Falkland cast a curious spell. The waking thoughts merged into dream visions and became a collection of sensory images and visual scenes. *The Castle of Otranto* has been called by Doughty " a vision or dream projected into real life "—really, it was an expression of Walpole's hidden dreams.

In 1721 was published *The Secret History of Pythagoras*. Part II. Translated from the original copy lately found at Otranto in Italy. By J. W. M. D. Its second edition came out in 1751. Walpole stated that " it was not till the story was finished that he looked up in the map of the kingdom of Naples for a well-sounding name and that Otranto was sonorous ". But there is a remarkable similarity between the manuscript device and the title of Walpole's tale, and it may be possible that Walpole had read the work. Miss Alice M. Killen, in her dissertation on *Le Roman Terrifiant ou Roman Noir* (1915), page 15, note ii, has pointed out the similarity between the Manfred of history and the Manfred of the first Gothic novel. The points of resemblance have been adroitly summarized in the admirable edition of the work by Oswald Doughty. It appears therefore that Walpole's past studies and scholarly interests had worked their way through the ' unconscious '.

As regards the " automatism of creative activity ", a point so much emphasized by the Surrealists, one finds that Walpole had plunged into the writing of his novel without premeditation ; it is a sample of " un-premeditated art " ; and he was always rather proud of the artless manner in which he had gone about his composition. In his letter to Cole on 9 March 1765 he mentions : " I began to write without knowing in the least what I intended to say or relate." One summer morn found him moved by the memory of a vivid dream ; during the day its influence was strong upon him, and with the deepening hours of twilight he took up his quill and started scribbling. Solitary in his castle, he sat night after night, scribbling and sipping coffee, wandering farther and farther into a fantastic and visionary world, escaping from the bitterness of grim realities. The summer nights one after another mingled with the dawn and Walpole, utterly fatigued and exhausted, sometimes with the last sentence incomplete, broke away and flung himself upon his bed. On the eighth night he laid down his quill. Now, if this was not " automatic writing " what else could it be ?

It has always been the function of art to stretch the mind beyond the limits of understanding. Herbert Read says in *The Meaning of Art* that " distance beyond may be spiritual, or transcendental, or perhaps, merely fantastical ". *The Castle of Otranto* belongs to the third category. Art in its wider sense is an extension of the personality ; while a personality without contradictions is incapable of creating a work of art. " The contradictions of the personality are resolved in the work of art," says Herbert Read, " that is one of the first principles of Surrealism." It is needless to point out here the inherent contradictions in the personality of Walpole. These have been admirably indicated by Lytton Strachey and Virginia Woolf.

Walpole's own method employed in his Gothic story is truly sur-realistic. His manner of ' telescoping ' different ages, settings, and characters, his strong manipulation of " the sense of contrast ", his use of dialogue and style, his story as it unfolds swiftly giving a nightmarish sensation : all these are methods of surrealism in particular. The scenes change with a dramatic swiftness, the incidents evoke a nightmarish sensation, and the whole story has a very dream-like insequence. The tale had its origin in the fantasy of an exhausted and repressed brain, and we do not fail to find the " unearthly impulse " of the original dream lingering in the narrative. The atmosphere of *The Castle of Otranto* is stamped by unreason and exaggeration of its events, and one does not fail to observe the nightmare juxtaposition of unrelated objects. The story sums up all the fantastic possibilities inherent in ' Surrealism ' : the fatal descent of the vast and *gigantic* black plumed helmet on the *little* prince has, besides its sensation of contrast, a sinister significance ; the portrait that walks sighing from the frame and vanishes into an upper chamber ; the statue that bleeds ; a skeleton wrapped in hermit's cowl ; the gigantic armour-clad foot in the gallery and the gigantic hand on the banister ; the immense Brobdingnagian sword carried by one hundred gentlemen with difficulty ; the nodding and waving plumes of the giant helmet ; the narrative unfolding a tale of unexpected paternities and dreadful injustices ; and, finally, Alfonso's enormous spectre bursting the Castle of Otranto asunder. It is all absurd and nonsensical and oddly exciting to read ; it evokes the same sensations as might the paintings of a Picasso, a Chirico, or a Chagall. It might also be likened to one of the early Flemish paintings depicting the burial of Christ, wherein the anguished grimaces of the emaciated creatures, their stiff, ungainly gestures seem to add a greater horror and poignancy to the scene.

The first ' surrealistic ' method that we observe in Walpole's technique is the method of ' telescoping '. He attempts to ' telescope ' age and characters. He wrote in the preface to the second edition of *The Castle of Otranto* that his aim was " to blend two kinds of romance, the ancient and the modern ". It is a telescoping of " the imagination and improbability " of the former with " the rules of probability " in the latter. He said that he wanted to make his characters think, speak, and act as they would do in extraordinary circumstances. He introduced the supernatural in contrast to the natural, represented real personages in unusual, unreal circumstances, and tried to picture realistically human nature and its reactions in different settings and environments. This is the grotesque method of which Chagall is a master.

The contemporary figures are placed in medieval settings. As the heroine or the hero move about the medieval scene, the castles and moats, vaults, turrets and galleries appear strange and awful to them. Walpole's Isabella is no more born to the medieval scene than are Pamela or Evelina. Uprooted from her proper society with contemporary emotional and intellectual pattern intact, thrust into a barbarous and primitive age, subjected to the various menaces of the Dark Ages, she serves as a projection of the nervous system of her own time, as a sensitive barometer of emotional reaction to horrors, and clearly, as transmitter of the thrills of their exposure. The effect thus is of a thing taken away from its own particular setting, an impression of " the grotesque " that justifies comparison with the paintings of Chirico.

The surrealist painters base their colours on the principle of contrast. The same sinister tones and overtones, a display of light and shade, effects of sound and silence, we find in *The Castle of Otranto*. There are contrasting situations and incidents displaying pitch-black darkness on the one hand, intermitted by thunder and lightning ; gloomy recesses and dark dungeons contrastingly presented to a gleam of moonshine or the ray of a flickering lamp. There are, besides the sublimity of description and moonlit effects, contrast presented in the theme itself : the emotion of 'fear' balanced against that of 'love'.

The third method in 'Surrealism' is a queer combination of the 'trivial' and the 'mighty', a mixture of the 'big' and 'small'. The 'gigantic' helmet descending on a 'little' prince, the gigantic hand in armour and the giant's foot, the spectre of the dilated Alfonso cracking the walls of the castle, a large portrait inspiring observers with fear, are some of the tricks used by Walpole. The statue bleeds, and the figure in the portrait walks away, and Walpole masters both the active and inactive agents of terror : the villain and the castle.

The Castle of Otranto is particularly surrealist in its dialogue, and the juxtaposition of the language and sentiments, of the *beau monde* with Gothic violence. Commenting on Walpole's strange combination of words and far-fetched allusions Macaulay said : " He coins new words, distorts the sense of old words, and twists sentences into forms which make grammarians stare. . . . His wit was, in its essential properties, of the same kind with that of Cowley and Donne. Like this, it consisted in an exquisite perception of points of analogy, and points of contrast too subtile for common observation. Like them, Walpole perpetually startles us by the ease with which he yokes together ideas between which there would seem at first sight to be no connection."

Few writers can have fluctuated more in critical extreme than the author of the first Gothic novel. Wilmarth Lewis finds that " time and patience are required to understand Horace Walpole ". To his own times, which knew nothing of his letter-writing, he was a brilliant historian and essayist. Byron, during the nineteenth century, stated that Walpole was a greater writer than any man living " be he who he may ". To Croker and Lord Liverpool, he was the most evil man that had ever lived, for Walpole had poisoned history at its source. Carlyle saw him as a light shining in darkness ; to Macaulay he was *pâté de foie gras* produced by an effete society. The latter pictured Walpole as a gossipy little dilettante, cold-blooded and sneering, whose mind was " a bundle of whims and affectations ", and whose features " were covered by mask within mask ". He went so far as to remark that the works of Walpole were " literary luxuries ", a product of " an unhealthy and disorganised mind ". To Macaulay, Walpole's works are " destitute of every charm ", which only can amuse without exciting. " He never convinces the reason, nor fills the imagination, nor touches the heart." Isaac D'Israeli in 1812 saw in Walpole " fancy and ingenuity ", and a " recourse to the *marvellous* in imagination ". He continues to say that " *The Castle of Otranto* and *The Mysterious Mother* are the productions of ingenuity rather than genius ; and display the miracles of Art rather than the spontaneous creations of Nature ". To Hazlitt, as far back as 1819, *The Castle of Otranto* appeared " dry, meagre, and without effect . . . done upon the false principles of taste ", shocking the senses and " having no purchase upon the imagination ".

The twin currents of ridicule and eulogy continue to flow down to the twentieth century. To C. S. Fearnside " Walpole lacks imagination ; his characters are wooden in motive and in action ". To Oswald Doughty " aesthetically *The Castle of Otranto* is a failure. . . . His (Walpole's) imagination was not sufficiently clear and intense for artistic creation. . . . Walpole tried but failed to re-create the enchanted castle of his subconscious dream world." To Alice M. Killen " he (Walpole) has carried his wonders too far, until they are almost ridiculous ". Walpole had, according to Miss Killen, no mastery over the half-shades that heighten the mysterious and the unknown ; rather he leads his readers rapidly from horror to horror, wonder to wonder, and does not prepare them, by thrills cunningly regulated, to receive the finishing stroke of super-stitious terror. But " it is a strange sort of niggardliness ", says the *Gentleman's Magazine*, " which denies the praise of genius to *The Castle of Otranto*. It exhibits picturesque fancy, invention and even . . . pathos." Mrs. Elizabeth Carter thought it " a great pity that Horace Walpole ever wrote anything but *The Castle of Otranto* ". And it is enough that in our own century we have had the praises of George Saintsbury, Lytton Strachey, and Bonamy Dobrée.

Although " Horace Walpole has been the object of hatred, adulation, condescension, and respect," there is no doubting the statement made in the Dedicatory Epistle to *Ivanhoe* by Sir Walter Scott that " Horace Walpole wrote a goblin tale which has thrilled through many a bosom ". As Stephen Gwynn remarked : " The book is a literary curiosity " ; and as Melville observed : " With *The Castle of Otranto*, Walpole struck an unexplored vein of romance." It is " literally an epoch-making book ", said Montague Summers, " in fine, a notable landmark in the history of English taste and English literature ".

Yet, does he require the patronage of these eulogies ? He needs " no more such laurels " but " shall be quite content with a sprig of rosemary thrown after him ". In 1773 he wrote to Madame du Deffand : " My dreams will never again give me a castle of Otranto. It is a sad thing to exchange dreams for accounts." And will it not be too harsh to bring his ' dreams' to ' accounts', and weigh his " midsummer fantasy " on " the balance of criticism " ? But there is no doubting one fact : that the tale had vast potentialities ; the seed sown by Walpole did flower and bear fruit, and then ran to seed again. *The Castle of Otranto* continues till today a towering achievement of art and beauty exciting curiosity and admiration.

CHAPTER IV

HISTORICAL-GOTHIC SCHOOL : THE HEIRS OF
'OTRANTO'

THE first offshoot from *The Castle of Otranto* is the Historical-Gothic school where, in an atmosphere of supernatural terror, is portrayed a distinct panorama of history or chivalry. Such works depict events and personages of a particular historical period presenting its manners and customs through fictitious characters, or they introduce local colour of the Middle Ages, diffusing over all an air of mystery and superstitious dread. Montague Summers states, in *The Gothic Quest* : " The Historical Novel—of a kind—flourished from the reign of Charles II until the beginning of the eighteenth century," and was most vigorously manifest during its Gothic phase when it was decked out in magnified splendour borrowed from the historical legends of the times. The glamour, the picturesqueness of past ages pervade the sensibility of this first branch of Gothic root.

Mrs. Barbauld objected to this mode of fiction which, according to her, obscured the steady and strong light of history with artificial colours and paraded with false pageantry the men and events of remote periods. She mentioned " a romance of which Edward the Black Prince is the hero, by Clara Reeve," where, " the manners of his court are drawn with such splendid colouring of heroic virtue, as certainly neither that court, nor any other deserved ". Commenting upon Sophia Lee's *The Recess*, she said that Historical-Gothic treatment has created " a prejudice against the character of our Elizabeth, arising from her cruelty to two imaginary daughters of Mary, Queen of Scots, who never existed but in the pages of a novel ". But such a method of weaving fictitious circumstances into the texture of history is not altogether deplorable for it makes the historical figures linger in the memory with all the vividness of dramatic characters.

The Castle of Otranto has a typically medieval scene where Frederic, Duke of Vicenza, arrives with his train of a hundred knights. Miss Reeve, in *The Old English Baron*, presents a more definite picture of feudalism : besides the historical colouring of Henry VI's times, there is a spectacular scene of medieval challenge of which the details are carefully

74

adjusted to historical usage. Even as late as 1826, in *Gaston de Blondeville*, Mrs. Radcliffe displays a rich profusion of historical chivalric pageantry with all its medieval costume and tournament and paintings on the tapestry of the castle hall. The arrival of King Henry's noble train at Kenilworth is accompanied with much pomp and splendour. But the work which can fairly claim to be the first specimen of Historical-Gothic romance distinct from *The Castle of Otranto* is *Longsword, Earl of Salisbury*, " An Historical Romance " in two volumes (1762), published anonymously, but written by Thomas Leland (1722–85), a Fellow of Trinity College, Dublin, who was a classical scholar and an erudite historian.

The scene of this novel is laid in the reign of Henry III. William, Earl of Salisbury, the famous ' Longsword ' of history, son of Henry II and the fair Rosamond, returns from adventures in France. He brings with him the daughter of an old friend whom he has rescued from robbers. Disguised as a Canterbury pilgrim, he lands on the Cornish coast just where his dearest friend Randolph is strolling, to whom he forthwith recounts his adventures during his long absence from England : shipwreck, imprisonment, attacks by robbers, treachery, attempted murder by an enemy, refuge with a friendly abbot, and eventually his escape. In an equally tedious fashion Sir Randolph tells the earl how Longsword has lost his wife, his son, and his lands and castle to his enemy Hubert de Burgh. The latter is an actual historical personage who in history defeated the French fleet under Eustace the Monk and had ruled England with an iron hand during Henry's minority. Longsword seeks shelter with his friend while the narrative unfolds the trials and sorrows of Ella, Countess Salisbury, who is the typical Gothic heroine— a personification of sensibility, grief, and tears. Subsequent events introduce Henry III, and the story moves with all complexities of plot until poetic justice is established and Longsword is reunited with his faithful wife and son.

Although crude in many respects, sometimes awkward and ill-jointed, this romance for the first time combines a real atmosphere of antiquity and authentic detail. It contains practically every ingredient of Historical-Gothic romance except supernatural machinery.

Fifteen years after *Longsword*, Clara Reeve attempted a synthesis of Leland's medievalism and Walpole's supernatural machinery in *The Champion of Virtue : a Gothic Story* (1777), which was republished in the following year as *The Old English Baron*. " This story is of a species which, though not new, is out of the common track." The setting is Lovel Castle in the reigns of Henry V and VI ; and the manners are supposed to indicate chivalrous times. The plot is simple and well connected : it turns upon the discovery of a murder and the consequent restoration of an heir to his title and estate. Sir Philip Harclay, returning to England after thirty years' absence abroad in French and Mohammedan wars, finds his own family extinct and himself a stranger in the castle of his dearest friend, now long dead. He is warned by the ghost of this friend in a dream that it rests with him to restore the hopes of the latter's house. In this dream he accompanies the apparition to his castle, hears dismal groans, and seems to sink down into a dark and frightful cave where he beholds the bloody armour of his friend. The scene then changes to a wild heath where preparations are being made for a combat. Next he is transported to his own house where he meets his friend "living, and in all the bloom of youth, as when he first knew him ".

This dream is fully verified by the sequel. Sir Philip's friend had been basely murdered by his next of kin, and buried in a chest under the floor of a closet in the Eastern apartment. His wife, terrified by the murderer into quitting the castle, was given out for dead, and a false funeral held. She died unrecognized in the fields near the castle, leaving a new-born child who was brought up as Edmund Twyford, the son of the peasants who found him and buried his mother's body. "It was reported that the castle was haunted, and that the ghosts of Lord and Lady Lovel had been seen by several of the servants. Whoever went into this apartment were terrified by uncommon noises, and strange appearances ; at length this apartment was wholly shut up, and the servants were forbid to enter it." Being haunted every night, the murderer at last sold the castle to his brother-in-law, the Lord Fitz-Owen, and left the country. The latter, the good lord of the story, attracted by the virtues and graces of young Edmund, brought him up with his own sons. Circumstances so shape that this youth is obliged to sleep for two nights in the Eastern wing, to testify to all whether it be haunted or not.

In the ghost-ridden suite is still preserved an old suit of armour, its breastplate stained with blood. As Edmund explores the chamber he finds the furniture decayed and falling to pieces, the fabrics moth-eaten ; the portraits of the rightful owners turned towards the wall, and the whole atmosphere a mournful reminder of the past. Suddenly Edmund's lamp is blown out, leaving him in utter darkness, and he listens to a hollow rustling noise as the door claps with a great violence, which is ascribed to the advent of Joseph, his old faithful friend.

The same night he dreams that steps ascend the staircase, the door opens, and a warrior in full armour enters, leading a beautiful but pale and wan lady. They approach the bed, declare him their son, and, clasping hands solemnly, bless him. The next night, as old Joseph and father Oswald are relating to Edmund all they know of the late Lord and Lady, not forgetting to mention Edmund's resemblance to the former, all three are startled by a violent noise in the rooms and underneath them like a clashing of arms and something falling with violence. Together they descend, and find a closet the door of which miraculously yields to Edmund alone. Joseph identifies the bloodstained suit of armour which belonged to the late Lord Lovel. Edmund, having interviewed the peasants and obtained certain proof of his lineage from the crested ornaments found with him, speedily departs and takes refuge with Sir Philip. The latter challenges the wicked lord, defeats him, extorts a confession, and then takes the necessary steps to reinstate Edmund. As Edmund arrives at his ancestral castle, the gates open by themselves accompanied by a sudden rising gust of wind, to receive the lawful master. The story ends in the triumph of virtue and in the righting of injured innocence and punishment of wrong : the defeated murderer is given a choice between banishment and the monastery ; the bones of Edmund's parents are interred with pomp, and he receives Emma as his bride.

The Old English Baron was written in prudish objection to the free use of the supernatural in *The Castle of Otranto*. Miss Reeve accepted Walpole's idea of the new type of prose fiction, but set out to correct his excesses. Her criticism of *The Castle of Otranto* was that with all its brilliant advantages " it palls upon the mind . . . and the reason is obvious, the machinery is so violent, that it destroys the effect it is intended to excite ". In the use of the marvellous she attempted to improve upon Walpole by reducing it to a minimum and keeping her ghost " within the utmost verge of probability ". Confined to a cupboard, his groans lead to the discovery of his skeleton and his murder. The *Gentleman's Magazine* (1778) noted with approval that " the author has endeavoured to preserve the effect . . . to avoid . . . the only fault in *Otranto*, viz., ' such a degree of the marvellous as excites laughter ' ".

Admitting that *The Old English Baron* " is the literary offspring of *The Castle of Otranto*," Miss Reeve gave her conception of the qualities

required in a novel which should unite the merits of the ancient Romance
and the modern Novel : " To attain this end, there is required a sufficient
degree of the marvellous to excite the attention ; enough of the manners
of real life, to give an air of probability to the work ; and enough of the
pathetic, to engage the heart in its behalf." Whereas Walpole sought
to combine fanciful events and natural characters, Miss Reeve requisitions
a touch of the marvellous merely to interest the reader. According to
Miss Reeve " the business of Romance is, first, to excite the attention ;
and secondly, to direct it to some useful, or at least innocent, end ".
She felt that the usual novel of manners was much too commonplace to
hold the attention, but she would not mind borrowing from it an air of
probability. She does not, like Coleridge, try to make the supernatural
natural, rather she aims in the spirit of her age to make it credible, with
added sentiment for an immediate appeal to the emotions ; thus seeking
to blend into one composite whole three different types of prose fiction :
the medieval romance, the novel of manners, and the sentimental
novel.

Walpole, as might be expected, was particularly severe in criticizing
The Old English Baron. In his letter to Jephson he declared : " I cannot
compliment . . . *The Old English Baron.* . . . It was totally void of imagination and interest ; had scarce any incidents ; and though it condemned
the marvellous, admitted a ghost. I suppose the author thought a tame
ghost might come within the laws of probability." Elsewhere he
deplored the " professed imitation of mine, only stripped of the marvellous, and so entirely stripped, except in one awkward attempt at a
ghost or two, that it is the most insipid dull-nothing you ever saw ".
And in another letter he indignantly exclaimed : " Have you seen *The
Old Baron : a Gothic story*, professedly written in imitation of Otranto,
but reduced to reason and probability ! It is so probable, that any trial
for murder at the Old Bailey would make a more interesting story."
Mrs. Barbauld's objections, if less vehement, were deprecatory ; she
found *The Old English Baron* " a novel of but a moderate degree of
merit ", in which " the chief fault . . . is, that we foresee the conclusion
before we have read twenty pages ". Montague Summers, who condones
the crudities and violent machinery in *The Castle of Otranto* because of
its glamour of medieval remoteness, condemns *The Old English Baron* as
a " dull and didactic narrative told in a style of chilling mediocrity ".
He unhesitatingly designates virtuous Edmund the hero " an unconscion-
able bore. The fair lady Emma ' with tears on her cheek, sweetly blushing,

like the damask rose, wet with the dew of the morning ', . . . a worthy
partner to this prig."

Yet, as so often happens, the public confounded the critics, and this
romance was so well received that thirteen editions appeared between
1778 and 1786. Readers still enjoyed fare that was diluted with reason
and sweetened with morality. To an audience which had not yet
relinquished eighteenth-century rationalism and was gradually becoming
attracted by Gothic charms, the furtive supernatural machinery of *The
Old English Baron* was less shocking than the bold enchantments of *The
Castle of Otranto*.

Clara Reeve was a disciple of Richardson, and a friend of his daughter,
to whom she dedicated this novel. She transplants Sir Charles Grandison
into the Middle Ages, and introduces the sentimental morality of middle-
class fiction against which Walpole had reacted. Despite adverse
criticisms, it may be said that Miss Reeve narrates a good story in which
the mystery is skilfully sustained. Her plot is neither rapid nor exhilarat-
ing, but it never actually stagnates. Apart from its thrill of terror, on the
whole its original title, *The Champion of Virtue*, sums up its true elements.
Miss Reeve's name is now more than partially forgotten, perhaps wholly
obscured by her far greater successor Ann Radcliffe. The timid compromise of the credible and marvellous may have robbed the story of its
wonders, yet Miss Reeve's use of the supernatural and romantic terror
paved the way for Mrs. Radcliffe.

Miss Reeve adopted Walpole's basic idea of a story conducted to its
climax by means of an agent of terror, but she invested the Gothic ghost
with superstitious legends familiar to every village rustic and confined
him to an Eastern apartment. Her ghost comes from the same family
as that in *Otranto* ; it is still a messenger of fate, and also a deeply interested
spectator of the progress of events, waiting for destiny to be accomplished
and sustaining an undiminished atmosphere of terror. Since Clara
Reeve's time no Gothic castle is complete without its " deserted wing ".
She also introduces presaging dreams, groans, clanking chains, and such
other Gothic machinery as she thinks comes within the range of probability. The rusty locks and the suddenly extinguished lamp may be a
heritage from Walpole, but the use of a " hollow rustling noise " and the
glimmering light, naturally explained later by the approach of a servant,
anticipates the methods of Mrs. Radcliffe.

Mrs. Radcliffe was especially indebted to the formative techniques of
Miss Reeve in producing genteel shudderings. The method and details

of a particular description in *The Old English Baron* may have given hints for Ludovico's vigil in *The Mysteries of Udolpho*. When Edmund in the haunted wing takes a survey of his chamber,

> the furniture, by long neglect, was decayed and dropping to pieces ; the bed was devoured by the moths, and occupied by the rats who had built their nests there with impunity for many generations. The bedding was very damp, for the rain had forced its way through the ceiling . . . he heard a hollow rustling noise. . . .

But the person coming through the narrow passage is Joseph with a bundle of faggots. Mrs. Radcliffe's methods are definitely forecast by certain passages :

> A second groan increased . . . all doors flew open, a pale glimmering light appeared at the door, from the staircase, and a man in complete armour entered the room.

Miss Reeve introduces another Gothic motif of identifying the hero : " a fine necklace with a golden locket and a pair of ear-rings," by which Edmund is discovered to be the heir of Lovel Castle. The mention of an old pilgrim who taught Edmund to read, recalls the later ' Gothic ' character of the Wandering Jew. In the hands of Miss Reeve, the noble peasant type of hero acquires definite traits :

> Edmund was modest, yet intrepid ; gentle and courteous to all, frank and unreserved to those that loved him ; discreet and complaisant to those who hated him ; generous and compassionate to the distresses of his fellow-creatures in general ; humble, but not servile, to his patrons and superiors.

Moreover, her commonplace simple details, easy and natural dialogue add a flavour of reality which was another gift to Gothic romance.

It is a matter worthy of note that the author of *The Old English Baron* is the first Gothic novelist to make use of dreams, that realm of mysterious subconsciousness which flows eternally like some dark underground river beneath the surface of human life. In Miss Reeve's work Sir Philip Harclay's dream about his friend the late Lord Lovel, or the dream of Edmund in which he sees his deceased parents, are definitely geared to the movement of the plot. With Ann Radcliffe, and almost all the succeeding Gothic novelists, dreams occupy an important place. Impending misfortunes, hidden indefinite crimes, are often revealed by dreadful nightmares and gloomy dreams. Small wonder therefore that modern Surrealists have found much congenial material in the Gothic novels.

Miss Reeve wrote two other historical novels : *The Exiles; or Memories of Count de Cronstadt* (1788) which has a German setting ; and her last work, *Memoirs of Sir Roger de Clarendon, natural son of Edward the Black Prince ; with Anecdotes of the times* (1793), which shows her sound scholarship in scenes and ceremonies and usages of the splendid reign of Edward III.

Another important work of this school is Miss Sophia Lee's *The Recess, or A Tale of Other Times* (1783–86). The title of this romance derives from a subterranean retreat within an abbey of Gothic magnificence in which the heroines are reared. Their secret chambers are reached through sliding panels and trap-doors leading to a subterranean passage. The author employs the old device of writing from an antique manuscript. She does not admit that she is writing an historical romance, but merely declares in the preface that she is modernizing history. *The Recess* is a collection of adventures astonishing and terrible and hence popular. It is not well written as regards either language or construction, being one monumental communication addressed to a certain Adelaide Mary de Montmorenci whom we never meet. Justly this work was criticized as " too uniformly gloomy " and as rendered tedious by the " long interpolated narratives ".

In *The Recess* Miss Lee was much indebted to Walpole, Reeve, and Baculard D'Arnaud. " Her work . . . constitutes a link between Prévost and Mrs. Radcliffe," says Ernest Bernbaum in *Modern Language Notes*, XLIII. Harriet Lee, in her Preface to the *Canterbury Tales*, observed that " *Cleveland*, written as I believe, by the Abbé Prévost, [is] the first novel of the type Sophia Lee chose to write ". Indeed, the substance and manner of *Cleveland* has been reproduced unchanged in *The Recess*. *Cleveland* narrates the misfortunes of Bridge and Cleveland persecuted by their father Cromwell. Having been reared in a cave, they sail to America and St. Helena, where they suffer strange vicissitudes of fortune. The chief incidents of the story include Cleveland's love for Fanny Axminster, and her abduction by Gelin. The plot of *The Recess* is parallel to *Cleveland* in recounting the misfortunes of Eleonora and Matilda, daughters of Mary, Queen of Scots. They are persecuted by Queen Elizabeth and courted by Essex and Leicester. Thus Elizabeth here takes the role of Cromwell in *Cleveland*. Williams, who attempts to abduct Eleonora, is Gelin, and the cave where the sisters are reared is

Rumney-hole. Queen Elizabeth, Lord Burleigh, the Earls of Essex, Leicester, and Southampton, Sir Philip Sidney, and other historical personages figure in the story. " It is hardly an exaggeration to say that in *The Recess* the personages for the most part act according to history." Harriet Lee noted that *The Recess* was " the first English romance that blended interesting fiction with historical events and characters, embellishing both by picturesque description ". Its use of supernatural machinery is confined to the presentation of an actual ghost in a dream, though on another occasion one of the persecuted heroines appears at the bedside of Queen Elizabeth who takes her to be an avenging spectre. Miss Lee's heightening of terror and anguish for artistic purposes had a marked influence on Historical-Gothic Romance. *The Recess* perhaps gave Walter Scott hints for *Kenilworth*.

Her translations of some of the stories of Arnaud appeared in the *Ladies' Magazine*. *Warbeck*, which she published in 1786, is a tale which resembles *Cleveland*, and is similar in tone and treatment to Leland's *Longsword, Earl of Salisbury*. In collaboration with her sister, Miss Harriet Lee, she wrote *The Canterbury Tales* (1797–1805), which contains twelve stories, out of which seven are related by travellers who find themselves snowbound in an inn at Canterbury, and beguile their stay by relating a story each. Five more stories were added later. There are definite ' gothic ' touches in these tales of which *Kruitzner* is a powerful piece.

Besides Clara Reeve and Sophia Lee, there were also a good number of minor writers who experimented in Historical-Gothic fiction. Between *Longsword* and *The Old English Baron* appeared an interesting work by William Hutchinson : *The Hermitage, A British Story* (1772), which shows an advance in medieval colouring in the description of Lord Albion's Castle with an unusual wealth of realistic detail. The author is guided by love of the past and the Middle Ages and makes a profuse introduction of the marvellous in the manner of *Otranto* ; he uses supernatural machinery in accompaniment with fierce lightnings and tremendous bursts of thunder, to punish the evil and succour the deserving.

Later, in 1787, Anne Fuller wrote *Alan Fitz-Osborne, an Historical Tale in 2 vols.*, a story greatly influenced by *Otranto*. It is dimly historical in its setting of the reign of Henry III with Alan the hero participating in the Barons' Wars. Meanwhile, his wife is murdered by an amorous villain, Walter Fitz-Osborne, who is then haunted by her pale and ghastly spectre. Her phantom stands by his bedside as the thunder crashes and she snatches from her wounded bosom a dagger gored in crimson from which gouts of blood fall upon the sheets. Miss Fuller also wrote *The Son of Ethelwolf, an Historical Tale* (1789).

The following works in the tradition of Historical-Gothic also deserve mention : James White's *Earl Strongbow ; or the History of Richard de Clare and the Beautiful Geralda* (1789) ; Agnes Musgrave's *Cicely ; or The Rose of Raby ; An Historical Novel* (1795), *Edmund of the Forest ; An Historical Novel* (1797), *William de Montfort, or The Sicilian Heiresses* (1808) ; and T. J. Horsley-Curties' *Ethelwina, or the House of Fitz Auburne* (1799), and *The Scottish Legend, or the Isle of St. Clothair* (1802).

The line of Historical-Gothic School finally culminated in Sir Walter Scott. He was a keen analyst of terror ; he perceived much in Gothicism that was highly useful, and constantly dressed up his historical novels with the romantic licence of Gothic sensationalism. Edith Birkhead points out that " the notes, introduction and appendices to Scott's works are stored with material for novels of terror ". In the general preface to *The Waverley Novels* he confessed he " had nourished the ambitious desire of composing a tale of chivalry which was to be in the style of *The Castle of Otranto*, with plenty of Border characters and supernatural incident ". In Walter Scott all that he admired in his Gothic predecessors is made more beautiful by truth. He projects the colouring of Gothic romance upon scenes of history, and although the terrors of the invisible world fill his canvas he creates romance out of the stuff of real life. The misty and unreal historical background of Gothic novels becomes arresting and substantial. Occasionally he alters specific historical fact to achieve narrative effects.

Walter Freye has attempted to show that Scott raised the Gothic novel from its decadence and made dry history live again in his tales. He traces Gothic elements in *Guy Mannering, Old Mortality, Montrose, The Monastery, The Abbot, The Betrothed*, and *Woodstock*. By quoting comparative passages he proves the influence of *The Monk* on *Marmion* and *The Vision of Don Roderick* ; and *The Mysteries of Udolpho* on *Rokeby* and *The Bride of Triermain*.

In *Guy Mannering* (1815) the prophecy and curse of Meg Merrilees, the ruin where she hides, and the strange fulfilment of Mannering's horoscope for young Ellangowan are peculiarly Gothic in effects. In *The Antiquary* (1816), when Lovel falls into an uneasy slumber in the Green Room at Monkbans, at midnight he is startled to find a green huntsman leaving the tapestry and turning into an old gentleman before his very eyes. In *Old Mortality* (1816), Edith Bellenden mistakes her lover for a ghost in purely Gothic manner. An atmosphere of horror and the sense of overhanging calamity prepare our minds for the super-natural in the opening of *The Bride of Lammermoor* (1819). In *Peveril of the Peak* (1823), Fenella communicates with the hero in prison, who mistakes her voice for that of an apparition. The incident has an air of Gothic mystery. Scott was an admirer of Mrs. Radcliffe's novels, and his *Woodstock* (1826) and *Anne of Geierstein* (1829) remind us of Mrs. Radcliffe in subject-matter and treatment.

Pure Historical Romances continued to be written during the Gothic epoch until the work of Scott eclipsed all previous attempts to such a degree that one is apt to forget his indebtedness to his predecessors. In a quick survey of the main landmarks of Historical-Gothic from *Longsword* to *Waverley*, a period of half a century, one may call attention only to important names and note an occasional milestone. There were other works which have historical settings but they are so dim and immaterial that they cannot be considered offspring of Gothic ancestry.

CHAPTER V

MRS. ANN RADCLIFFE : THE CRAFT OF TERROR

It is a curious coincidence of literary history that the stars that reigned in the year of the nativity of *The Castle of Otranto* (1764) saw the birth of Mrs. Ann Radcliffe (*née* Ward), in whose works we perceive the Gothic fiction approaching its meridian. Not much is known about her life, except that she was the wife of an Oxford graduate, and that she wrote her weird and mysterious tales beside a blazing fire in a quiet room to enliven her long, solitary winter evenings. Extraordinarily fascinating stories flowed from her pen which, with all their faults, unmistakably bear the stamp of genius. The name of this potent enchantress, who touched the secret springs of fear and extended the domain of romance, was felt as a spell by her admirers, and to this day her blood-curdling terrors freeze many a midnight reader.

Yet she was known only by her works. The *Edinburgh Review* (May 1823) declares : " She never appeared in public, nor mingled in private society, but kept herself apart, like the sweet bird that sings its solitary notes, shrouded and unseen." She spent a life in the quiet shade of domestic seclusion, unheeded amidst the bustle of the world, confining her activities to domestic duties and homely pleasures. " She was more than repaid by the enjoyments which were fostered in the shade ; and perhaps few distinguished authors have passed a life so blameless and so happy." It is curious that no biography of this celebrated lady has been written, nor any attempt made to draw aside the veil from the personal course of her peaceful existence. She probably attended Sophia Lee's school at Bath, and perhaps the only reference we get about her person is given by Charles Bucke in an interesting footnote to a curious work, *On the Beauties, Harmonies, and Sublimities of Nature*, stating that " her countenance indicated melancholy. She had been, doubtless, in her youth, beautiful." We are not yet made aware of any of those amusing foibles which usually chequer the lives of successful authors : " here are no brilliant conversational triumphs ; no elaborate correspondence with the celebrated, or the great ; no elegant malice ; no anecdotes of patrons or rivals ; none of fashion's idle pastime, nor of controversies, nor idle business ". The report, long current, that she was driven insane by her own ghostly creations is unfounded, but she certainly possessed to a high degree sensibility and sensitiveness of temperament, qualities she bequeathed to her exquisite heroines. " At the time *The Italian* appeared, probably no author was so generally admired and so eagerly read as this young woman," says Clara Frances McIntyre in *Ann Radcliffe in Relation to her Time*, but in the high period of her fame she chose to lay by her pen. Probably she was disgusted to see her mode of composition profaned by a host of servile imitators, who, unable to achieve her merits, rendered her defects more obvious.

It is perhaps not altogether wise to judge the greatness of an author by the pleasure he or she affords the readers, " but the invention of a story, the choice of proper incidents, the ordonnance of the plan, occasional beauties of description, and, above all, the power exercised over the reader's heart by filling it with the successive emotions of love, pity, joy, anguish, transport, or indignation, together with the grave, impressive moral resulting from the whole, imply talents of the highest order, and ought to be appreciated accordingly ", Mrs. Barbauld remarks, and the works of Mrs. Radcliffe reveal all these, together with a conscious craftsmanship and a structure of high quality, although, as Dr. J. M. S. Tompkins puts it in *The Popular Novel in England*, " they are the day-dreams of a mind at once fastidious and audacious, capable of energy and languor, responsive to beauty and to awe, and tremblingly sensitive to imaginative fear ". She awed and enraptured the public mind by hints of things unseen, by employing pure and innocent enchantments. She describes the various passions with a glowing pen, leads us through enchanting pastoral scenery, and by the charm of all her pages holds her readers spellbound until the end of the tale. It is therefore interesting to trace the development of her genius and assurgent powers from the pallid *Castles of Athlin and Dunbayne* (1789) to the rich and sombre colouring of *The Italian* (1797).

The Castles of Athlin and Dunbayne (1789) was inspired by Sophia Lee's *Recess* (1785), and is the Gothic-historical successor to *The Castle of Otranto* (1764). The story shows the unmistakable stamp of Clara Reeve's *The Old English Baron* (1777), having a " noble peasant ", a usurping villain and his victims, for chief characters ; but Mrs. Radcliffe introduces *two* heroes and *two* heroines both at the mercy of the villain. She retains the garrulous domestic servants of Walpole and Reeve, while the stock sensibility of the characters is just the same. The heroines are, once more, all blushes—a shade deeper than the Matilda, Isabella or

Emma of Radcliffe's predecessors—and more full of tender tremors, more softly timid.

This immature and interesting work is of no great length and may be regarded as an essay, a first step ; but, with the exception of the super-natural, it contains in embryo all notable elements of Mrs. Radcliffe's romances. The slight sketch of Baron Malcolm " mighty in injustice, cruel in power ", was to be the ancestor of fierce, picturesque characters like Montoni and Schedoni. We can also trace in this work some germs of that taste and talent for the wild, mysterious, and romantic which she was to employ with such powerful effect. Although it is a wild tale with improbable, strained, disconnected, and confused incidents, where incredible events follow each other in quick succession, yet there is in its atmosphere a feeling for nature, a power of imagery which anticipates finer things to come.

The *Monthly Review* (LXXXI—1789) failed to perceive the merit of the work and wrote :

> To those who are delighted with the *marvellous*, whom wonders and wonders only, can charm, the present production will accord a considerable degree of amusement. This kind of entertainment, however, can be little relished but by the young and unformed mind.

But descriptions like the following foreshadow her future achievements :

> . . . whose broken arches and lonely towers arose in gloomy grandeur through the obscurity of evening. It stood the solitary inhabitant of the wastes—a monument of mortality and ancient superstition, and the frowning majesty of its aspect seemed to command silence and veneration. The chilly dews fell thick. . . . The awful solitude of the place, and the solemn aspect of the fabric, whose effect was heightened by the falling gloom of evening, chilled her heart with horror.

There are also hints of her future technique of heightening curiosity :

> They perceived a faint light . . . paused awhile in silence . . . expectation to listen if anything was stirring. . . . All was involved in the gloom of night, and the silence of death prevailed.

The setting of this tale is " in the most romantic part of the High-lands of Scotland " during the dark ages, but there is no effort to describe either the manners or scenery of the country. However, the picture of the castle itself is striking. It is described as :

> built with Gothic magnificence, upon a high and dangerous rock. Its lofty towers still frowned in proud sublimity, and the immensity of the pile stood a record of the ancient consequence of its possessors.

The novelist does not name a specific period as the setting, but endeavours to maintain an atmosphere of feudalism and the Middle Ages, by constant references to fortified castle sieges, armed vassals, dank dungeons, and threats of arbitrary executions. In spite of the goodly number of old towers, dungeons, keeps, subterranean passages, and hairbreadth escapes, the story has little veracity ; and it appears as if the author had caught a glimpse of the regions of romance from afar, and formed a dreamy acquaintance with its recesses and glooms. The story lacks historical accuracy, but then most of the descriptions evolve not from original sources in ancient documents, but from the author's own imagination.

Her characters are made sensitive to the influence of scenery, as when the imprisoned Earl finds the view of distant hills a " source of ideal pleasure ". They dwell among picturesque landscapes bathed in faint moonlight and swept by tumultuous gusts of wind. A shipwreck occurs on the coast in the atmosphere of stormy blasts, broken clouds, white foam, and " deep resounding murmurs of distant surges " of which Mrs. Radcliffe was particularly fond. Nor do we miss the parting sun trembling on the tops of the mountain and the softer shades falling upon the distant countryside, or the sweet tranquillity of evening that throws an air of tender melancholy over the mind, hushing sorrows for a while. She strikes here a new note in romantic fiction, and appears to be undoubtedly influenced by the fashionable enthusiasm for Ossian.

Although Mrs. Radcliffe does not introduce either the supernatural agency or superstitious terror in this romance, yet she raises terror and anguish to romantic heights by " dreadful silence " and horrors of darkness and loneliness, by the prolonged fear of death and by harrowing descriptions of hairbreadth escapes, by alternate suffusions of hope and the chilly touch of fear. She maintains this atmosphere of sublimated fear by obvious devices : obstacles are multiplied in order to depict a further interval of despair, an additional thrill of hope ; and the total impression is forceful. Bleak winds howl mournfully with the falling shades of night ; a ray of light darts through the gloom of the damp vapours of a dungeon ; the hushed silence of death prevails in subterranean labyrinths.

Her next work, *A Sicilian Romance* (1790), marks a notable advance in exuberance and fertility of imagination, and as the *Monthly Review* (September 1790) stated, it contains " romantic scenes and surprising events exhibited in elegant and animated language ". The descriptions are fanciful and the narrative impressive, and Mrs. Radcliffe obtains a bird's-eye view of all the surface of that delightful region of romance, picturing its winding vales, delicious bowers, and summer seas, but is unable to introduce the reader individually into the midst of the scene, to surround him with its luxurious air, and compel him to shudder at its terrors.   The softer blandishments of her style, which were scarcely perceptible in her first work, are now spread forth to captivate the fancy. Her genius, which felt cramped in the bleak atmosphere of the Highlands, in her first novel, now blossomed forth in the luxurious climate of the sweet south.   Indeed, the title of this work evokes an atmosphere of idyllic " Sicilian fruitfulness ".

The tale unfolds the life-story of the stern Marquis of Mazzini, who has newly married a second wife, and would force his daughter Julia, who loves the Count de Vereza, to wed the Duke of Luovo.   Many of the incidents relate to Julia's flight from her father, only to be captured and brought back merely to escape once more.   The flight of Julia, the heroine of this romance, is like a strain of " linkèd sweetness long drawn out ", as one after another a series of delicious valleys open out before us, and " the purple light of love is shed over all ".

The opening is a fine piece of word-painting, impressive and pregnant with mystery.   It describes a traveller halting before the sombre and decaying ruins of the Castle of Mazzini.   He obtains hospitality at a neighbouring monastery, where he is allowed access to the library, and from an ancient manuscript extracts the story of those deserted walls. The story transports us to the latter part of the sixteenth century and is said to be founded on facts recorded in a manuscript preserved in a convent library in Sicily.

Mystery pervades the castle ; in the deserted chambers doors are heard to close at night, and an occasional sullen groan disturbs the heavy, ominous silence.   These noises proceed from none other than Mazzini's first wife, who is not dead, as given out, but secretly imprisoned. Eventually Mazzini's second lady, who has been faithless, poisons him and stabs herself.   Julia and her lover are united, and all retire to Naples, leaving the castle to solitude and ruin.

Suggestions and stray hints thrown out here and there show the novelist's first grasp of the masterly power of presenting terrific incidents and scenes in later works.   A light flickers behind the closed windows of the deserted rooms, the confession of Vincent is checked by death, groans are heard from beneath Ferdinand's prison, or a figure is perceived stealing among the vaults. The author is gradually learning to awaken the throbs of suspense by mysterious suggestions, and makes powerful use of subterranean passages, trap-doors with flights of steps descending into darkness, Gothic windows that exclude the light, the sobbing wind, and the wild haunts of Sicilian banditti.

Adventures are heaped upon adventures in a quick and brilliant succession, and the reader is hurried from scene to scene, through stirring incidents, in a state of bewildered excitement and curiosity. The escapes, recaptures, encounters with banditti, appear to have no credible sequence. The work has distinct traces of defects natural to an unpractised author. It led Scott to remark that " the scenes are inartificially connected, and the characters hastily sketched without attempts at individual distinctions ; being cast in the usual mould of ardent lovers, tyrannical parents, with domestic ruffians, guards, and the others ".

Hippolitus enters a ruin by moonlight, for shelter ; hears an anguished voice, and perceives through the shattered casement a man being plundered by a group of banditti. The man, curiously enough, turns out to be Ferdinand, his intended brother-in-law. Later Hippolitus discovers himself in a vault, and hearing a groan from some inner apartment, opens the door to find a fainting lady, whom he recognizes as his mistress. Once again, in his flight with Julia, he is led into a " dark abyss " which happens to be the burial-place of the victims of the banditti, interspersed with graves and strewn with rotten carcases. He climbs to a grating and witnesses a combat between the robbers and officers of justice ; escapes with his lady through a trap-door into the adjacent forest, only to be pursued by her father's party, and as he fights at the mouth of a cavern, she loses her way in the recesses, till by accident they are conducted into a dungeon where her mother, given out as dead for fifteen years, lies imprisoned. And all these incidents, exciting and improbable, are narrated in a few pages. There are in this story incidents enough for two such works as *The Mysteries of Udolpho*.

The *Monthly* and the *Critical* reviews discovered in *A Sicilian Romance* much merit, despite its "numerous improbabilities and hairbreadth escapes ". The imagery and the scenery relieve the tension created by fast-moving action, and the total effect is like that of a splendid Oriental tale. This book is not only " a link in the line uniting the ancient and modern class of romance, but also is the parent of a new and fresh style ". This work led Scott to remark : " Fielding, Richardson, Smollett, even Walpole, though writing upon an imaginative subject, are decidedly prose authors. Mrs. Radcliffe has a title to be considered as the first poetess of romantic fiction."

There is a gradual improvement in the novelist's technique : the sufferings endured are more prolonged ; the escapes attended with more difficulty and consequent suspense. Poetic justice and moral virtue triumph as usual. Here she also employs superstitious terror, and introduces phenomena ostensibly supernatural, but later explained away, a device which becomes a distinguishing mark of her work. The mysterious lights and noises that disturbed the castle of Mazzini she traces to natural causes, the secret of which is skilfully kept unrevealed until almost the end of the tale. There is, also, in this romance, emotional background as in the first novel, with moonlit romantic scenes, of fearsome forests and caverns, of stones and long reverberating peals of thunder, as circumstances demand.

The Romance of the Forest (1792), is a far better planned and regulated work, in which we are aware of the first dawn of her mature powers. She begins her conquest of the fanciful and enchanted land of romance, although her range is yet small, and her persons limited. She harnesses her fancy to the pattern of a regular tale, and all the time keeps a masterly grip upon the reins of the story. She concentrates on a smaller field of incident, and exhibits a skill in handling materials and introducing to the imagination her tissue of mystery and terror. She displays the faculty of controlling the wild images which float around her, and investing them with consistency and truth.

Our interest is awakened by the very first hurried midnight flight of La Motte and his family to an unknown destination ; then sustained by incidents following in quick succession—the heroine introduced in extraordinary circumstances ; the charming forest scenes surrounding the deserted abbey of St. Clair offering a delicious asylum to the persecuted outlaw ; his fears of discovery, his clandestine visits to the tomb ; the vast solitudes of Fontanville ; its wood-walks and valley glades glistening with morning dew. Mrs. Radcliffe shows especially a greater skill in her presentation of the desolate abbey. She touches the imagination with descriptions of the decaying ruins of ancient grandeur which evoke the eerie aspects, the weird abode of " powers unseen, and mightier far than we ". She seizes upon the popular taste for scenic description which Gray and Rousseau encouraged. The impressions of the sylvan scene are delineated in poetic language. Extremely beautiful are her descriptions of the luxuriant woods, the huge-girthed oaks, the romantic glades and avenues, the tangled mazes and far-stretching vistas, the rippling stream winding past the grassy lawns, the delightful flowers, and " the sweet melody of feathered songsters mingling with the music of the waters in one harmonious cadence ".

The time of the story is the seventeenth century, the author's preliminary statement being that " the striking story of Pierre de la Motte and the Marquis Phillipe de Montalt " is from the " proceedings in the Parliamentary Courts of Paris during the 17th century ". The trial of the former is one of the exciting parts of the romance, and possibly the first instance of the court-room scene found in so many novels since.

" The story turns upon the machinations of a profligate villain and his agent against an amiable and unprotected girl, whose birth and fortunes have been involved in obscurity by crime and perfidy." She wears the usual costume of innocence, purity and simplicity, and her troubled mind receives solace in contemplating the grandeur of nature. Most of the interest in the story is afforded by the vacillations of La Motte's character, and he is the centre round which the plot gravitates. His heart disapproves each time he is on the point of becoming an agent in atrocities. He is " a needy man who has seen better days ", expelled with contempt from the world, and condemned by circumstances to seek asylum in a desolate abbey full of mysteries. He avenges himself by playing the gloomy despot within his own family. But a more powerful agent appears on the scene to dominate this dark and irresolute spirit.

There are no hints of the supernatural as yet. The book is certainly romantic rather than macabre, yet mysterious shadowings are by no means wanting. An incidental allusion to a skeleton in the chest of the vaulted chamber ; the dagger spotted with rust ; the faded manuscript of the prisoner, which Adeline reads by the fitful light of the lamp, and which later proves to be written by her own father, excite in us the apprehension of some secret crime, and adds to the mystery and terror. These carefully prepare us for the sad life-story of the Marquis, in as much as these grim relics in the end establish the real identity of Adeline, whose parentage is cleverly shrouded in mystery up to the very end.

The *Critical Review*, commenting on this book in 1792, said : " We have the ruined abbey, a supposed ghost, the skeleton of a man secretly murdered, with all the horrid train of images which such scenes and such circumstances may be supposed to produce. They are managed, however, with skill, and do not disgust by their improbability ; everything is consistent and within the verge of rational belief : the attention is uninterruptedly fixed, till the veil is drawn." The *Monthly Review*'s comments were equally favourable. Skilful handling of the apparently marvellous had won over the critics.

Yet, in spite of all explanation, the effect of the illusion is retained, and certain scenes stand out even when the tale is ended. Such is the description of sin-laden La Motte with terrors of guilt weighing upon his conscience, who shrinks from entering the uncanny abbey where the beautiful tapestry hangs in shreds, giving rise to a vague feeling of rapidly accumulating dread ; or when Adeline in her solitary chamber in the abbey dares not raise her eyes to the glass lest she find a face other than her own reflected in it ; or her escape with a man whom she supposes to be the servant she had trusted and who startles her with a strange voice, to find herself on horseback in a dark night, carried away by an unknown ruffian ; or the luxurious pavilion of the Marquis, to which we are introduced after a frightful journey through a storm ; or the scene where the Marquis, after a series of dark solicitations, understood by La Motte as pointing to Adeline's dishonour, proposes her death. The latter is a fine piece of dramatic effect :

> La Motte now stepped hastily towards the bed, when, breathing a deep sigh, she [Adeline] was again silent. He undrew the curtain, and saw her lying in a profound sleep, her cheek, yet wet with tears, resting upon her arm. He stood a moment looking at her ; and as he viewed her innocent and lovely countenance, pale in grief, the light of the lamp, which shone strong upon her eyes, awoke her, and perceiving a man, she uttered a scream.

This very situation was later developed in *The Italian* when Schedoni entered the midnight chamber of Ellena.

Although the narrative of *The Romance of the Forest* is well constructed, and the intricacies of the plot excite a deep interest in the story, this work is more admired for its idyllic charms than for its thrills. It does excite and gratify a pleasant curiosity, but fails to dilate the imagination or curdle the blood. Darker threads are, however, woven into the fabric. In plot and atmospheric suggestion this novel marks a great advance on the former two, but although perhaps faultless in execution, it remains an attempt of an inferior order to *The Mysteries of Udolpho* or *The Italian*.

The Mysteries of Udolpho (1794), the most popular of Mrs. Radcliffe's works, exhibits all the potent charms of this " mighty enchantress ".

The title alone arouses curiosity. " The very name was fascinating, and the public, who rushed upon it with all the eagerness of curiosity, rose from it with unsated appetite. . . . The volumes flew, and were sometimes torn from hand to hand," says Scott. Edition after edition was called for and rapidly exhausted. Joseph Warton, then Headmaster of Winchester, took it up one evening and sat up the greater part of the night for he found it impossible to sleep until he had finished the book. Sheridan and Fox both speak of it in terms of the highest praise. Judged as pure romance, it must be accorded a prominent place in fiction. " Of all the romances in the world, this is perhaps the most romantic." It is a book which it is impossible to read and forget. Its noble outline, its majestic and beautiful images harmonizing with the scenes exert an irresistible fascination. It gradually rises from the gentlest beauty towards the terrific and the sublime.

In *Udolpho* Mrs. Radcliffe works on a broader canvas, on a larger and more sublime scale, enriches the characteristic traits of her genius, and perfects all her peculiar machinery. She has now conquered the enchanted land of romance and appears quite familiar with its massive towers and solemn glooms. Scott refers to her as " waving her wand over the world of wonder and imagination ". She presents the objects of beauty and of horror through a haze, which sometimes magnifies and sometimes veils their true proportions. The story abounds with more frequent instances of mysterious and terrific appearances. The intrigue is elaborated in a vaster framework, the villains are darker and fiercer, the castles more gloomy, the mysteries more impenetrable, the terrors more dreadful, while the beautiful young heroine, virtuous and innocent, endures a persecution crueller than before. The events are more agitating, the scenery wilder and more terrific. The scale of the landscape is equally different ; the quiet, limited, woodland scenery of *The Romance of the Forest* forms a contrast with the splendid, highly wrought descriptions of Italian mountain grandeur in *Udolpho*. Some readers may prefer the simplicity of *The Romance of the Forest* to the more highly coloured extravagance of *The Mysteries of Udolpho*, but the majority have appreciated the latter's superior magnificence of landscape and dignity of character presentation. It is impossible to convey to one who has not read Mrs. Radcliffe an idea of the sustained atmosphere of romantic terror that pervades this book, her masterpiece. Even *The Italian*, her next romance, although it is a stronger piece of work in plot and characterization and displays more purely intellectual powers, is less enchanting and has not the same moonlit glamour of love and romance.

The story opens with a picture of domestic repose in the home of St. Aubert, who is leading a life of retirement in a beautiful spot, away from the fevered bustle of the world, soothing his mind with elegant and tranquil pleasures. Mrs. Radcliffe portrays a life of poetry, a dream-like existence, in lovely surroundings of flowery turf and balmy air, the limpid murmuring stream meandering along the wood-walks of a romantic glen. Then there unfolds before us the mountain grandeur of the Pyrenees and the exquisite journey of St. Aubert and his daughter through the richly coloured vintage scenes ; and then his death near the woods of a chateau, where strains of unearthly music float along the air

Emily is consigned to the care of her aunt, who marries the desperate Montoni, and then the clouds start gathering thick and we get the first forebodings of approaching terror. " Montoni, a desperado, and Captain of condotierri, stands beside La Motte and his Marquis like one of Milton's fiends besides a witch's familiar." Under the gloomy influence of this unfaithful and oppressive tyrant, both become inhabitants of time-stricken towers, and witnesses of scenes bordering upon the supernatural and the horrible.

Before the work of terror begins, the author describes the luxuries of Venice with delicacy and lightness. We fluctuate between examples of pathos and gaiety ; Mrs. Radcliffe presents entrancing glimpses of Venice, the city of islets, palaces and towers, sketching its voluptuous society, and with a deft hand treats of its tremulous twilight—midnight revels, and moonlight scenes under romantic skies of the sunny south. Nothing is more picturesque than the ascent of the Apennines, where ranges of mountains unfold one after another in gloomy stateliness, till we reach a lost horizon skirting the inmost valley and shut off from the world, and Montoni breaking a long pause of silence utters the words : " This is Udolpho ! "

There is a mystic vagueness about the lovely landscape setting of Udolpho seen for the first time. Its gloom at nightfall, the ominous picture of its sombre exterior and shadow-haunted halls prepare us for the worst when we enter its portals. Our anticipation is a queer mixture of pleasure and fear, as we shudder at the impending events within its walls. Mrs. Radcliffe prepares each tragic denouement by sketches and panoramic views, which provide a backcloth for the enactment of the awe-inspiring horrors that follow in quick succession at Udolpho.

Drawn with consummate power and skill, the picture of the castle prepares the mind for the crimes and horrors of which it has been the mute witness. Massive in its austere grandeur, a castle of awe and gloom, beneath its dark battlements awful scenes are enacted. " Udolpho is a veritable hall of terrors ; its veiled portrait, the ghostly utterances which alarmed Montoni's companions . . . and the visitant of the battlements, make up a medley of horrors which might well daunt the bravest heart." Certain startling and appalling scenes of brawls and wild revelry stand out prominently. Through its halls and shadowed corridors prowl armed bandits, at whose evil banquets the Venetian glass cracks as the poisoned wine hisses into it poured out by the host ; and in whose inmost chambers are hidden horrors not to be guessed at nor named. At every turn something eerie and uncanny heightens our nervous tension ; mysterious appearances, lurking shadows, gliding forms, inexplicable groans and mysterious music appal us and convey wonderfully the tricks of feverish imagination. The moaning wind, a rustling robe, a half-heard sigh, the echo of distant footsteps, and a voiced watchword on the platform below, startle us and keep our curiosity at full stretch. Thrilling are the experiences of Emily in her lonely chamber near the haunted room. And even when she escapes from this terrible castle after her aunt's death, she is still pursued by the demons of Mrs. Radcliffe's imagination.

After Madame Montoni is worried into the grave by her monstrous husband, the scene shifts to Chateau le Blanc, where the mysteries are more touching and dreadful. The haunted chamber of the Marchioness who died twenty years before is visited by Emily. Her experiences are most affecting and fearful when she moves into the faded magnificence of the vast apartment ; the black pall lying on the bed, as when it decked the corpse ; the robe and other ornaments of dress carelessly strewn round about ; her veil, which no hand had since touched, dropping to pieces : all is solemn and spectral in its effect till the pall moves and a face rises from beneath it. The same chamber was the scene of Ludovico's vigil, described in a passage which may be regarded as a masterpiece of supernatural suggestion :

> Ludovico . . . in his remote chamber, heard now and then the faint echo of a closing door as the family retired to rest, and then the hall clock at a great distance strike twelve . . . he looked suspiciously round the spacious chamber. The fire on the hearth was now nearly expiring ; . . . but he soon added fresh wood, not because he was cold, though the night was stormy, but because

he was cheerless ; and having again trimmed his lamp, he poured out a glass
of wine, drew his chair nearer to the crackling blaze . . . and again took up
his book.

The mind of the reader is keyed up for some strange, impending
catastrophe by the admirable ghost story which Ludovico is represented
as perusing to amuse his solitude, as the scene closes upon him.

The romance is rich in striking effects, but its shortcomings are many
and obvious. Although the thread of mystery becomes more and more
intricate, and the author admirably manipulates her effects, so that the
solution is held back until the last moment, the superstitious horrors are
assigned to apparently very simple causes, and explained away by circumstances provokingly trivial. Appearances of the most impressive kind
continually present the idea of supernatural agency, but they are at
length accounted for by natural means. Mrs. Barbauld remarks : " They
are not always, however, *well* accounted for ; and the mind experiences
a sort of disappointment and shame at having felt so much from appearances which had nothing in them beyond ' this visible diurnal sphere '."
The black veil concealed a waxen image ; that wild, floating strain of
unearthly music proceeded from an insane nun who wandered about
the woods ; the words which startled Montoni and his comrades at their
guilty carousals, were uttered by a captive wandering through a secret
passage ! The power, effect, and the sweetness of the spell is thus rudely
broken.

None the less the pall that moves in the funeral chamber, or the
curtain which no one dares draw, strongly evoke our interest, and we
feel the quickest throbs of curiosity. We have been affected so repeatedly,
the suspense has been so long protracted, and the expectation raised so
high, that no explanation can satisfy, and no imagery of horrors can
equal the vague shapings of our imagination.

The *Monthly Review* remarked on " an interesting air of *mystery*
over the story " and " the pleasing agitation of uncertainty concerning
several circumstances ", and added that : " Without introducing into
her narrative anything really supernatural, Mrs. Radcliffe has contrived
to produce as powerful an effect as if the invisible world had been obedient
to her magic spell ; and the reader experiences in perfection the strange
luxury of artificial terror, without being obliged for a moment to hood-
wink his reason, or to yield to the weakness of superstitious credulity."
Other reviews : *Critical*, Ser. 2, XI (1794), 402 ; the *British Critic*, IV
(1794), 110 ; and the *European Magazine*, XXV (1794), 443, were

equally favourable. The peak of interest in Gothic fiction had been reached.

The Italian (1797), is probably her finest work, the high-water mark of her achievement. The story is more skilfully constructed, has a greater unity of plan and concentration than *The Mysteries of Udolpho*, while her pictures are more individual and distinct, her figures more terrible, and her situations more thrilling and vivid. Although the Inquisition scenes during the later chapters are unduly prolonged, the story is coherent and free from digressions. Mrs. Radcliffe did not copy nor repeat herself. " She selected the new and powerful machinery afforded her by the Popish religion, when established in its permanent superiority, and thereby had at her disposal monks, spies, dungeons, the mute obedience of the bigot, the dark and dominating spirit of the crafty priest—all the thunders of the Vatican, and all the terrors of the Inquisition," says Scott. These materials became, in the hands of Mrs. Radcliffe, a powerful set of agents, which supplied means and motive for evoking scenes of terror. And what better actors could be found for such a tale of terror " than these mysterious figures, muffled in their cowls and scapularies, bound by awful vows, dark and threatening, with all the terror and all the power of the church behind them ? " Little, or rather nothing, was known of their orders, their rules, their devotions, their aims ; and it provided scope for the most frantic fantasies.

The story commences in an impressive manner ; unlike the tender and beautiful beginning of *The Mysteries of Udolpho*, it at once excites anxious curiosity and inspires us with awe. An Englishman on his travels, walking through a church, sees a dark figure stealing along the aisles. He is informed that it is an assassin, and that such deeds are common in Italy. His companion then points to a confessional in an obscure aisle of the church. " There," says he, " in that cell, such a tale of horror was once poured into the ear of a priest as overwhelmed him with astonishment, nor was the secret ever disclosed." Mrs. Barbauld, commenting on this fine opening of the story, said : " This prelude, like the tuning of an instrument by a skilful hand, has the effect of producing at once in the mind a tone of feeling correspondent to the future story." The introductory passage may be likened to the dark and vaulted gateway of an ancient castle, leading to a tale of its mysterious walls ; and as the narrative proceeds we are given intimations of veiled and secret terrors.

The story develops in a series of dramatic, haunting scenes, which

stand out in bold relief : the strangely effective overture, which describes
the Confessional of the Black Penitents ; the midnight adventures of
Vivaldi and his lively impulsive servant, Paulo, amid the ruined vaults of
Paluzzi ; the machinations of Schedoni and the Marchioness for Ellena's
murder, and particularly the scene where the Confessor makes palpable
to the Marchioness the secret wishes of her heart for Ellena's death ;
Ellena's imprisonment in the convent of San Stephano on the hills and
her escape with Vivaldi ; the melodramatic interruption of the wedding
ceremony, and the meeting of Ellena and Schedoni on the lonely seashore ; and her terrible sojourn in Spalatro's cottage by the sea when
her lover has been seized by the Holy Office. The dreary horrors of the
fisherman's cottage are admirably described : the awful conversation
with the ruffian when the deed is planned ; the long and hideous preparations as Schedoni equips himself to strike the blow ; his strange relentings
and his bitter remorse. Edith Birkhead says, " the climax of the story
when Schedoni, about to slay Ellena, is arrested in the very act by her
beauty and innocence, and then by the glimpse of the portrait which
leads him to believe she is his daughter, is finely conceived and finely
executed ".

Walter Scott observes that " The fine scene, where the monk, in the
act of raising his arm to murder his sleeping victim, discovers her to be
his own child, is, of a new, grand, and powerful character, and the
horrors of the wretch, who, on the brink of murder, has but just escaped
from committing a crime of yet more exaggerated horror, constitute
the strongest painting which has been under Mrs. Radcliffe's pencil, and
are well fitted to be actually embodied on canvas by some great painter ".
Eventually we meet the terrific Schedoni imprisoned by the Inquisition
counterplotted and betrayed by an associate who had once enjoyed his
confidence. The presentation of the trials in the halls of the Inquisition
is said to have been written under the influence of ' Monk' Lewis. Remarking on the Inquisition scenes that " contain the solid substance of a
formidable reality ", and go to make this novel a powerful work,
Montague Summers said : " The masterly way in which Mrs. Radcliffe
has made use of the Inquisition, and the restraint which she has exercised
in depicting the scenes in the cells and sombre halls of that tribunal, are
most noticeable. The Inquisition itself has, of course, been employed in
many subsequent novels, but never with such decorum and effect."

The episodes in the vast prisons and dungeons of the Inquisition are
fraught with fear of bodily torture almost eclipsed by an apprehension of

the supernatural, and Mrs. Radcliffe deepens the horror of this gloom by a whisper of things yet more terrible and evokes fear of the unseen. The Monk, who haunts the ruins of Paluzzi, and who reappears in the prison of the Inquisition, speaks and acts like a being from the world of spectres. The circumstances are contrived with admirable effect to heighten, vary, and prolong the feeling of curiosity and terror. Apparently endless agony of physical torture in the dungeons of the Inquisition is awfully suggested by the author's solemn and weighty style. Mrs. Barbauld, one of her contemporaries, suggested that " if she wishes to rise in the horrors of her next, she must place her scene in the infernal regions. She would not have many steps to descend thither from the courts of the Inquisition." In these violent, romantic scenes the genius of Mrs. Radcliffe shows greater power and eloquence, hitherto unrealized. Coleridge reveals in the *Critical Review*, June 1798, that although he did not prefer *The Italian* to *The Mysteries of Udolpho*, he realized " there are, however, some scenes that powerfully seize the imagination, and interest the passion ".

This novel added a unique portrait to the gallery of Gothic fiction : Schedoni, the masterly plotter and murderer. According to Scott he is " a strongly drawn character as ever stalked through the regions of romance, equally detestable for the crimes he has formerly perpetrated, and those which he is willing to commit ; formidable from his talents and energy ; at once a hypocrite and a profligate, unfeeling, unrelenting, and implacable ". He is a character agitated by passion and will, whose actions are the mainspring of the plot. The wooing of Ellena by Vivaldi, is overshadowed by this dark and mysterious character, an interesting study in psychology, whose dominating figure is invested with an air of mystery. His spirit and personality envelop the entire atmosphere of the tale.

Gaston de Blondeville (1826), Mrs. Radcliffe's last and posthumous work, written in the winter of 1802, and inspired by her visit to the ruins of Kenilworth Castle, was not intended for publication. She found her subject fascinating ; it struck her imagination and quick sensibility, and she became interested in exploring the history of that old castle. After this novel, she undertook no work of magnitude ; her pecuniary resources had become very ample, and there was neither enthusiasm nor excitement left in her to divert her energies to an extended romance.

Although all her works are set in a distant age, she never achieved historical accuracy. It is only in her last novel that she made use of old chronicles or attempted a reconstruction of history.

The story purports to have been taken from an old manuscript dated 1256, dug up in the churchyard of what had once been a Priory of Black Canons. The book shadows forth an age of chivalry, has far more colour than Leland's *Longsword* (1762), Miss Reeve's *The Old English Baron* (1777), or Miss Sophia Lee's *Recess* (1785). Its scene is Kenilworth Castle, at the time of the " Court of Henry III keeping festival in Arden ". It narrates a love story, and includes the description of a splendid tournament which recalls the lists of Ashby-de-la-Zouche in *Ivanhoe*. The spectre in a " pale sad light " glides up the stairs before Gaston, the King's favourite, who has murdered him three years before ; and when justice is not immediately done " three drops of blood " fall on his robe ; and, when the chain of the murdered man is put into his hands, they spread until the whole of one side of his garment is crimson. The volume is curiously divided into eight days (eight parts or chapters) and the influence of Scott is very evident. The story is rather tedious, and unworthy of her powers, and Mrs. Radcliffe is far from her best here. There is a certain langour in the narrative, as though it had been written with effort. The story is neither characteristic of Mrs. Radcliffe nor of her followers, on whom it had no influence, as it was not printed until 1826.

The only merit of this work is that here Mrs. Radcliffe makes the first use of supernatural machinery. In this very romance she gratified herself by introducing a true spectre. And the manner in which the supernatural agency is conducted, deepens the general regret that she had not employed it in her longer and more elaborate productions. " Only in *Gaston de Blondeville* does she introduce a spectre which is not explained away, but stalks unabashed through Kenilworth Castle. The story is in fact a reversion to the methods of Walpole's *Otranto*," says McKillop in the *Journal of English and Germanic Philology* (1932).

Her ingenuity fostered a new style of romantic fiction distinct from the poetical marvels of conventional tales of magic and chivalry or the realistic manner of Richardson and Fielding. Yet the wondrous and the credible are both woven into her fabric : the gossamer dreams of bygone times across the grim realities of her own days. She had not the art of stimulating the fancy by deft, light sketches of life and manners. Her most powerful effects are gained by the passion of fear, and this base emotion is raised to the dignity of romance. In the silence of nature we listen to echoes from beyond the grave, and with a tremulous eagerness we follow the sequence of events. She fascinates and appals us at the same time, and stirs up those secret springs of mortal apprehension which join our earthly existence and our spiritual self. This art is not melodramatic, but is very similar to the essence of tragic power, " which is felt not merely in the greatness of the actions, or sorrows, which it exhibits, but in its nice application to the inmost sources of terror and pity ".

She approached the terrible with all the tremors of a highly strung nervous system, by working upon the sensations of natural and super-stitious fear and making artistic use of obscurity and suspense, which remain the most fertile sources of sublime emotion. She skilfully selected and described scenes and figures precisely tuned to the feelings she sought to awaken. Thus her talent consisted in " defining the indefinable and giving a body to a phantom ".

She excited the imagination by supernatural apprehensions, by phantom effects and half-heard sounds. In her hands the gusts of wind, the creaking door, even the sound of a common footstep became sources of terror and mystery. The crude machinery of Walpole's story— secret trap-doors, sliding panels, spiral staircases, and subterranean vaults—in her hands became artistic instruments to evoke an atmosphere of suspense and beauty.

She was skilful in producing terror by awakening a sense of mystery. The sequence of her narrative is so managed that it moves our minds to a feeling of impending danger, and we hold our breath in suspense. Her vast, antique chambers have about them a sense of unearthly presences ; where an ominous silence prevails ; where echoing footsteps die away in prolonged gloom, and where phantoms lurk in dark corridors, and whispers come from behind the tapestry, as it flutters in the gusts of wind. " She alarms with terror ; agitates with suspense, pro-longed and wrought up to the most intense feeling ; by mysterious hints and obscure intimations of unseen danger ", according to Mrs. Barbauld.

Strange occurrences that seem not of this world's ordering surprise our prudence : she knows the chord of feeling she must touch. Instead of exhibiting a succession of magnificent glooms, which only darken the imagination, she whispers some mysterious suggestion to the soul ; and in nothing is her supremacy so clearly shown as in the wise and daring economy with which she has employed the instruments of fear : " A

low groan issuing from distant vaults ; a voice heard among an assembly
from an unknown speaker ; a little track of blood seen by the uncertain
light of a lamp on a castle staircase ; a wild strain of music floating over
moonlight woods ; as introduced by her, affect the mind more deeply
than terrible incantations, or accumulated butcheries." The delicacy
of means by which effects are evoked is remarkable : a sigh, a
vanishing light, an unfamiliar tone of voice, the shadow of a cloaked
and striding figure. " The skill of the writer, applying itself justly to
the pulses of terror in our intellectual being, gives tragic interest to
the enquiry, makes the rusted dagger terrible, and the spot of blood
sublime."

Mrs. Radcliffe, a mistress of hints, associations, silence, and emptiness,
only half-revealing her picture leaves the rest to the imagination. She
knows, as Burke has asserted, that obscurity is a strong ingredient in the
sublime ; but she knew the sharp distinction between Terror and Horror,
which was unknown to Burke. " Terror and horror ", says McKillop,
" are so far opposite, that the first expands the soul, and awakens the
faculties to a high degree of life ; the other contracts, freezes and nearly
annihilates them . . . ; and where lies the great difference between terror
and horror, but in the uncertainty and obscurity, that accompany the
first, respecting the dreaded evil ? " Sounds unexplained, sights in-
distinctly caught, dim shadows endowed with motion by the flicker
of the firelight or the shimmer of the moonbeam invoke superstitious
fear.

" To the warm imagination," she writes in *The Mysteries of Udolpho*,
" the forms which float half-veiled in darkness afford a higher delight
than the most distinct scenery the Sun can show." To describe is to
limit and circumscribe the operations of the reader's imagination, but
to suggest is to stimulate it by the intimation of a grandeur or a terror
beyond the compass of words. Isaac D'Israeli said, " It is by concealing
that we exhibit objects to the imagination," and it is this process of
elevating by obscurity which forms an important part of Mrs. Radcliffe's
aesthetic. McKillop observes : ". . . The strong light which shows
the mountains of a landscape in all their greatness, and with all their
rugged sharpnesses, gives them nothing of the interest with which a
more gloomy tint would invest their grandeur ; dignifying, though it
softens, and magnifying, while it obscures." Thus, things and incidents,
set in the shadow of Gothic masonry, half-lit by perpetually failing
lamps, acquire a monstrous hue.

She developed this principle of suggestive obscurity to a fine art. Throughout her romances half-revealed objects, hints, and traces lead the mind into realms of vague sublimity. The beauty of her heroines is half-obscured in veils, and black cowls hide the face of her villains. Her landscapes and scenery are bathed in mist or pale moonshine ; her castles and abbeys are first impressed upon us in an atmosphere of twilight ; her settings are mostly half-explored buildings never fully known even to their inhabitants who wander as in a dream along unfamiliar cloisters and crumbling staircases.

She excites impatient curiosity by the impressive commencement of her works and the ingenuity of her narrative. Her plots deserve much admiration. Characterization " was not the department of art on which her popularity rested," says Scott, " the public were chiefly aroused, or rather fascinated, by the wonderful conduct of a story, in which the author . . . called out the feelings of mystery and awe, while chapter after chapter, and incident after incident, maintained the thrilling attraction of awakened curiosity and suspended interest ". Coleridge, reviewing *The Mysteries of Udolpho*, remarked that " curiosity is a kind of appetite, and hurries headlong on, impatient for its complete gratifica-tion ". As Walter Scott put it : ". . . it is not until the last page is read, and the last volume closed, that we feel ourselves disposed to censure that which has so keenly interested us. We become then at length aware that there is no uncommon merit in the general contrivance of the story ; that many of the incidents are improbable, and some of the mysteries left unexplained ; yet the impression of general delight which we have received from the perusal, remains unabated, for it is founded on recollec-tion of the powerful emotions of wonder, curiosity, even fear, to which we have been subjected during the currency of the narrative." Nothing interrupts the swift progress of the tale which grips us entirely.

Edith Birkhead draws a telling analogy ; her " tantalising delays quicken our curiosity as effectively as the deliberate calm of a raconteur, who, with a view to heightening his artistic effect, pauses to light a pipe at the very climax of his story ". The account of Ellena's experience in a lonely house by the seashore, and Spalatro's refusal to murder her because he is haunted by a supernatural warning and has seen the hallucina-tion of bloody hands, or of Schedoni's entrance into Ellena's room at midnight, dagger in hand, ready to kill her—are all moments of extreme tension, heightening the reader's curiosity and keeping it upon the stretch of mystery and wonder. Scott notes that " to break off the narrative, when it seemed at the point of becoming most interesting—to extinguish a lamp just when a parchment containing some hideous secret ought to have been read—to exhibit shadowy forms and half-heard sounds of woe, were resources which Mrs. Radcliffe has employed with more effect than any other writer of romance ".

Her artistic use of suspense was different and distinct from the method of Richardson and Fielding who shaped the incidents in their novels to fit into a general plan or design.   Also, in the picaresque fiction, the novelist had introduced action for its own sake, but Mrs. Radcliffe used ' action' for complicating the tissues of plot and then resolving them. For the first time, reading was an exercise to be undertaken with bated breath, and it was to this tension that Coleridge referred in the *Critical Review* when he called *The Mysteries of Udolpho* " the most interesting novel in the English language ".

She sedulously explains by natural agency each marvel of her story. And although she holds a masterly sway over the terrors that she employs, the mysteries accounted for by mere physical causes have been supposed " to make the cause totally inadequate to the effect ".   Her mask of reasonableness imposed on romanticism led Coleridge to remark : ". . . mysterious terrors are continually exciting in the mind the idea of a supernatural appearance, keeping us, as it were, upon the very edge and confines of the world of spirits, and yet are ingeniously explained by familiar causes ; curiosity is kept upon the stretch from page to page, and from volume to volume, and the secret, which the reader thinks himself every instant on the point of penetrating, flies like a phantom before him, and eludes his eagerness till the very last moment of protracted expectation ".

The *Quarterly Review* (May 1810) commented : " We disapprove of the mode, introduced by Mrs. Radcliffe, and followed by Mr. Murphy and her other imitators, of winding up their story with solution, by which all the incidents appearing to partake of the mystic and marvellous are resolved by very simple and natural causes . . . we can believe, for example, in Macbeth's witches, and tremble at their spells ; but had we been informed, at the conclusion of the piece, that they were only three of his wife's chambermaids disguised for the purpose of imposing on the Thane's credulity, it would have added little to the credibility of the story, and entirely deprived it of its interest."

It is perhaps the vice of her method that scenes of raised excitement, where suspense is continually heightened by mystery and unexpected incidents, are followed by patches of flat explanation. A variety of startling phenomena resolved into petty deceptions and gross improbabilities, disappoints the fancy and shocks the understanding of the reader. " To arouse feelings of pleasurable awe and fear in the mind of a reader by a tale of terror, and then at the end to turn on him and cry ' April Fool ', as it were, is literary false pretence . . . her [Mrs. Radcliffe's] erroneous method of treating the supernatural is an indelible blot upon her artistry," said the *Contemporary Review* in February 1920.

What Walpole left inexplicable, and Reeve laboured to make credible, Mrs. Radcliffe reduces to a fascinating illusion. She would have gained artistically had she left its existence a possibility : the simplicity of her explanations destroys the mystery. The supernatural continually fascinates, but in the end is proved to be a cheat. The smugglers are made responsible for the disappearance of Ludovico and the shaking of the black pall, and Laurentini di Udolpho is remarkably still alive. As Coleridge summed up : " Curiosity is raised oftener than it is gratified ; or rather, it is raised so high that no adequate gratification can be given it ; the interest is completely dissolved when once the adventure is finished, and the reader, when he is got to the end of the work, looks about in vain for the spell which had bound him so strongly to it."

Thus it has been argued that when explanation falls short of the expectation of the reader, the interest terminates on the first reading of the volumes, and cannot recall a second excited perusal. But " Mrs. Radcliffe's plan of narrative, happily complicated and ingeniously resolved, continues to please after many readings ". " Even when she has dissolved mystery after mystery, and abjured spell after spell, the impression survives, and the reader is still eager to attend again, and be again deluded. After the voices heard in the chambers of Udolpho have been shown to be the wanton trick of a prisoner, we still revert to the remaining prodigies with anxious curiosity, and are prepared to give implicit credence to new wonders at Chateau le Blanc." So unnerved are we by the mysterious shadows, the vanishing lights, the unaccountable groans or even by the rustle of an unseen robe, and our vitality gets so low, that every little sound appals us, and being completely absorbed in the atmosphere of her romance, we do not question what she would have us believe. " The ' explained supernatural ' still leaves unexplained the tendency of the human mind to reach out beyond the tangible and the visible ; and it is in depicting this mood of vague and half-defined emotion that Mrs. Radcliffe excels," says McIntyre. Her suggested

mysterious terrors, and the feelings they arouse until the moment of
explanation, make one feel the full impression of the world of shadows
although she stops short of anything really supernatural. She may dismiss
her alarming circumstances in a matter-of-fact way ; nevertheless she
sends a chill down our spine.

Why then must she thus give the lie to the imagination of her readers ?
McKillop has summed up an important point in Mrs. Radcliffe's theory
" that the poet of the supernatural should avoid shocking the understanding. . . . Mrs. Radcliffe's practice in her own romances is of course
much more rationalistic. . . ."

Secondly, the supernatural explained was not a technique entirely
new : Smollett had already made use of it in his *Ferdinand Count Fathom*
(1753) ; and the vague presentiments of terror in the novels of Mrs.
Charlotte Smith foreshadowed this method. Mrs. Radcliffe probably
realized that Walpole's enchanted sword and gigantic helmet, or
the portrait walking out of its frame, strained human credulity. She
therefore sought, like Clara Reeve in *The Old English Baron* (1777), to
compose works in which the seemingly supernatural could be reasonably
explained.

Thirdly, the credulous readers of the eighteenth century, Scott
remarked, ". . . compel an explanation from the story-teller ; and he
must either at once consider the knot as worthy of being severed by
supernatural aid, and bring on the stage his actual fiend or ghost, or
like Mrs. Radcliffe, refer to natural agency the whole materials of his
story ".

Lastly, Dr. Tompkins justifies the author's method : " The reader is
not invited to unpick a knot but to enjoy the emotion of mystery ; the
knot, indeed, is not unpicked at all ; at the appointed hour an incantation
is breathed over it, and it dissolves, for the methods of an enchantress
are not those of Sherlock Holmes."

One cannot doubt the importance of her novels as a contribution to
fiction. The discussion of the social and intellectual problems, in the
manner of the eighteenth-century novelists, was not the centre of her
interest. Firstly, by her insight into the workings of fear she contributed
to the development of the psychological novel. She was perhaps the
first English novelist to dissect the human motives in a character. Edith
Birkhead points out, " Mrs. Radcliffe's psychology is neither subtle nor
profound, but the fact that psychology is there in the most rudimentary
form is a sign of her progress in the art of fiction ". We watch as if

under an irresistible spell every movement of Spalatro's haggard countenance until the low sound of his stealthy footsteps dies away.   There are some wonderful studies of character physiognomy in Schedoni :

> His physiognomy . . . bore the trace of many passions, which seemed to have fixed the features they no longer animated. . . . His eyes were so piercing that they seemed to penetrate with a single glance into the hearts of men, and to read their most secret thoughts.

Or again :

> His visage was wan and wasted ; his eyes were sunk, and become nearly motionless, and his whole air and attitude exhibited the wild energy of something—not of this earth.

When Schedoni meets Ellena on the seashore :

> He was silent, and still gazed upon her ; but his eyes, when she had ceased to struggle, assumed the fixed and vacant stare of a man, whose thoughts have retired within themselves, and who is no longer conscious of surrounding objects.

Certain emotions as well are reflected in the physiognomy :

> The Confessor was silent, and his countenance assumed a very peculiar character ; it was more terrible than usual, and overspread with a dark cadaverous hue of mingled anger and guilt.

Schedoni, advanced in years, exhibits a more severe physiognomy, " furrowed by thought, no less than by time, and darkened by the habitual indulgence of morose passions. . . . Cheerfulness had once played upon his features."   When he lies in the dungeons of the Inquisition :

> . . . his countenance, upon which the little light admitted through the triple grate of the dungeon gleamed, seemed more than usually ghastly ; his eyes were hollow, and his shrunk features appeared as if death had already touched them.

Even while presenting her minor characters, Mrs. Radcliffe does not forget to throw light on physiognomy.   When the old porter opens the door of the porch in the lonely house by the seashore in *The Italian*, she describes him as one

> . . . whose visage was so misery struck . . . the lamp he held threw a gleam athwart it, and showed the gaunt ferocity of famine, to which the shadow of his hollow eyes added a terrific wildness.

Her second gift to fiction was her " power of masterly dialogue used as a means of revealing character and of advancing the action ". Her dialogues are characterized sometimes by shrewdness as in the dialogue between the Marchesa and Schedoni in the choir of the convent of San Nicolo, or by emotional tension, as in the dialogue between Schedoni and Spalatro, when the latter refuses to murder Ellena :

> " Give me the dagger then," said the Confessor. . . . At the foot of the staircase, he again stopped to listen.
> " Do you hear anything ? " he asked, in a whisper.
> " I only hear the sea," replied the man.
> " Hush ! it is something more ! " said Schedoni, " that is the murmur of voices ! "
> They were silent.

Thirdly, as Miss McIntyre pointed out, Mrs. Radcliffe's " most important contribution is a matter not of theme, but of structure ". Miss A. A. S. Wieten also comments on " a change in the structure of the novel in the direction of the dramatic ". Although it was Walpole who made the first formative attempt to give a new turn to the plot by adding a dramatic technique, Mrs. Radcliffe carried that method to a higher artistic development, making a much finer use of the principle of suspense, which was rather of a nightmarish nature in Walpole's goblin tale. The novels of the Victorian times are a blend of the picaresque and dramatic methods, and the latter element predominates.

Fourthly, allied to her dramatic technique is her art of spotlighting individual scenes. Dibelius has pointed out Mrs. Radcliffe's use of individual scenes that stand out prominently in the reader's mind even after the tale is ended. This method is a feature of her genius which distinguishes her from Fielding and Smollett. In *The Mysteries of Udolpho* and *The Italian* certain pictures effectively impress themselves upon the mind : the scene where Emily's aunt is interred ; the duel between Montoni and the count following that scene of dramatic tension at Udolpho where Emily sits at dinner among the fierce guests, and the poison rises hissing in Montoni's glass ; Emily and Dorothée's visit to the apartment of the dead Marchioness ; or Ellena in her gloomy chamber startled from her sleep to find Schedoni ready to plunge a dagger into her heart.

This technique was adopted by the future generation of novelists. Scott owed to Mrs. Radcliffe his strong feeling for stressing the individual scene.

Fifthly, the technique of suspense was refined by her pen. In the works of Richardson and Fielding the interest of the novel was geared to the chief character, while Mrs. Radcliffe developed suspense until it predominated over character and became the main motif of the story. Suspense is the chief ingredient in the short story today, from the master-pieces of Poe to the cheap stuff that floods the modern magazines. Poe, in his aim of producing certain emotional effect, and in his method of exciting suspense, seems to have been influenced by Mrs. Radcliffe. Also the detective thrillers with prolonged mystifications, and uncon-vincing solutions, have much in common with Radcliffian technique. As Dr. Tompkins put it : " She satisfied the detective interest in her readers."

Her other two gifts to literature were ' romantic scenery ' and the ' villain-hero '. Since these were her most important contributions, they seem to merit a detailed treatment.

Dr. Tompkins saw in Mrs. Radcliffe " the focus of all the romantic tendencies of her time ". " She collected, combined and intensified them, harmonizing her work by picturesque beauty and quickening it with fear and awe." Her passion for the mysterious, the weird and eerie, was intensified by her love of romantic scenery, and a romantic passion for night and solitude pervades her pages. Her vivid glimpses of such landscape are as impressive as her terrible agencies of dread.

Her quick and accurate eye with a masterly power of observation captured all the naked grandeur of the external world, and fixed ever in beautiful images and scenes the varying tints or fleeting shadows of nature, spreading before our vision lovely fairy prospects. She looked at scenes with the eye not of a philosopher, but a landscape painter. There is nothing in her like the chaotic beautiful images which we get later in Lewis and Maturin, nor anything like the remembered fragments of a gorgeous dream as in *Vathek*. Rather, she had an eye for sad colour, and her ' musing eye ' loved to rest upon scenes of gloomy grandeur. She produced her spectral effects among settings like the large romantic ruins of abbeys and Gothic buildings with their broken casements dimly shadowed under starlight, as the nocturnal winds moan and howl through their ruined turrets. Her wider canvas includes bleak and solitary heaths, gloomy forests, and craggy precipices, over which is diffused a shimmer of haze and colour.

Artists are of two kinds : some distinguish their pictures by precision and correctness of outline, while others revel in the force and vividness of their colours. Mrs. Radcliffe belongs to the latter group. Her immediate inspiration was undoubtedly *Ossian* ; she appears to have been affected by the showers and sunbeams and flying mists that clothe the Ossianic hero and foreshadow his destiny. She was deeply read in poets, Tasso being her favourite author ; and in the lyrical interpretation of nature she appears to be in line with Charlotte Smith. The writings of Gray, Thomson, and Rousseau touched a responsive chord in her nature, and she certainly owes a great deal to the inspiration of Thomson in her poetical treatment of landscape. It was probably from Gray that she inherited her sensitiveness to the quieting influence of nightfall. D. Murray Rose has compared her to sentimentalists like Mackenzie and Sterne.

Her fine local colour is imaginary : descriptions of foreign scenery in the journals of travellers furnished raw material for her transmuting genius. Perhaps she also called to her aid her own personal recollections of English mountains and lakes. Her contemporaries thought that her fancy-portraits were exact descriptions of scenes which she had been privileged to visit, which was not a fact. The *Edinburgh Review* wrongly stated that Mrs. Radcliffe accompanied her husband to Italy, when he was attached to one of the British Embassies, and that " it was on that occasion she imbibed the taste for picturesque scenery, and the obscure and wild superstitions of mouldering castles, of which she has made so beautiful a use in her romances ".

She lays the setting of her romances in one of the Mediterranean countries where passions grow luxuriantly like summer weeds ; where ruined and desolate monuments of antiquity and massive remnants of the Middle Ages stand as mute witnesses of time ; and where the despotic power of feudal tyranny and Catholic superstition conveniently exercise their sway. Mrs. Barbauld tells us, " Switzerland, the South of France, Venice, the valleys of Piedmont, the bridge, the cataract, and especially the charming bay of Naples, the dances of the peasants, with the vine dressers and the fishermen have employed her pencil ". To places where she had never been she sent her heroines, basing the settings on works of landscape painters. The flight of Julia takes place in the wild beauties of Sicily, Adeline visits Switzerland and Languedoc, and Emily tours in the Pyrenees and crosses the Alps. Udolpho is set among the Apennines, and for a while there are glimpses of enchanting Venice. When she attempts to describe places she never visited, like a true lover she invests nature with imaginary loveliness. Thomas Green, in his

Diary of a Lover of Literature, wrote : ". . . to paint from the imagination, and to copy nature, are such different achievements, that I was surprised, I confess, to find that she had succeeded so well, and failed so little."

Travelling was the romance of her life, and she wrote copious diaries of her several tours, which are strewn with rich descriptions. One is impressed with the clarity of her images and the boldness and simplicity of her strokes ; we are not overwhelmed by any incrustation of sentiment or perplexing dazzle of fancy such as ordinarily colour the diary of descriptive tourists. " She seems the very chronicler and secretary of nature ; makes us feel the freshness of the air ; and listen to the gentlest sounds." She discriminates the shifting aspect of nature with a delicacy and exactness. " No aerial tint of a fleecy cloud is too evanescent to be tinged in her transparent style. Perhaps no writer in prose, or verse, has been so happy in describing the varied effects of light in winged words." Coleridge failed to appreciate this when he said that " in the descriptions there is too much of sameness ; the pine and the larch trees wave, and the full moon pours its lustre through almost every chapter ".

She adored all that was picturesque : majestic mountains, verdant landscapes, beautiful moonlit nights, tranquil lakes, music heard at evening beside the water's edge. Following Rousseau's example, she loved to describe the simple joys of rustic life, and many a passage from her romances recalls the *Nouvelle Héloise*. Famous are the descriptions of the golden clouds of sunset and the break of early dawns ; impressive are the pictures of Gothic castles with ramparts gilded by the rays of the sinking sun ; romantic are the moonlit woods, with their mysterious and weird atmosphere ; colourful are the fertile plains laden with fruits and blossoms ; and frightful are those deserted mountain passes infested with banditti. ". . . never had mountains and spectral music, defenceless beauty and the Inquisition, ruined manor vaults, pilgrims and banditti been adorned with so much unfamiliar gorgeousness ; never had there been such ample provision for the romantic mood, so pure in quality and so respectable in form," says Dr. Tompkins.

In contrast to Mrs. Charlotte Smith's landscapes, which remain definite and local, Mrs. Radcliffe's scenes are far from true and accurate but painted with a broad careless sweep. Mrs. Smith's sketches are so graphic that even the smallest detail can be painted on canvas by any artist. Mrs. Radcliffe, on the other hand, supplies the most vigorous and noble ideas while she leaves the distinct and accurate outline to the imagination of the painter. Scott observes, " as her story is usually enveloped in mystery, so there is, as it were, a haze over her landscapes, softening indeed the whole, and adding interest and dignity to particular parts, and thereby producing every effect which the author desired, but without communicating any absolutely precise or individual image to the reader ". One such description is of the Castle of Udolpho. The towers of Udolpho, wreathed in mist and obscurity, afford a noble subject for the painter, " but were six artists to attempt to embody it upon canvas, they would probably produce six drawings entirely dissimilar to each other. . . ." The description of Udolpho is a fine specimen of Mrs. Radcliffe's particular talents :

> Towards the end of day the road wound into a deep valley. Mountains, whose shaggy steeps appeared to be inaccessible, almost surrounded it. . . . The sun had just sunk below the top of the mountains . . . whose long shadow stretched athwart the valley ; but his sloping rays, shooting through the opening of the cliffs . . . streamed in full splendour upon the towers and battlements of a castle that spread its extensive ramparts along the brow of a precipice above. The splendour of these illuminated objects was heightened by the contrasted shade which involved the valley below . . . the whole edifice was invested with the solemn duskiness of evening. Silent, lonely, and sublime, it seemed to stand the sovereign of the scene, and to frown defiance on all who dared to invade its solitary reign. As the twilight deepened, its features became more awful in obscurity.

This lovely first glimpse of the castle of Udolpho charmed Sir Walter Scott, Leigh Hunt, and others ; the description possesses a sort of mystic vagueness which leaves only an impression of the castle as a pile of enormous proportions.

Such a lack of distinctness in her pictures may have been caused by her attempt to blend a landscape actually seen by her with a landscape borrowed from elsewhere. She looked at the grandeurs and beauties of creation through a soft and tender medium. And, as she painted nature with the hues of romance, some of its graces were heightened while some of its delicate varieties were lost.

Atmosphere and scenery provide the whole focus of interest in the novels of Radcliffe, while the characters, like the figures in a landscape, are subordinated to effective scenes. The function of characters is to focus and enhance the sentiment of the scene : they are distinguished only by such features as are appropriate to their setting of dark battlements

or rocks and trees. The scenes reflect the emotions of her characters ; the gloom darkens when the incidents move towards a tragic
catastrophe, and a warm sunshine spreads with the moods of happiness
and security. " A flexible harmony of colour accompanies the action ;
it is beneath a lowering sky and beside a wind-ruffled lake that Ellena
walks on her fateful marriage morning, while the changing aspects of
the Fontanville forest keep pace with Adeline's changing fortunes, as its
lawn darkens with the coming storm and its trees are stripped by the
wind," says Dr. Tompkins. The chief interest perhaps does not lie in the
characters of Emily and Montoni, or in the conflicts of Vivaldi or
Adeline ; it is the southern landscape that enchants us, whose cumulative
effect is heightened in the happy musings of lovers or in their terror-
stricken flight. The castles and the convents remain complete expressions
of the victim as well as the tyrant. " The *raison d'être* of her books is not
a story, nor a character, nor a moral truth, but a mood, the mood of a
sensitive dreamer before Gothic buildings and picturesque scenery."

The plot and characters centre round this mood, and the spirit of the
grim places like Udolpho or Fontanville Abbey speak through Emily or
Adeline. They receive and transmit the faintest tremors that possess these
grim and deserted abodes. Those that fill up the canvas are characters
lacking individual features, representative of certain class or types, coming
to life with the strokes of Mrs. Radcliffe's brush. They are the gloomy
and tyrannical baron, an aged and garrulous maid who has locked up in
her heart many a secret of the family legend, a gay and easy valet, or a
heroine endowed with all perfection exposed to an interminable succession
of misfortunes, struggling against the tide of adversity, and hurried downward by its torrent.

Wieten has pointed out that Mrs. Radcliffe uses " the terrible forces
of nature to reflect the dark passions of man ". She establishes thus a
concord in literature between man's mood and the changing aspect of
nature, and gives an appropriate setting not only to the evil emotions,
but also to the feelings of joy or content or love. The love of landscape
is reflected in all her heroines, who purify their souls in the beauty of
frequent dawns and sunsets, and draw fortitude and patience from the
divine order of nature. The dominating force of atmosphere over passion
is the cumulative effect of the landscape. At times, terror is obscurely
reflected in the victim's mind. Changes in the moods of nature harmonize
with the terrors of the heroine. The savage wildness of the mountain
scenery or the dim shades of unexplored forest vistas exclude human aid

and darken solitude. Lord Ernle, in his study *The Light Reading of our Ancestors* (1927), says : " The wind howls, whistles or moans ; the clouds lower ; the roll of the thunder is ominous ; the flash of the lightning intensifies the blackness of the night by its momentary glare. Again and again hope seems dead, or is snatched back to life from the very verge of despair." Descriptions infected with picturesque terminology, yet beautiful in their artifice, flood the romances with colour, besides enhancing the emotions of the principal characters.

The use she made of nature, and more specifically nature in its most terrifying aspects, is a heritage of the great English drama. Consciously or unconsciously, Mrs. Radcliffe, like Shakespeare, put into practice the doctrine of " beauty in horror and the horrible in the beautiful ". The most thrilling incidents in her novels do not occur without the elements being unleashed in all their fury : the stormy midnight when La Motte is obliged to flee from Paris in *The Romance of the Forest*, or the atmosphere when Adeline found the time-yellowed manuscript, or in *The Italian* when Schedoni goes to murder Ellena. ". . . at times immoderate in using scenery to suggest or accompany emotional moods, the excess may be pardoned in the discoverer of a novelty which was of a great potential value."

The horrid graces of wildness have been ascribed by B. Sprague Allen to the " influence of Salvator Rosa on the cultivation of a taste for wild scenery in England ". He adds that " It was the philosopher's influence combined with that of the Italian painters which made beauty visible where it had not been perceived before ". Towards the middle of the eighteenth century the arts and the general aesthetic sensibility of England were subjugated to a new passion ; the yearning for the ' picturesque ', quickened by a fresh perception of natural grandeur. The " acute sensibility " reflected in the literature and the very psychology of the age was immeasurably reinforced by a study of the pictures of Claude Lorrain, Gaspar (Dughet) Poussin, or Salvator Rosa, while the impulse towards melancholy and horror was inspired by a deliberate endeavour to construct by means of ruins, cypress trees, weeping willows, and temples, situations of varied emotional appeal. In *The Times Literary Supplement*, 1 December 1927, we read : " The qualities exhibited in their work . . . are the predilection for ' landscape '—that is, for wide prospects, richly filled with the works of nature and of man, and revealed by dramatic contrasts of light and shade ; the use of ' roughness and sudden variation joined to irregularity ' to gain striking effects of form and colour ; the taste for vast architectural masses, and for the associations of grandeur and terror evoked by such objects as palaces, castles, crags, gnarled tree trunks or lonely hovels." Such was, indeed, the kingdom of the picturesque which exercised its influence on the romances of Mrs. Radcliffe, whose art was the product of emotion deeply stirred by contact with nature.

On the whole the grand and imposing in nature appealed more strongly to her than the mildly sweet. Mrs. Radcliffe goes in for vastness of natural scenes ; the wide horizon of the sky and the vastness of the sea affect her more. She is particularly enchanted by the music of the wave or the sound of a distant surge. The soul dilates in the contemplation of such vast scenes over which there is an aura of holiness. Such scenes are uncommonly beautiful, for they deepen the awfulness of sound and silence. Speaking of Adeline in *The Romance of the Forest*, Mrs. Radcliffe says :

> Of all the grand objects which nature had exhibited, the ocean inspired her with the most sublime admiration. She loved to wander along on its shores, and, when she could escape so long from the duties or the forms of society, she would sit for hours on the beach, watching the rolling waves, and listening to their dying murmur, till her softened fancy recalled long lost scenes.

Indeed, the grandeur and immensity of the view astonished and overpowered Mrs. Radcliffe. Once more there is a reference to the pauses of the surge breaking loud and hollow on the shore as a profound stillness reigns in the fisherman's cottage in *The Italian* whenever the murmur of the waves sink :

> The moon, rising over the ocean, showed its restless surface spreading to the wide horizon, and the waves, which broke in foam upon the rocky beach below, retiring in long white lines far upon the waters.

Certain passages in her diary constantly refer to her love of the sea, and to scenes of extreme wildness, grandeur, and solitude :

> How sweet is the cadence of the distant surge ! It seemed, as we sat in our inn, as if a faint peal of far-off bells mingled with the sounds on shore, sometimes heard, sometimes lost : the first note of the beginning, and last of the falling peal, seeming always the most distinct. . . . This chiming of the surge is when the tide is among the rocks, and the wind, blowing from the sea, bears and softens all the different notes of the waves to a distance, in one harmonious cadence ; as in a concert, your distance from the orchestra blends the different instruments into a richer and softer harmony.

Again, while sailing from Cowes after sunset, she exclaims :

> how impressive the silence ! . . . like a song of peace to the departing day !
> . . . Everyone who gazed upon this scene, proud or humble, was a step nearer
> the grave—yet none seemed conscious of it. The scene itself, great,
> benevolent, sublime, powerful, yet silent in its power—progressive and
> certain in its end, steadfast and full of a sublime repose : the scene itself spoke
> of its Creator.

For Mrs. Radcliffe nature is a manifestation of Divine grandeur and her
attitude contains all the germ of that philosophy of nature which was
later so well expounded by the Romantic poets. The sense of religious
exultation that we get in her painting of wild landscapes easily points
the way to Wordsworth, for both feel the regenerating power of nature.

Her passion for romantic scenery, and her poetic treatment of landscapes, opened up new resources to the art of the novelist. She enlarged
the scope and domain of prose fiction by liberating fancy and quickening
colour. She filled it with goodly imagery and captivated the senses,
which made Scott consider her " the first poet-novelist, if rhythm is
not always an essential characteristic of poetry ". At another place,
while referring to her pictures " now pleasing and serene, now gloomy
and terrible ", he said that these were " scenes which could only have
been drawn by one to whom nature had given the eye of a painter, with
the spirit of a poet ". She was indeed a " prose poet ", " the first to
introduce the poetic element into the English novel ", thus making
an appreciable contribution to the realm of fiction. The inclinations of
her poetic sensibility foreshadow the period of the coming Romantic
Revival.

Her scenery is as gloomy as her tale, and her personages are those at
whose frown that gloom grows darker. Her villain-heroes correspond
to the scenery ; their wicked projects are dark, singular, and atrocious ;
and their guilt is tinged with a darker hue, so that they seem almost to
belong to an unearthly sphere of powerful mischief.

Mrs. Radcliffe has drawn her villains from the Italy of the Elizabethan
dramatists and not from the Italy of history. Malcolm, the Marquis of
Mazzini, La Motte and the Marquis de Montalt, Montoni or Schedoni
—all have the spark from Elizabethan villains like D'Amville in *The
Atheists' Tragedy*, or Francisco in *The Duke of Milan*, or the Cardinal in
The Duchess of Malfi. The villain-hero or " the dominating figure in
the story of a man of great power, stained with criminal designs " was
a type developed by Marlowe and later Elizabethans. The villain-heroes

of Mrs. Radcliffe are characterized by the same domineering, relentless personality, and selfish aims. Two of them are usurping brothers, a common character in Shakespeare and other Elizabethans.

Miss C. F. McIntyre has pointed out that " Mrs. Radcliffe . . . was the person really responsible for the revival of Elizabethan villain ". She gives credit to Walpole for having created a tyrant " cruel and calculating, but having little individuality ", but she holds Mrs. Radcliffe responsible for transmitting this character to later romanticists. " The Elizabethan villain-hero did not cease to exist when the Elizabethan playwrights had finished their work. . . . The so-called ' Gothic ' novelists, and especially Mrs. Radcliffe as their strongest representative, brought him forward again, and handed him on to later Romanticists like Byron and Shelley."

These sinister personages, with their passion-lined faces and gleaming eyes, are the pivot of all her romances, and her presentation of the type gains in power and vigour as they slowly evolve from Malcolm in *The Castles of Athlin and Dunbayne* to Schedoni in *The Italian*.

Malcolm, master of Dunbayne, is " proud, oppressive, revengeful ", " mighty in injustice and cruel in power ". He seizes his brother's estate, murders him and expels his son ; having murdered the Lord of Athlin he tries to murder the latter's son Osbert, and even attempts to compel the daughter Mary to become his mistress.

The tyrannical Marquis of Mazzini in *A Sicilian Romance* wishes to force his daughter to marry someone she does not love, and also imprisons his wife in the dungeons of his castle. In *The Romance of the Forest* we meet the dispirited La Motte. Although the vacillations in his criminal purposes makes him only too human, he is overshadowed by a darker figure.

In *The Mysteries of Udolpho* we meet Montoni, with his forbidding and mysterious air, whose dark personality harmonizes with the gloom of Udolpho. He possesses that vigour and vitality, and those essentials of character which were later developed in Schedoni. According to Eino Railo, Montoni is " the lonely, stalwart, saturnine and black-browed man of beautiful countenance, whose spiritual life is in the grip of some secret influence and who, by reason of his intelligence and strength of will and the volcanic nature of his passions, stands out from his surroundings as an independent individual. In this respect Mrs. Radcliffe . . . has . . . a vision of something superhuman, of a superman with uncommon qualities, whose soul and actions are dominated by passions unknown to the ordinary mortal, passions verging on the demoniac." His selfish treatment of Emily and her aunt at Udolpho, his speedy assumption of authority immediately after his marriage, his cruel treatment of his antagonist in the duel, his personal bravery and suffering—all are the traits of Elizabethan villain. " As he wanders through the passages of his dilapidated castle, silent and darkly defiant, brooding over some secret thought, yet noble and beautiful in appearance, or sits cold and mocking amongst his accomplices, gambling or drinking, he achieves in some way an effect of romantically majestic proportions which attracts our interest owing to its novelty."

" In 1797 Mrs. Radcliffe's *The Italian* added another figure to the Gothic gallery—the masterly plotter and murderer, Schedoni." Mrs. Radcliffe throws on him just enough of that dubious light which mystery requires :

> . . . as he stalked along, wrapped in the black garments of his order, there was something terrible in his air, something almost superhuman. His cowl, too, as it threw a shade over the livid paleness of his face, increased its severe character, and gave an effect to his large melancholy eyes which approached to horror.

His imposing, austere figure stained with darkest crimes becomes the medium for Mrs. Radcliffe to explore the mysteries of the human soul and its darker motives. His character has strong traces of Milton's Satan and affinities with Shakespeare's Cassius. He approximates fully to the type of Elizabethan villain-hero, and at times rises to a pitch of real tragic conflict, as during his inward struggle when about to murder Ellena. " The conflict between his design and his conscience was strong, or perhaps, it was only between his passions."

Mr. Clarence Boyer, in his *The Villain as Hero in Elizabethan Tragedy*, has pointed out six Machiavellian qualities in Marlowe's Barabas : egotistical, cruel, faithless, remorseless, murderous, and lastly a poisoner, all of which qualities are profusely evident in Schedoni. His egotism is evident in his assured bearing before the Marchesa and his contemptuous treatment of Vivaldi whom he plans to employ as minister to his own ambitious ends. Schedoni is as outrageously selfish as any of Marlowe's heroes. His cruelty emerges when he advocates Ellena's death, and as Mr. Boyer observes : " has no regard whatever for human beings, but sweeps them away as though they were so many flies ". He is faithless in his dealings with the Marchesa. And he dies without any real remorse, for his behaviour toward his supposed daughter is inspired by natural affection rather than by repentance for evil intentions. He is murderous, as well as a poisoner, a fact which appears three times in the story. Firstly, at his suggestion Ellena is supplied with poisoned food ; then, he hands over his poisoned dagger to the peasant who has been his guide, and finally he poisons both himself and the revengeful monk Nicola who betrayed him. Schedoni's skilful handling of the Marchesa has the stamp of Shakespeare's Iago.

Schedoni works out his purposes with almost superhuman powers ; and even when unseen, we feel his will directing his awful energies. The spell is broken only when he is brought within the range of human emotion moved by an anxiety for the safety and marriage of his supposed daughter. We feel the incongruity ; as if a spectre were moved to tears and human pity. " At one touch of human pathos the enchantment would have been dissolved, as spells are broken by a holy word, or as the ghost of Protesilaus vanished before the earthly passion of his enamoured widow."

Maturin's Melmoth, and the heroes of Scott and Byron, are descended from Mrs. Radcliffe's villains. The same world-weariness pervades them ; with gleaming eyes and passion-wrought faces they resemble Walpole's Manfred and Mrs. Radcliffe's villain-heroes. Lord Ernle says, " Byron modelled his scowl on that of Schedoni, and *Lara* and the *Giaour* owed much to the really powerful description of that monastic villain in *The Italian*." Selfish and unscrupulous, brave and rash, they are possessed of great personal strength ; their sinister personality and fierce manner strikes dread all round, while a veil of dark mystery hangs over their early life. ". . . the Byronic hero was a glorified man of feeling, with a dash of devilry in his composition. His ' fierce dilating eye ', inherited from Mrs. Radcliffe's villains, was more magnetic and compelling than the ' suffused orb ' of sensibility. His deeply lined countenance was undisputed evidence of a stupendous capacity for emotion." The " Byronic hero " of the early nineteenth century was a gift from the Elizabethan plays passed on by Mrs. Radcliffe. Byron's heroes are egotistic in lust for power, and in arms against the world as were Marlowe's heroes. Moreover, their lust for wandering and adventure suggests the spirit of the Renaissance.

This agent of terror, oppressed with agony, was bequeathed to the nineteenth century. Scott, commenting on Mrs. Radcliffe's villain-heroes, says : " To draw such portraits requires no mean powers. And although they belong rather to romance than to real life, the impression which they make upon the imagination is scarce lessened by the sense."

Mrs. Radcliffe drew on diverse materials, assembled the scattered hints, and shaped them with her characteristic method. It is, however, difficult to distinguish how far these transpositions into the romantic key were deliberate, and how far an unconscious alchemy of memory. Two dissertations by Wieten and by McIntyre have unsuccessfully attempted to explore the sources of her masterly creations, while Dr. Tompkins has appended a small list to *The Popular Novel in England* (Constable, 1932).

Every page of Mrs. Radcliffe's work is bedewed with the tear of sensibility, every volume is damp with it. And she herself provides the key to this sentimentality, melancholy, and excessive emotion : her chapters are prefaced by quotations from Shakespeare, Milton, Thomson, Warton, Gray, Collins, Mason, and others. " English literature had discovered the sentimental possibilities of nature extremely early, developing it in *The Seasons*, ' graveyard ' and ' night ' poetry, odes, *Pamela* and *Clarissa Harlowe, Ossian* and other similar products." Sentimentalism infused itself into general literature about the middle of the century, as a protest and reaction against the emotional coldness of the classical age. It announced itself in Richardson, Rousseau, and the youthful Goethe. Mrs. Radcliffe has been compared to sentimentalists like Mackenzie and Sterne, while in her attitude towards nature and in her imaginative force she seems to have been influenced by Rousseau. Her heroines are descended from Richardson's Pamela or Clarissa, but placed in more romantic situations. Mr. Foster thinks that the Radcliffian novel was a product of sensibility having its origin in Prévost, despite the usual opinion that the French influence on the English novel between 1750–1800 is almost negligible.

Mrs. Radcliffe's debt to Smollett, Leland, Walpole, Clara Reeve, and Sophia Lee, is fairly obvious : Smollett had given inklings of ' Gothicism' in *Ferdinand Count Fathom* ; Leland had attempted *Longsword*, ' a historical romance ' ; *The Castle of Otranto* had hinted at dramatic technique ; Reeve's *The Old English Baron* influenced *The Mysteries of Udolpho* ; and Miss Lee in *The Recess* gave studies of female sensibility heightened by fear. The cult of suspense was developed by other writers of the 'eighties who preceded Mrs. Radcliffe. Elizabeth Blower in *Maria* (1785) and A Lady of Distinction in *Helena* had described Gothic passages through which the heroine wanders at midnight alarmed by supernatural apprehensions.

But probably the greatest debt Mrs. Radcliffe owed was to her contemporary, Mrs. Charlotte Smith, who " wrote sentimental adventure stories furnished with landscapes, castles and ghosts ". Professor Foster quotes certain similar passages from the works of both these novelists.

The *Analytical Review*, July 1788, p. 327, noted how the methods and plans in Mrs. Smith's *Emmeline* (1788) influenced the novels of Mrs. Radcliffe. The same journal in December 1789, p. 484, while reviewing Mrs. Smith's *Ethelinde* (1789) commented upon its atmospheric preparation for the appearance of the ghost, illustrating the combination of states of high sentimental tension with melodramatic terror, a technique which became fine art in the hands of Mrs. Radcliffe. The innocent beauty of Emmeline, set in its Gothic frame, foreshadows Adeline and Emily, and the situation in *Ethelinde* (1789) where the heroine invokes her father's spirit and seems to feel it near, has an affinity with Mrs. Radcliffe's future technique.

Professor Foster feels that *The Romance of the Forest* owed much to Mrs. Smith's *Celestina*, which was perhaps published early in 1791, for it was reviewed in the *Analytical Review* the same year in August. *The Romance of the Forest* must have seen print later, being first mentioned in the *Critical Review*, April 1792. Montague Thorold, the servile lover in *Celestina*, foreshadows the unrequited lover Louis La Motte in *The Romance of the Forest*. " Montoni's marriage with Emily's aunt is not unlike Roker's marriage of Leonard (Roker is the vile lawyer in *The Old Manor House*). The ghosts of Bangy Castle (Bangy is the Villeroi chateau in *Udolpho*) prove to be the smugglers of *The Old Manor House*, while the recovery of Ludovico reminds one of the banditti scene in *Desmond*."

Mrs. Piozzi's *Observations and Reflections made in the course of a Journey through France, Italy, and Germany* (1789) seems to be a direct source for her descriptions in *The Mysteries of Udolpho*. She may have used two other books : one by Ramond de Carbonnières, *Observations faites dans les Pyrénées* (1789), and the other P. J. Grosley's *New Observations on Italy and its Inhabitants* (1769). " She drew on them both in *The Mysteries of Udolpho* (1794), on Ramond for the Pyrenean scenes of the first and fourth volumes, and on Grosley for Emily's journey into Italy, while memories of Grosley recurred in her next and last book, *The Italian* (1797)." It was in Grosley's book that " she found . . . the hint for the veiled figure at Udolpho ".

" The scenes that Salvator Rosa dashed " were also her model.

Dr. Manwaring, in her *Italian Landscape in Eighteenth Century England* (Milford), has illustrated in detail the deepening glow of " Italian light on English walls " during the period.   The pictures of Claude and Salvator, or paintings even by their imitators and forgers, were very popular, along with a passion for building or enlarging great mansions, each with its ambitious picture gallery ;   the word ' picturesque ' from the Italian *Pittoresco*, meaning first ' pictorial ', was naturalized in the English language to denote an agreeable wildness or horror.   The picturesque prospect, like the ruin, was but the means of being " agreeably terrified ".   M. Praz, writing in *The Times Literary Supplement*, 13 August 1925, says, " the tortured precipices and storm-riven trees of the ' bandit ' Salvator Rosa were the most powerful force in this development of taste, but Claude's ' unreal Arcadian scenes ', as Dr. Manwaring terms them, with their insubstantial vistas and ruins smilingly returned to Nature, were scarcely less potent as a romantic stimulus."

The idea of explaining away the supernatural might have occurred to Mrs. Radcliffe from Schiller's popular romance *Der Geisterseher* (1789), in which the elaborately contrived marvels of the Armenian, who was modelled on Cagliostro, were but the feats of a juggler and had a physical cause.   Professor Foster, however, traces this method to Prévost who " tells some genuinely supernatural tales, but his usual method is to explain a phenomenon which seemed mysterious as something very natural.   This is Mrs. Radcliffe's *surnaturel expliqué*.   The ghost which appeared before Fanny Cleveland in the chateau of Corogne is really Don Thadeo bound up in white surgical bandages, we are told, after sharing sympathetically the emotional torment of the poor Fanny who thought it her dead brother."   Professor Foster holds that Mrs. Radcliffe did not know Prévost at first hand, but she knew him through Charlotte Smith, Sophia Lee, Clara Reeve, Madame De Genlis, and Arnaud.

G. Buyers, in an article in *Englische Studien*, XLVIII, pp. 350 ff., has suggested that Schiller's *Geisterseher* influenced the portrait of Montoni in *The Mysteries of Udolpho* (1794).   According to Miss McIntyre, the peculiar physiognomy of the Armenian was transmitted to Schedoni in *The Italian* (1797).   But as the first English translation of *Der Geisterseher* appeared only in 1795, it cannot be said to have influenced *The Mysteries of Udolpho*, unless Mrs. Radcliffe was able to read it in the original. L. F. Thompson, in his article on *Ann Radcliffe's knowledge of German*, states that " . . . a perusal of her *Journey through Holland and Germany*, undertaken in 1794 in the company of her husband, points to her being able to obtain an adequate knowledge of a German book before the publication of Udolpho ". Miss Killen has suggested that " after the publication of *The Forest* . . . Mrs. Radcliffe seems to have spent some of her time studying the German literature of outlaws and brigands ". Mrs. Elwood, in her " Memoirs of Literary Ladies ", declares, on the authority of a contemporary of Mrs. Radcliffe, that Ann Radcliffe professed great admiration for the ' Brigands ' of Schiller. Another German source of Mrs. Radcliffe was perhaps Benedicte Nauberts' *Herman of Unna* (ascribed in the translation to Cramer) which appears to have suggested the kidnapping of the heroine to a mountain convent and her meeting there with her unknown mother.

Besides the influence of German literature which was then becoming popular in England, the other great influence on Mrs. Radcliffe was Shakespeare and other Elizabethans. She quotes Shakespeare more frequently than any other author, and many of her scenes are reminiscent of Shakespearean tragedy. Yet her method of inspiring awe and exciting curiosity has more the impress of later Elizabethans than of Shakespeare, especially in " their inclination toward the sensational and the gruesome ".

Miss C. F. McIntyre, in her article *Were the ' Gothic Novels ' Gothic ?*, has shown Radcliffe's indebtedness to Elizabethan drama, in her picturing of the violent and bloody scenes, and in the use of revenge motive. In *The Italian*, Vivaldi finds a heap of bloody garments in the ruins of Paluzzi, while the two abductions of Ellena, first, when she has to leave her servant tied to a pillar, and second, when Vivaldi is seized by the powers of Inquisition, are examples of violence. Miss McIntyre states that poisoning was a characteristic crime during the Renaissance ; Massinger's play, *The Duke of Milan* (1623), reveals a characteristic treatment of the theme, where the Duke draws poison from the painted lips of his dead duchess. The part that poisoning plays in Mrs. Radcliffe's novels shows another Renaissance influence upon her works. In *A Sicilian Romance* the Marquis mixes poison in the food for his imprisoned first wife, who, however, escapes, and the Marquis is poisoned by his faithless second wife. In *The Romance of the Forest* the Marquis himself resorts to poison when his crimes are about to be exposed. In *The Mysteries of Udolpho*, sister Agnes, formerly Laurentini di Udolpho, had goaded the Marquis. di Villeroi to poison his wife. And then there is that colourful scene when poison rises hissing in Montoni's glass at the Udolpho banquet.

The revenge motive is displayed in Mrs. Radcliffe's first romance *The Castles of Athlin and Dunbayne*. The Earl of Athlin was foully murdered by Malcolm, a neighbouring chief, and " when Osbert learned the story of his father's death, his young heart glowed to avenge the deed ". In *The Italian*, Nicola, goaded by the spirit of revenge, works to expose the crimes of Schedoni, his former friend. The plot of Mrs. Radcliffe's posthumous tale, *Gaston de Blondeville*, is typically Elizabethan: the kinsman of a murdered man accusing his murderer, and the spectre of the murdered man appearing to support the charge and execute vengeance.

Some of her passages and situations are strikingly reminiscent of *Macbeth* and *Hamlet* : the former being a Tragedy of Blood and the latter a Tragedy of Revenge.

The ravings of the dying nun Agnes recall *Macbeth* :

> " What ! there again," said she . . . " come from the grave . . . do not smile so piteously."

Also the hallucination of Spalatro in *The Italian* :

> I have never been at peace since. The bloody hand is always before me ! and often of a night, when the sea roars, and storms shake the house, *they* have come, all gashed as I left them, and stood before my bed ! I have got up and run out upon the shore for safety.

And again :

> " Frenzy ! would it were, signor ; I saw that dreadful hand—I see it now—it is there again !—there ! "

The dispute between Schedoni and his associate Spalatro in the cottage by the seashore as to who shall murder Ellena, concludes with Confessor's words :

> " Give me the dagger then . . . "

Again, when the guests from the table at Udolpho rise in confusion, when Montoni's story of Laurentini's disappearance is interrupted by a mysterious voice, the picture suggests the breaking up of the banquet scene in *Macbeth*. Or when Emily enters Udolpho, the sounding of the portal bell reminds us of Shakespeare's " knell that summons thee to heaven or hell ", or of the raven that " croaks the fatal entrance of Duncan " under the battlements of Inverness.

The influence of *Hamlet* is traceable in the scene where the mysterious figure is seen on the terrace outside Emily's window. The conversation reminds us of the opening of *Hamlet*.

Therefore " one is justified in recognizing the Elizabethan influence upon Mrs. Radcliffe in her decidedly dramatic structure ; in her general choice of theme, especially her attitude toward death and toward the supernatural. . . ."

What Vernon Lee said of the works of later Elizabethans—Webster, Ford, Tourneur, and Marston, may well be applied to the atmosphere of Mrs. Radcliffe's works :

> The world of these great poets . . . is the darkened Italian palace, with its wrought-iron bars preventing escape, its embroidered carpets muffling the footsteps ; its hidden, suddenly yawning trap-doors ; its arras-hangings concealing masked ruffians ; its garlands of poisoned flowers ; its long suites of untenanted darkened rooms. . . .

Mrs. Radcliffe had studied certain old chronicles, and she may also have depended on oral legends clustering round ancient abbeys for the background of her stories. Ghostly legends fascinated her, and she probably amassed a hoard of traditions when she visited English castles during her tours with her husband. Her settings and characters may well have come from folk-lore. " The Gothic castle, suddenly encountered in a dark forest is boldly transported from fairyland and set down in Italy, Sicily, or Spain."

Mrs. Radcliffe's individual style of composition has never been equalled, but her success drew forth a host of imitators. A long list of such imitations has been appended to Miss McIntyre's thesis. " Every pen essayed to catch something of her style, to write of some peerless heroine persecuted by wicked marquis or villainous monk, imprisoned in a terrific castle or mouldering abbey, scared by apparitions and illusions caused by cracking doors, unaccountable noises, sudden gleams of light where no person could be walking, until at last Matilda, or Rosalia, or Imogene is rescued by her lover, and as the story closes with this happy bridal it is discovered that the very castle or abbey where she had been secretly detained is part of her own domain now restored to her by the death of a cruel and treacherous relative." Her imitators produced only cumbrous caricatures, in which the terrors have no decorum, and the explanations are almost farcical. All have some variation of plot and characters, and a ghost of whatever sort is always explained away. A

glance at the titles of their works reveals nothing but " Mysteries ",
" Dark and Fatal Secrets ", " Abbeys " and " Old Castles ".

Most of the shilling shockers of the Victorian age fell into two general
groups : " The first . . . in the footsteps of such novels as *The Monk*,
and *The Italian*. . . . The second group . . . followed the lead of *The
Castle of Otranto* and *The Mysteries of Udolpho*." Even here Mrs. Radcliffe
dominated the twin currents of disintegration.

All successful followers had to call to aid other means to make their
works interesting. ' Monk ' Lewis added sickly voluptuousness to his
terrors, while Maturin, full of " rich conceits ", approached the borders
of forbidden speculations and paradoxical morals. But greater names
owed allegiance to Mrs. Radcliffe. As Montague Summers puts it :
" Honoré de Balzac thought her romances admirable, and many of his
first efforts were directly inspired by her pages. In some of his maturer
work their influence still prevails, as it often does in Dumas, Victor Hugo,
Eugène Sue, Joseph Petrus Borel, Baudelaire—and when I have said
Balzac and Baudelaire what more can I add ? "

Martha Hale Shackford, in her article *The Eve of St. Agnes and The
Mysteries of Udolpho*, has pointed out Keats's indebtedness to Mrs. Radcliffe.
Quoting comparative passages of " indefinable likenesses in spirit and
atmosphere " from the two works, she writes :

> The setting of Mrs. Radcliffe's story possessed many elements that seem
> revived by Keats. There was the solid grandeur of an ancient Gothic castle,
> with shadowy galleries, mysterious staircases, moonlit casements, and
> gorgeous apartments hung with arras glowing with medieval pageantry.
> The feudal life with old retainers serving an arrogant master and his carousing
> friends is pictured in both works.

To Miss Wieten her influence was potent on Tennyson, " in subject,
form, and partly in treatment ". " She shadows forth Wordsworth and
Tennyson's intense joy in nature, as well as Shelley's and Swinburne's
love of liberty and abhorrence of restraint."

" Gothic romance gained its firm hold on the reader's interest about
1791, the year in which Mrs. Radcliffe attained her first outstanding
success." Romance, as exhibited by her, " tricked antique ruff and
bonnet ", has yet eyes of youth ; and the beauty is not diminished by
the folds of the brocade, or the stiffness of the damask stomacher. Her
powers of originality, her high degree of excellence and capacity for rich
invention, has won universal applause. Scott said that she has never
been excelled or even equalled in " appealing to those powerful and

general sources of interest, a latent sense of supernatural awe, and curiosity concerning whatever is hidden and mysterious ". Hazlitt remarked that " in harrowing up the soul with imaginary horrors, and making the flesh creep and the nerves thrill with fond hopes and fears, she is unrivalled among her countrymen ". Coleridge, while reviewing *The Mysteries of Udolpho*, wrote :

> Thine too these golden keys, immortal boy !
>   This can unlock the gates of joy,
> Of horror that, and thrilling fears,
> Or ope the sacred source of sympathetic tears.

Such are the presents of the Muse to the infant Shakespeare, and though perhaps to no other mortal has she been so lavish of her gifts, the keys referring to the third line Mrs. Radcliffe must be allowed to be completely in possession of.

Charles Bucke spoke of her as one " bred in the schools of Dante and Ariosto, and whom the Muses recognize as the sister of Salvator Rosa ". Bucke may have had in mind Mathias' well-known compliment to Mrs. Radcliffe : " She was the Mighty Magician of ' The Mysteries of Udolpho ' bred and nourished by the Florentine Muses in their sacred solitary caverns, amid the paler shrines of Gothick superstition, and all the dreariness of enchantment." André Chenier in his ' Observations ' upon the English romance writers, ranks her next to Shakespeare, while Dr. Nathan Drake has called her " the Shakespeare of Romance writers ".

She has also been called " The Great Enchantress " and Montague Summers refers to " the sombre and sublime genius of Ann Radcliffe ". " Her works, in order to produce their greatest impression, should be read . . . at that delightful period of youth, when the soft twilight of imagination harmonizes with the luxurious and uncertain light cast on their wonders. By those, who come at such an age to their perusal, they will never be forgotten."

In Mrs. Radcliffe's work there is the finest flowering of the novels of Terror. She eclipsed for a while the geniuses of Richardson, Fielding, and Smollett, but her own star dimmed at the ascendancy of Walter Scott, the Ariosto of the North.

CHAPTER VI

THE SCHAUER-ROMANTIK : OR CHAMBERS
OF HORROR

IN the sunset glory of its Schauer-Romantik phase the Gothic novel blazes forth in all its lurid violence and sensationalism. During its transition from Mrs. Radcliffe towards the intense school of ' Monk ' Lewis, Maturin, and others, it undergoes a gradual development of spirit and temper, wherein we observe a " crashing crescendo of emotion ". " As we proceed from decade to decade, we find that the earlier novels depict, cultivate, and satisfy the gentle emotions ; that the craving for stronger and deeper ones gradually arises, until in the end the most violent and tragic passions are demanded," says Ernest Bernbaum. Completely abandoning all restraints, it " outrageously oversteps the modesty of nature and indulges in a farrago of frightfulness ".

The chords of terror which had tremulously shuddered beneath Mrs. Radcliffe's gentle fingers were now smitten with a new vehemence. The intense school of the Schauer-Romantiks improvised furious and violent themes in the orchestra of horror. Edith Birkhead says, " the villain's sardonic smile is replaced by wild outbursts of diabolical laughter, his scowl grows darker and darker, and his designs become more bloody and more dangerous, his victims no longer sigh plaintively, but give utterance to piercing shrieks and despairing yells ; tearful Amandas are unceremoniously thrust into the background by vindictive Matildas, whose passions rage in all their primitive savagery ; the fearful ghost ' fresh courage takes ', and stands forth audaciously in the light of day ; the very devil stalks shamelessly abroad in manifold disguises. We are caught up from first to last in the very tempest, torrent, and whirlwind of passion." The contrast between the work and personalities of Mrs. Radcliffe and ' Monk ' Lewis serves to illustrate the two distinct streams of the Gothic novel : the former representing the Craft of Terror, the latter and his followers comprising the Chambers of Horror. As Michael Sadleir¦ aptly observes : ". . . the Radcliffians are like persons who sit about a blazing fire on a stormy night. . . . Into the firelit refuge of the Radcliffian novelist the follower of Lewis would fain intrude, haggard, and with water streaming from his lank hair, shrieking, perhaps, as would befit a demon of the storm ; then, when he had struck the company to silent fear, he would wish to vanish again into the howling darkness."

The difference between Terror and Horror is the difference between awful apprehension and sickening realization : between the smell of death and stumbling against a corpse. Professor McKillop, quoting from Mrs. Radcliffe, said that " obscurity [in Terror] . . . leaves the imagination to act on a few hints that truth reveals to it, . . . obscurity leaves something for the imagination to exaggerate ". Burke held that " To make any-thing very terrible, obscurity seems in general to be necessary ", and added that, ". . . darkness, being originally an idea of terror, was chosen as a fit scene for such terrible representations ". Burke did not distinguish between the subtle gradations of Terror and Horror ; he related only Terror to Beauty, and probably did not conceive of the beauty of the Horrid, the grotesque power of something ghastly, too vividly imprinted on the mind and sense.

Terror thus creates an intangible atmosphere of spiritual psychic dread, a certain superstitious shudder at the other world. Horror resorts to a cruder presentation of the macabre : by an exact portrayal of the physically horrible and revolting, against a far more terrible background of spiritual gloom and despair. Horror appeals to sheer dread and repulsion, by brooding upon the gloomy and the sinister, and lacerates the nerves by establishing actual cutaneous contact with the super-natural. " Seeing a supernatural visitant is terrible, hearing him is direful, smelling him is loathsome, but having him touch you is the climax of horror," says Dorothy Scarborough. The same feeling is expressed by Mrs. Barbauld : " Solitude, darkness, low-whispered sounds, obscure glimpses of objects, flitting forms, tend to raise in the mind that thrilling, mysterious terror, which has for its object the ' powers unseen and mightier far than we '." The very vagueness and uncertain origin of this terror suggests an indefinable presence which might manifest itself suddenly ; there is an utter inability to judge or cope with the extent of the power this presence can exercise, probably for evil and malignant ends. But when the grand cause of terror manifests itself, it excites horror. No longer wrapt up in the shades of its own incomprehensible obscurity, its revealed loathsomeness is awful, striking, and horrible, so that strength, violence, pain, and terror are ideas " heterogeneously yoked " together thus making a combined attack upon the mind. ' Horror ' approaches violence in its intensity ; ' Terror ' when sufficiently violent embodies horror.

Horror itself has been finely described in two holy scriptures. The following passage from the *Book of Job* illustrates the nature of Horror :

> In thoughts from the visions of the night, when deep sleep falleth upon men, fear came upon me and trembling, which made all my bones to shake. Then a spirit passed before my face. The hair of my flesh stood up. It stood still . . . an image was before mine eyes ; there was silence ; and I heard a voice. . . .

And the effect of horror is what Arjuna felt in the *Bhagvadgita* :

> My limbs quail, my mouth goes dry, my body shakes and my hair stands on end.

The Craft of Terror was finer in its working, and keener in its effect. Dr. Tompkins says, " Beauty refines terror, connects it with dignified associations and prevents it from verging on disgust ; terror in turn heightens beauty, like the thundercloud impendent over so many scenes in eighteenth-century engravings." The Schauer-Romantiks inverted the rules of fear, and used romance " as a mere maquillage for horror ". Coleridge remarks : " Situations of torment, and images of naked horror, are easily conceived ; and a writer in whose works they abound, deserves our gratitude almost equally with him who should drag us by way of sport through a military hospital, or force us to sit at the dissection table of a natural philosopher. . . . Figures that shock the imagination, and narratives that mangle the feelings, rarely discover *genius*, and always betray a low and vulgar *taste*." But Coleridge went too far while making this comment. His delicate sensibility could not probably bare itself to the petrifying gaze of Medusa, or comprehend her cold, destructive beauty.

Each writer of the intense school contributed a grotesque and gruesome theme of horror to the Schauer-Romantik phase of the Gothic novel. They wrote stories of black-magic and lust, of persons in pursuit of the *elixir vitae*, of insatiable curiosity and unpardonable sins, of contracts with the Devil, of those who manufacture monsters in their laboratories, tales of skull-headed ladies, of the dead arising from their graves to feed upon the blood of the innocent and beautiful, or who walk about in the Hall of Eblis, carrying their burning hearts in their hands. Such morbid and fantastic creations like Beckford's *Vathek*, Godwin's *St. Leon* and *Caleb Williams*, Lewis's *The Monk*, Mrs. Shelley's *Frankenstein*, Polidori's *Vampyre*, or Maturin's *Melmoth the Wanderer*, show that the Schauer-Romantiks really had their own private catalogue of subjects to inspire their work, and furnish their Chambers of Horror. The Chambers of Horror are of infinite variety ; each cavern has something new to reveal ; they have new themes and new techniques, and novel methods to shock the nerves.

It is a commonplace of criticism to presume that the horror-romantic phase of Gothic fiction was initiated by Lewis's story, *The Monk* (1795), but there are one or two interesting precursors of this work. The most important is *Vathek* (1786), the wild fantasy of William Beckford, an eccentric and colourful personality. The author states in his preface that *Vathek* is a " story so horrid that I tremble while relating it, and have not a nerve in my frame but vibrates like an aspen ". This work is included under the category of " Gothic novel " since its air of mystery arises from supposedly unnatural causes, while a sense of horror is heightened for artistic effect. Some portions of the narrative read like a nightmare, or at least the quivering stretches of a bad dream, while a sombre sense of fatality and mortal tragedy brood over it like ominous doom. Its gorgeous style and stately descriptions, its exaltation of both poetic and moral justice, relate it to the Gothic romance. The machinery of magic, and the horror of the final scene, place it in the Schauer-Romantik with ' Monk ' Lewis and his followers.

The opening of the story immediately evokes fantasy and awe. Vathek, grandson of Haroun Al Rachid, has a Faustian spirit thirsting after infinite knowledge, seeking to compass " even sciences that did not exist ". He builds the palace of five senses and a lofty tower of fifteen hundred stairs connected with it by a subterranean passage. The settings are resplendent with gorgeous arras, and we are dazzled by a myriad wonders. Here his mother, Carathis, a frisky old lady, indefatigable in wickedness and obsessed with the darker side of magic, pursues her occult studies. She instigates her son to abjure Mahomet and, under her influence, he sets out in quest of the palace of subterranean fire. A devilish Giaour prophesies that Vathek shall sit on the throne and revel in the treasures of the pre-Adamite Sultans. But Vathek disobeys the injunction not to enter any house, visits an Emir, and falls in love with his bewitching daughter Nouronihar. Her father, wishing to separate them, gives a sleeping potion to Nouronihar, and announces that she is dead. But Vathek stumbles on her hiding-place, and together they elope to the palace of subterranean fire.

The episodes hurry us at a breathless pace into abodes of horror : a temple adorned with a pyramid of skulls festooned with human hair, a cave inhabited by reptiles with human faces, and a chamber where carpets of a thousand kinds and colours hang from the walls, fluttering as if stirred by human creatures writhing beneath their weight. There Vathek and Nouronihar find inexhaustible wealth and power for a few days followed by an eternity of torture in the Hall of Eblis.

The last few pages of *Vathek*, with its Oriental, exotic, and resplendent horror, must have inspired the genius of future writers such as Rider Haggard, who penned novels like *She* and *Ayesha*. The atmospheric effects and colouring of the scene where Vathek and Nouronihar approach the Hall of Eblis, leave a dark and solemn impress on the mind :

> . . . they advanced by moonlight till they came within view of the two towering rocks that form a kind of portal to the valley, at the extremity of which rose the vast ruins of Istakar . . . the horror of which was deepened by the shadows of night. . . .
>
> A death-like stillness reigned over the mountain and through the air ; the moon dilated on a vast platform the shades of the lofty columns which reached from the terrace almost to the clouds . . . of an architecture unknown in the records of the earth, served as an asylum for the birds of night, which, alarmed at the approach of such visitants, fled away croaking.

Then follows the description of the

> ruins of an immense palace, whose walls were embossed with various figures. In front stood forth the colossal forms of four creatures, composed of the leopard and the griffin, and though but of stone, inspired emotions of terror.

And as the human steps approached

> the mountain . . . trembled . . . the rock yawned, and disclosed within it a staircase of polished marble, that seemed to approach the abyss. . . . Their steps accelerated to such a degree that they seemed not walking but falling from a precipice.

The baleful hall of Eblis, " the abode of vengeance and despair ", is pictured in the full effulgence of infernal majesty. It conveys to us the horror of the most ghastly convulsions and screams that may not be smothered. Here everyone carries within him a heart tormented in flames, to wander in an eternity of unabating anguish :

> In the midst of this immense hall, a vast multitude was incessantly passing, who severally kept their right hands on their hearts, without once regarding anything around them : they had all the livid paleness of death. Their eyse, deep sunk in their sockets, resembled those phosphoric meteors that glimmer

by night in places of interment. Some stalked slowly on, absorbed in profound reverie ; some, shrieking with agony, ran furiously about like tigers wounded with poisoned arrows ; whilst others, grinding their teeth in rage, foamed along more frantic than the wildest maniac. They all avoided each other ; and, though surrounded by a multitude that no one could number, each wandered at random unheedful of the rest, as if alone on a desert where no foot had trodden.

A list of the demonic relics gathered by Carathis to equip her infernal ceremonial sends a chill down the spine :

> By secret stairs . . . she first repaired to the mysterious recesses in which were deposited the mummies that had been wrested from the catacombs of the ancient Pharaohs. . . . Under the guard of fifty female negroes, mute, and blind of the right eye, were preserved the oil of the most venomous serpents, rhenoceros' horns, and woods of a subtile and penetrating odour procured from the interior of the Indies, together with a thousand other horrible rarities.

The description of oblations by Carathis, in this setting of infernal exhalations, presents a nightmarish scene of horror :

> Phials of serpent's oil, mummies, and bones, were soon set in order on the balustrade of the tower. . . . The sparks had already kindled the dry wood ; the venomous oil burst into a thousand blue flames ; the mummies dissolving, emitted a thick dun vapour ; and the rhenoceros' horns, beginning to consume, all together diffused such a stench. . . . The oil gushed forth in a plenitude of streams. . . . At last the fire became so violent, and the flames reflected from the polished marble so dazzling . . .

To balance such nightmarish horrors, Beckford pictures certain gorgeous scenes of Oriental splendour :

> The pavement, strewed over with gold dust and saffron, exhaled so subtle an odour as almost overpowered them. . . . Infinity of censers . . . were continually burning. Between the several columns were placed tables, each spread with a profusion of viands, and wines of every species sparkling in vases of crystal. A throng of genii and other fantastic spirits of either sex danced lasciviously at the sound of music which issued from beneath.

Beckford's pictures have a definite precision of outline. He does not throw vague hints and suggestions, nor does any shadow veil his description of peculiar horrors. Edith Birkhead says, " the quaint dwarfs perched on Vathek's shoulders, the children chasing blue butterflies, Nouronihar and her maidens on tiptoe, with their hair floating in the breeze, stand out in clear relief, as if painted on a frieze ". Against the background of glittering splendour and colour flit a host of unearthly figures—wrinkled astrologers, hideous Giaours, gibbering negresses, and restless forms pacing with their hands on burning hearts. Oliver Elton finds that " Beckford, like Blake, was a dreamer, as defiant, as full of stubborn vitality . . . revelling in things that are strange, costly and transitory ". He was deeply saturated in the history and romance of the East, a fact well corroborated by the scholarly and voluminous annotations of his editor Henley. Authorities cited are D'Herbelot, *The Arabian Nights*, *The Koran*, *Tales of Inatulla* (Persian), *Anacdotes Arabes*, Habeser's *State of the Ottoman Empire*, Ockley's *History of the Saracens*, Richardson's *Dissertations on the Languages, etc., of the Eastern Nations*, Dr. Cooke's *Voyages and Travels*, Dr. Pocock's *Travels*.

During the two years preceding the publication of *Vathek*, interest in the Orient had been awakened by Sir William Jones's researches into Oriental languages (1784), and Sir Charles Wilkins's translations from *The Mahabharata* (1785). " *Vathek* (1786), generally recognized as the best English imitation of a genuine eastern tale . . . [was] . . . stimulated by an early and continuous reading of eastern stories, particularly of *The Arabian Nights*." Beckford also borrowed some materials from the *Moghul Tales* and *The Adventures of Abdalla, son of Hanif*, which were translated into English in 1729. Probably the Eastern Tales of Voltaire and Count Hamilton also left some impress on Beckford.

The Orient has always fascinated the western mind by its glamorous reality—" a reality that the popular travel books continued to emphasize throughout the period 1775-1825 ". Beckford's *Vathek* is not only a pseudo-Oriental tale ; in it " the Near East was portrayed in a manner unlike anything before in English literature ". The East came back once more to fertilize the fancy of the West, and contribute its mite towards the development of Gothic Romance.

William Godwin (1756–1836), in his *Caleb Williams* (1794) and *St. Leon* (1799), creates an atmosphere of an altogether different type of horror. He is not a master of hints or suggestions, gloom, or weird lights. He displays his horrors in a manner that is credible but intense, like the human body seen in the monotonous brightness of an operation theatre.

Flickering, subterranean torchlight illumines *Vathek*, but Godwin's settings are flooded with clear sunshine. There are no unearthly groans, or phosphorescent flares to enhance the scene of mystery and horror. There are images of excruciating pain, convulsive throbs, and intervals of death-like, insupportable sickness. These horrors comprise a realistic, feverish dream of human existence, and narrate the bruises and ill-treatments inflicted by the world upon a single human being.

Godwin's interest in the supernatural was too mild, only extending so far as it afforded him insight into the " credulity of the human mind ". His characters are not supernatural but human, although they display fiend-like qualities of mind. With an almost morbid skill Godwin applies his " metaphysical dissecting knife " to his characters. His sufferers are creatures of the real world, around whom there plays no weird light of fantasy. While analysing remorse or self-torture, he rises to a cold vehemence in his descriptions.

The *Adventures of Caleb Williams* unfolds a story of the tortures, oppressions, and horrors a poor man may endure at the hands of the powerful and rich. It depicts things as they are : horrors that arise from " domestic and unrecorded despotism, by which man becomes the destroyer of man ". In the hands of Godwin relentless Fate becomes the symbol of a psychological nightmare.

The narrative has a sombre, dreary power and relates Falkland's diabolical pursuit of Caleb Williams. Incidents are conceived not in a series of disconnected episodes, but as part of an involved psychological situation. Falkland, who is impelled by a perverted sense of honour, murders Tyrell, and allows two innocent individuals to be hanged for the crime. He guards his secret, being tortured by his consciousness of guilt. Caleb Williams, urged by a fatal curiosity, discovers the hidden murder committed by his patron, who is a being of the superman type. Falkland employs all resources which law can lavish on men of wealth and position to inflict horrors upon his inquisitive secretary, and deprives him of credit and character, so that he may retain him in his power. Caleb is subjected to years of hunted misery, is plunged into dungeons, and haunted everywhere he goes. This provides an opportunity for Godwin to display pictures of ghastly physical horrors.

Caleb Williams narrates his experience, when he attempted to escape from the cell :

> I had got to the top of the wall. . . . He . . . threw a large stone, which grazed me in its flight. Alarmed at my situation, I was obliged to descend on the other side without taking the necessary precautions, and in my fall nearly dislocated my ankle. . . . I endeavoured to rise after my fall, but the pain was so intense that I was scarcely able to stand, and, after having limped a few paces, I twisted my foot under me, and fell down again.

But that is not all. Godwin shows especial fascination for ghastly details, and can undoubtedly produce an atmosphere heavily charged with relentless physical horror :

> In the morning they . . . fixed a pair of fetters upon both my legs, regardless of the ankle, which was now swelled to a considerable size, and then fastened me with a padlock to a staple in the floor of my dungeon. . . . The pain of the fetter was intolerable. I endeavoured in various ways to relieve it, and even privily to free my leg ; but the more it was swelled, the more was this rendered impossible. . . . The whole mass of my blood was already fevered by the anguish I had undergone.

This gives the author an opportunity of commenting on English social atrocities :

> Is that a country of liberty where thousands languish in dungeons and fetters ? . . . visit the scenes of our prisons ! Witness their unwholesomeness, their filth, the tyranny of their governors, the misery of their inmates !

He further enumerates the horrors of the prison :

> We talk of instruments of torture ; Englishmen take credit to themselves for having banished the use of them from their happy shores ! Alas, he that has observed the secrets of a prison, well knows that there is more torture in the lingering existence of a criminal, in the silent, intolerable minutes that he spends, than in the tangible misery of whips and racks !

Picturing the solitary cheerless darkness of the English prison house, Caleb Williams says :

> Our dungeons were cells, 7½ feet by 6½, below the surface of the ground, damp, without window, light, or air, except from a few holes worked for that purpose in the door. In some of these miserable receptacles three persons were put to sleep together.

The chain permitted the prisoner to move only about eighteen inches to the right or left, and in extreme mental agony Caleb Williams says :

> A thousand times I could have dashed my brains against the walls of my dungeon ; a thousand times I longed for death.

The suggestion of horror rises to a pitch of intensity when Caleb seeks refuge in a hamlet :

> Leave you ! No : I will thrust through your ribs, and drink your blood ! —You conquer me ?—Ha, ha !—Yes, yes ! you shall !—I will sit upon you, and press you to hell ! I will roast you with brimstone, and dash your entrails into your eyes ! . . .

Godwin's *St. Leon, A Tale of the 16th Century* (1799), " is of the miraculous class ", to quote the author, its aim being to " mix human feelings and passions with *incredible* situations, and thus render them impressive and interesting ". This book may very well be called what St. Leon once named it, " a history of his sensations ". Although the author is fascinated by the occult and dabbles in the supernatural, he does not attempt to create an atmosphere of mystery. Like the former work, this novel provides psychological interest by its portrayal of the gradual ruin wrought in the happiness and affections of the possessor of the philosopher's stone and the elixir of life. *St. Leon* is the study of a mind torn by painful remembrances, and agitated by terrible forebodings.

Descended from an old and distinguished French family, St. Leon is a conspicuous figure at the court of Francis I, and has made his mark at the siege of Pavia. He has gambled away his fortunes, and seeks refuge in a Swiss Canton with his wife and four children. Ensuing poverty having brought in its trail every variety of misfortune, a mysterious stranger appears and reveals to him the secret of the philosopher's stone and the elixir of life. Through possession of this fatal secret follows the loss of honour, family, friends, and almost life, when in the end he becomes a victim of the Inquisition. He is taken in a procession to the pious *Auto de Fé*, held to celebrate the return of Phillip II to his devoted subjects. St. Leon narrowly escapes being a victim ; he concocts and drinks the elixir of life and becomes young again. Cursed with immortality, he wanders all over Europe an outcast, abhorred and shunned of men, for he is the ruin of all with whom he comes in contact.

St. Leon's imprisonment in the dungeons at Constance, his escape from the *Auto de Fé* at Valladolid are ' gothic ' in character. The scene of the *Auto de Fé* abounds in physical horror :

> I saw the galleries and accommodations that had been erected for the spectators : I saw the windows and roofs of the houses crowded with beholders. The shrieks of the sufferers I could not hear ; they were drowned in the infernal exultations of the multitude. . . . I discerned some of the condemned, fixed as they were upon small boards, near the top of stakes about four yards high, and therefore greatly above the heads of the assembly, while the flames, abundantly fed with faggots and dry fuel, climbed aloft, and seemed eager to embrace their victims. . . . There were thirty of these death-devoted frames.

The brutal murder of Hector the negro, St. Leon's servant, at the hands of an infuriated mob, provides a gruesome scene :

> The mob had burst into the house ; they seized him alive. They dragged him out in the midst of them ; they insulted over him, as the special favourite

of the infernal king.   They inflicted on him every species of mockery and of torture ;   they killed him joint by joint, and limb by limb.

The aged stranger, who bestows on St. Leon the philosopher's stone and the elixir of life, has the piercing eye familiar to readers of the Gothic novel :

> His eye-beam sat upon your countenance, and seemed to look through you.   You wished to escape from its penetrating power, but you had not the strength to move.   I began to feel as if it were some mysterious and superior being in human form, and not a mortal with whom I was concerned.

The character of Bethlem Gabor, rugged, ferocious, and brutal like the typical ' gothic ' figure, has

> a mystery in his carriage, a something not to be explained, a shell that no human forces could penetrate, that was mortal to confidence, and might quail the stoutest.

His personality is akin to Mrs. Radcliffe's Schedoni, in his love of solitude, and superhuman aspects, which inspire dread all round :

> He was more than six feet in stature . . . and he was built as if it had been a colossus, destined to sustain the weight of the starry heavens.   His voice was like thunder. . . .

This book inspired Maturin's *Melmoth the Wanderer* (1820), Shelley's Rosicrucian tale of *St. Irvyne* (1811), and suggested to Bulwer Lytton his *Strange Story*.   " The first novelist of the United States . . . Charles Brockden Brown, acknowledged Godwin as his master, and found in his work ' transcendent merit '."

Godwin had neither gift nor inclination to conjure with Gothic properties.   But he did extend the range of the Gothic novel by introducing ' criminal ' and ' alchemical ' elements.   *Caleb Williams* is the first spirited story of crime and detection, which Hazlitt considered as " one of the best novels in the language ".   The story is planned backwards, and the method of narrative influenced Conan Doyle and other writers of detective fiction.   Moreover, in these two novels Godwin broke new ground in creating an atmosphere of ghastly physical horror.

Now let us shift our focus towards the fantastic and sombre genius of Matthew Gregory Lewis, who painted his grim and ghastly themes in dark and lurid colours.   His inflamed imagination and violent exaggeration of emotion suggest adolescence, yet he thrills his readers and makes their flesh creep. This author of remarkable talent makes horrors come crowding thick upon us, and often crudely resorts to the physically horrible, through images and descriptions of loathsome corruption, mouldering cerements, and festering relics of death and the grave. Yet, so great is the interest of his unadorned narrative, with its quick succession of events, that such bold exaggeration seems only fitting.

Of all the tales of horror, *The Monk* (1796) is probably the most extravagant. " Lewis had enlivened his sensational story of rape, incest, murder, magic, and diablerie, with an obvious sensuality."   " These puerile effusions dashed down within the space of ten weeks ", are not altogether contemptible : *The Monk* remains a romance of extraordinary fascination and power.

No summary can possibly reproduce the colouring given to the story of *The Monk*. Ambrosio is an abbot of the Capuchin monastery at Madrid. A son of mystery, his parentage unknown, as a child he had been found on the monastery steps, and accepted by the monks as a gift of Heaven. When the story opens he is a young man of about thirty, famed for devoutness and rigid austerity, whose spiritual pride makes him an easy prey to temptation.

Rosario, the youngest novice of the house, becomes a particular favourite with Ambrosio ; and one evening, when they are together in the gardens, Ambrosio discovers to his horror and amazement that his companion belongs to the fair sex. The lady is Matilda de Villanegas, daughter of a noble house, who had dared to penetrate the cloistral walls out of her passionate love of Ambrosio. Her radiant beauty reminds him of the Madonna's picture, which had been the object of his increasing adoration ever since its purchase by the monastery some two years ago. After a brief but fierce struggle Ambrosio yields to overwhelming temptation and seeks satisfaction in Matilda's wanton embraces.

Once he has been seduced from the paths of virtue, he appears the most rampant of fornicators. Soon tired of his first mistress he resolves to enjoy the young and innocent Antonia, a lovely maiden of fifteen, and to accomplish this he consents to resort to black magic inspired by Matilda. The monk takes part in impious rites at midnight in the dark vaults of the monastery. He is soon involved in a labyrinth of crime : sorcery, matricide, rape, incest, murder, all follow in swift succession. " The Monk . . . degenerates into an uglier fiend than the gloomy imagination of Dante would have ventured to picture."

His iniquities are accidentally unmasked, and with his accomplice he is plunged into the vaults of the Inquisition. In terror of a fiery death at the stake, just as the door of the dungeon is grating on its hinges to lead him to his doom, he sells his soul to the devil to secure his escape, signing a parchment Deed with the usual iron pen dipped in his own blood.

The fiend enters with thunder and lightning, snatches up his victim, and wafts him up to the wild and dizzy heights of the Sierra Morena, where in a moonlit Salvator Rosa landscape of torrents, cliffs, caverns, and pine forests, to the sound of the weird nocturnal wind, he hurls him down the steep mountain-side to fall bruised and mangled beside a brook. A fearful hurricane arises ; the river swells and carries away the dead body of the despairing monk.

The sub-plot comprises more than one-third of the whole novel, and relates the story of the unhappy nun Agnes and her lover Raymond. The narrative opens with a ' robber ' episode in a forest between Luneville and Strasbourg : Raymond is sheltering in a cottage belonging to a group of bandits, but frustrates their murderous plans, having received timely warning whispered into his ears by the wretched wife of a member of the gang. He finds the bed-sheets stained with the blood of previous unfortunate travellers ; he skilfully evades the draught of poisoned wine, feigns stupefied slumber, and escapes. During this adventure he also rescues the Baroness Lindenberg from the robbers' den, and while visiting her castle falls in love with her niece Agnes, who is destined for the cloister in accordance with the vow of her parents.

For more than a century the eastern tower of the castle had been haunted by the spectre of " the bleeding nun ", who married and murdered an ancestor of the Lindenbergs. Every fifth year, on the night of the fifth of May, she could be seen descending the tower stairs, her nun's habit spattered with blood, with lamp and dagger in her hand, on her way to the gloomy cavern, where she had murdered her husband and was herself later murdered. For many years past it had been the custom to leave the gates open between one and two o'clock on this night for her exit and return.

Agnes sees her only chance to escape by personating the bleeding nun. Raymond is ready with a carriage and keeps the appointment. As the clock strikes one, from the portals of that moonlit castle with its ruined towers and ivied battlements, issues the spectre of the bleeding nun, with dagger and lamp in hand. He flies to meet her, and conducts her to the carriage, which sets off with astonishing swiftness. After a mad career through woods and over chasms, in the midst of a furious tempest, the carriage suddenly overturns, and Raymond falls stunned on the ground. When his consciousness returns he finds himself in the neighbourhood of Ratisbon, an inconceivable distance to have traversed, and with no trace of " the bleeding nun ".

The following night, scarcely has the stroke of ' one ' died away when heavy footsteps sound on the stair, and the spectre presents itself to his horrified gaze, this time with neither lamp nor dagger but with lifted veil disclosing " an empty skull, and a hollow grin ", and vanishes after printing an icy kiss upon his lips. Every night at precisely the same hour, invisible to all but Raymond, the horrid visitant repeats her cold embrace and utters words in sepulchral tones, while the afflicted lover fades away into a shadow of himself.

A curious stranger offers to release him ; this is the Wandering Jew, who bears the burden of eternal life, and cannot stay at one place for more than a fortnight. With magic books and spells, in Raymond's bed-chamber he awaits the dreaded visitor, who, struck by the blazing cross on the magician's forehead, reveals that her unquiet visits will cease if Raymond will bury her bones still mouldering in the fatal cavern. Raymond fulfils this condition, recovers his health, and ranges through heaven and earth seeking his lost love Agnes. Agnes enacted the persona-tion of " the bleeding nun " a minute too late, and was captured and immured in St. Claire's convent. Finding her out, he plans for her escape, when their correspondence is detected, and the cold and virtuous Ambrosio condemns the guilty Agnes to captivity in a frightful dungeon.

This romance is well constructed except for the management of the sub-plot, which touches the main plot at only two vital points : the detection of Agnes's guilt by Ambrosio, and the detection of his guilt on the occasion of her rescue. None the less, the story of Raymond and Agnes is by itself a complete series of episodes.

Lewis invents and combines incidents and situations with a dramatic skill, and depends upon clear, forceful expression for his effects. Although Antonia is as helpless as " a plaster statue demolished by an earthquake ", the figure of Matilda has more vitality. Ambrosio's character, too, has been drawn with a certain psychological skill, and there is real insight in the account of the Monk's struggle between religion and passion. The first review of The Monk appeared in the Monthly Mirror (June 1796) and it was entirely laudatory : " The stronger passions are finely delineated and exemplified in the progress of artful temptation working on self-sufficient pride, superstition, and lasciviousness. . . . The whole is very skilfully managed, and reflects the highest credit on the judgement and imagination of the writer." Even Coleridge, the most bitter critic of *The Monk*, realized that " the whole work is distinguished by the variety and impressiveness of its incidents ; and the author everywhere discovers an imagination rich, powerful, and fervid ".

The motto from Horace on the title page of *The Monk* sums up Lewis's peculiar machinery of horror :

> *Somnia, terrores magicos, miracula, sagas,*
> *Nocturnos lemures portentaque.*

("Dreams, magic terrors, spells of mighty power,
witches, and ghosts who rove at midnight hour.")

Earlier Gothic machinery included flickering candles, glimmering and disappearing lights, haunted chambers, mysterious manuscripts, obscure heroes, and other similar properties. But the " intense school " of ' Monk ' Lewis introduced stalking spectres, devils, evil spirits, sorcerers and demons, magic mirrors, enchanted wands, phosphorescent glow, and other paraphernalia associated with black magic. Here Spanish grandees, heroines of dazzling beauty, bravoes and forest banditti, foolish duennas and gabbling domestic servants, monks, nuns, inquisitors, move in a world of midnight incantations, poisonings, stabbings, and ministrations of sleeping potions ; in an atmosphere of thunder, lightning, storm, sulphurous fumes, and miracles. "The inventory of his arsenal of natural effects is complete ", and yet he wantonly gloats over scenes of matricide and unconscious incest.

The conjuration of spirits and pacts with the devil may have been inspired by a current interest in cabbalism, and Lewis became an undeterred exponent of horror-romantic-realism by his own conjuring of sepulchral horrors, sometimes achieving his frightful effects through the medium of dreams. We read in the *Critical Review* for February 1797, " the sufferings which he describes are so frightful and intolerable, that we break with abruptness from the delusion, and indignantly suspect the man of a species of brutality, who could find a pleasure in wantonly imagining them ".

In the following extract, which reveals Matilda conjuring up a demon, we may observe the author's portrayal of the seductions of magic :

> The monk beheld her with anxious curiosity. Suddenly she uttered a loud and piercing shriek. She appeared to be seized with an excess of delirium ; she tore her hair, beat her bosom, used the most frantic gestures,

and drawing the poniard from her girdle, plunged it into her left arm. The blood gushed out plentifully ; and, as she stood on the brink of the circle, she took care that it should fall on the outside. The flames retired from the spot on which the blood was pouring. A volume of dark clouds rose slowly from the ensanguined earth, and ascended gradually till it reached the vault of the cavern. At the same time a clap of thunder was heard, the echo pealed fearfully along the subterraneous passages, and the ground shook beneath the feet of the enchantress. . . .

Ambrosio started, and expected the demon with terror. . . .

A passage from the episode of Agnes de Medina, the incarcerated nun, adequately illustrates Lewis's method of charnel-house horrors. The physical tortures of the fallen nun are described in revolting detail :

My blood ran cold as I gazed upon this melancholy abode. The cold vapours hovering in the air, the walls green with damp, the bed of straw so forlorn and comfortless, the chain destined to bind me for ever to my prison, and the reptiles of every description, which . . . I descried hurrying to their retreats, struck my heart with terrors. . . .

Fettered in such a hidden dungeon of the monastery, cut off from light and human society, Agnes lingers through the final chapters of her existence. No one hears her voice, no friendly word replies to her speech ; a deep unbroken silence immures her :

Thus did I drag on a miserable existence. . . . The cold seemed more piercing and bitter, the air more thick and pestilential. My frame became weak, feverish, and emaciated. I was unable to rise from the bed of straw, and exercise my limbs in the narrow limits to which the length of my chain permitted me to move. Though exhausted, faint, and weary, I trembled to profit by approach of sleep. My slumbers were constantly interrupted by some obnoxious insect crawling over me. Sometimes I felt the bloated toad, hideous and pampered with the poisonous vapours of the dungeon, dragging his loathsome length along my bosom. Sometimes the quick cold lizard roused me, leaving his slimy track upon my face, and entangling itself in the tresses of my wild and matted hair. Often have I at waking found my fingers ringed with the long worms which bred in the corrupted flesh of my infant. . . .

And in the vicinity lies a human head which worms are devouring :

I was oppressed by a noisome suffocating smell ; . . . my hand rested upon something soft ; I grasped it and advanced it towards light. Almighty God ! what was my disgust ! my consternation ! In spite of its putridity, and the worms which preyed upon it, I perceived a corrupted human head, and recognised the features of a nun who had died some months before. . . .

At times Lewis reveals a morbidity akin to that of Webster and Tourneur, especially in the passage where the enraged mob kills the haughty prioress :

> . . . the rioters still exercised their impotent rage upon her lifeless body. They beat it, trod upon it, and ill-used it till it became no more than a mass of flesh, unsightly, shapeless, and disgusting.

Finally, the description of the dead body of the monk ends the book :

> Myriads of insects were called forth by the warmth ; they drank the blood which trickled from Ambrosio's wounds ; he had no power to drive them from him, and they fastened upon his sores, darting their stings into his body, covered him with their multitudes, and inflicted on him tortures the most exquisite and insupportable. The eagles of the rock tore his flesh piecemeal, and dug out his eyeballs with their crooked beaks.

This pitiless accumulation of gross, incidental detail is different from previous apprehension of horror in bygone murders and hoarded skeletons.

By his brutal emphasis on gross detail, Lewis stands apart from Mrs. Radcliffe and her followers. He does not possess that fine instinct for reticence, rather his gift is " the negation of reticence ". Mrs. Radcliffe was a mistress of suggestions, hints and terrors that stalk unseen. She had produced only a mild titillation of the spine. Lewis's ghosts are real, and his loathsome horror reaches to the raw nerves. " In Mrs. Radcliffe's stories, the shadow fades and disappears just when we are close upon the substance . . . Lewis's wonder-world . . . hurls us without preparation or initiation into a daylight orgy of horrors." Mrs. Radcliffe represents the rational and sentimental side of Gothic romance. Her delicate method of presentation is beyond the power of Lewis, who nevertheless admired and strove to emulate such situations in her novels where the reader with quickened pulse breathlessly anticipates a startling development. Lewis carries this technique to its extreme form, inducing more rapid palpitations. His incidents come in quick kaleidoscopic succession, like the disjointed phases of a delirium or nightmare. The description of the midnight visitant, " the bleeding nun ", to the chamber of Raymond, adequately illustrates his method :

> She lifted up her veil slowly. What a sight presented itself to my startled eyes ! I beheld before me an animated corpse. Her countenance was long and haggard ; her cheeks and lips were bloodless ; the paleness of death

was spread over her features ; and her eyeballs, fixed steadfastly upon me, were lustreless and hollow.

I gazed upon the spectre with horror too great to be described. My blood was frozen in my veins. . . .

. . . the apparition seated herself opposite to me at the foot of the bed. . . . Her eyes were fixed earnestly upon mine. . . . My eyes were fascinated, and I had not the power of withdrawing them from the spectre's.

. . . At length the clock struck two. The apparition rose from her seat, and approached the side of the bed. She grasped with her icy fingers my hand, which hung lifeless upon the coverture, and pressing her cold lips to mine. . . .

Walpole's *Otranto* contained a crude accumulation of terror-striking incidents. The Gothic novel, in his hands, was remarkable only for its ' gothic' and ' mysterious' character, for Walpole sought in the Middle Ages what was most frightening and most savage. Clara Reeve attempted to moderate the extravagances of her predecessor, while in the hands of Mrs. Radcliffe the Gothic novel gave genteel shivers and suggested the uncanny. And now " with one blow Lewis had swept away all the previous effusions of the ' Gothic' school, for in a series of horrors, each more ghastly than the one which preceded it, he had ' out-Walpoled' Walpole. . . . With this novel [*The Monk*] he became . . . ' the high-priest' of the ' intense' school."

Lewis also wrote a number of melodramas extending the domain of horror to the stage, but that falls beyond the orbit of this book. However, in passing, one may refer to characteristic examples—*The Castle Spectre* (1798) and *The Captive* (1803). " Never did Covent Garden present such a picture of agitation and dismay. Ladies bathed in tears—others fainting—and some shrieking with terror—while such of the audience as were able to avoid demonstrations like these, sat aghast with pale horror painted on their countenances."

The structure of Gothic romance is based on a principle of contrast. Walpole had produced his effects by surrealistic contrast of light and shade ; Mrs. Radcliffe evoked sensations through her artistic use of sound and silence ; Lewis's world is a macabre juxtaposition of charnel-house horror and lust. His desire to heighten the tone also accounts for the voluptuousness of some descriptions. Commented on by Montague Summers : " his pictures of voluptuous passion are necessary to the narrative ; the violence of the orgasm but serves to balance and throw in high relief the charnel horrors. The comeliest forms of man and maid entwined in quivering embrace that Aretine might have imaged in his shameless sonnets, the long rapture of warmed honeyed kisses such as Secundus sung, the full swift pulse of life, beauty, love, desire, all these are suddenly shadowed by the dark pall of mortality ; those eyes that sparkled with lust's flame must fade and close in night, those hands whose touch was as a draught of heady wine must palsy, grow cold, and decay, the worm must pasture on those corrupting limbs where lover's teeth once bit the white flesh in frenzy of sadistic appetite."

The Monk has been called a " most notorious exemplar of the ' Gothic ' school of romance ". But the author certainly owes no few fronds of his deathless wreath, be it of laurel or of yew, to the gross charges of blasphemy and indecency which were vehemently hurled against this book. It is not worth while to repeat the resounding scandal which was caused by the first edition of The Monk. To us it seems ineffably puerile that anyone could be disturbed by these mild erotics. But, immediately, the prigs and prudes rose up, " Fierce as ten Furies, terrible as Hell ", and bawled " Blasphemy !   Obscenity ! " from the house-tops. " Never was such a clamour, such an outcry, heard since Troy Town fell, or the geese hissed upon the Capitol, for at the noise one might have believed that the very pillars of religion and decency were shaken to the dust and crumbled away, that the reign of Cotytto had returned, that the altars of Priapus were set up in St. Paul's," Montague Summers says. Scenes between Ambrosio and Matilda, not unusual in a modern novel, were pronounced horribly smutty ; and various references to the Bible, which if delivered some fine Sunday morning from the Metropolitan pulpit by a Midland bishop would be greeted as the flower of cultured scholarship, were considered impious in the highest degree.

The Monthly Review severely reprehended " the vein of obscenity which corrupted the entire narrative ". The Scots Magazine was indignant and regretted that youth should be exposed to the evil influence of such romances. The Analytical Review found fault with the author's parallel plots and the two catastrophes. The European Magazine said that it " had neither originality, morality, nor even probability to commend it ". Moore thought it " libidinous and impious " ; Mathias stated that " novels of this seductive and libidinous tendency excite disgust, fear, and horror ". Coleridge, with full conviction, pronounced his judgement that " The Monk is a romance, which if a parent saw in the hands of a son or daughter, he might reasonably turn pale ". He called it " a poison for youth, and a provocative for the debauchee " ; wherein " the shameless harlotry of Matilda " and " the temptations of Ambrosio " are described with " libidinous minuteness ".   One wonders what he would have said of *Lady Chatterley's Lover* and *Ulysses* !

Coleridge raves and rants and flings abuses on the author : " If it be possible that the author of these blasphemies is a Christian . . . if he be an infidel . . . to pour contempt on the only book . . . the Bible in conjuring up the spirit of uncleanliness. . . . He extracts pollution from the word of purity . . . and turns the grace of God into wantonness."   The Attorney-General was moved by a society for the suppression of vice to obtain an injunction against the sale of the book.   The persecution failed to materialize, but Lewis had in the meantime removed what he supposed objectionable, expunging, so he wrote to his father, " every syllable on which could be grounded the slightest construction of immorality ".

Thus *The Monk* received little credit for its merits, and curiously the notion that this work is " a deliberate and unabashed portrayal of lust " continues to dominate critical minds down to this day.   Even as late as 1890 the *Imperial Dictionary of National Biography* condemned this work as " shamelessly voluptuous ".   E. A. Baker, while writing the *History of the English Novel* in 1934, notes that Lewis " betrays the perverted lusts of a sadist ", and refers to his " morbid appetite ".   He finds Ambrosio's crimes described with " gluttonous fullness ", and the episode of Agnes and Raymond pictured with a " revolting frankness ".

It must not be supposed, however, that *The Monk* was a solitary instance of its kind.   " The author was encouraged to write it from example and the public was led to read it from habit."   " Other fictions of a hardly less objectionable tendency had prepared the way for *The Monk*," says his biographer, who proceeds to point out the pernicious effect of the " sentimental novel " on this later type of fiction : " this very school—one, the avowed intention of which was to hold by virtue for imitation, and vice for scorn and hatred—sowed the first seeds of that distorted taste which received the novel of *The Monk* with avidity ".   Lewis did not offend the taste of the majority of his readers ; he wrote for the generation whose grandparents had discussed *Clarissa Harlowe* in clubs, assemblies, and over coffee-cups.   His work is after all only the logical outcome of analysis of feeling pushed to its ultimate conclusion.   He portrayed passion as the sentimentalists did emotion. That his book was read with eagerness and discussed without reserve is shown by several anecdotes told at length by his biographer in his *Life and Correspondence*.

The Monk is the outcome of diverse sources, whose cosmopolitan character make it an interesting study. It was nourished by all that Lewis could find most extravagant and most fantastic in English, German, and French literature, though all his various ingredients were flavoured with a certain individuality. Better than any other, he represents the juncture of the native and foreign streams. " He contributed to the English tradition, lent materials to German and French writers for development in their respective countries, and finally capitalized on the results of the international circulation when native and foreign elements were reunited in England."

Certain influences from his childhood shaped and coloured the lurid imagination of Lewis. A considerable portion of his early life was spent at a very ancient manor, Stanstead Hall, in Essex. One wing of this great mansion had long been closed, and it was common belief that those uninhabited rooms were frequented by supernatural visitants. His head was stuffed with necromantic legends by the housekeeper. As he passed the massive and carved folding-doors, he would glance, all trembling, in their direction and hasten his steps lest they should fly open and some unearthly apparition with clanking chain issue forth. Also the favourite reading of his mother consisted of tales of goblins and of the supernatural, and undoubtedly she related such stuff to her eldest child. With a histrionic and highly impressionable boy such as Matthew Lewis, these early memories of gloom and ghastliness are of considerable importance, and his experiences of early childhood must have coloured them to an appreciable extent.

His favourite reading was Glanville's *Sedducismus Triumphatus, or a Full and plain evidence concerning Witches and Apparitions* (1681). " Throughout his life he seems to have made a hobby of the literature that arouses violent emotion and mental excitement, or lacerates the nerves, or shocks and startles." Between beginning and completing *The Monk* Lewis had steeped his mind in *Werther* and the recent marvels of German imaginative literature. " His depredations on German literature are . . . serious and extensive." How vitally German Romanticism energized English literature need not be emphasized.

The *Critical*, reviewing the *Bravo of Venice* in 1805, said : " Novels have commonly been divided into the pathetic, the sentimental, and the humorous ; but the writers of the German School have introduced a new class, which may be called the *electric*. Every chapter contains a shock ; and the reader not only stares, but starts, at the close of every paragraph. . . ." The best embodiment of the German influence and its fusion is *The Monk* of Lewis, with its distinguishing features of luridness, extravagance, and crude sensationalism ; the spectre nun and charmed moonshine are not wanting.

Lewis stayed in Germany for eight months in 1791, and was particularly attracted towards the School of " Sturm und Drang ". Lewis's command of the German language is evident for " to him . . . Byron owed his knowledge of Goethe's *Faust*, having heard Lewis translate parts of it viva voce ". Lewis had read the works of Goethe and Schiller : " he translated Goethe's *Das Veilchen* and read it to the author personally " ; and it is almost certain that Part I of *Faust* had contributed to the conception of *The Monk*.

In the writing of the ballads with which he has strewn his novel, Lewis is more indebted to German poetry than he admits. In his advertisement he states, " The Bleeding Nun is a tradition still credited in many parts of Germany ". In the introductory remarks to the 1822 edition of Lewis's *Castle Spectre*, the editor, while referring to Lewis's intimate acquaintance with German literature, says that the whole story of the *Bleeding Nun* is borrowed, and much of the language too, from a tale in the *Volksmarchen*, called *Die Entführung* ; and that the catastrophe of the Monk Ambrosio is almost word for word from a tale in Veit Weber's *Sagen der Vorzeit*, called *Die Teufel's Beschworöng*.

Lewis's *Bravo of Venice* (1804) is a short romance from a German source, an " outlaw story " patterned after Schiller's *Die Räuber*. The hero is one Abellino, the " noble bandit ", who hovers in the background of the web of love and intrigue surrounding Rosabella, the beautiful daughter of the Doge of Venice, and in the disguise of a bandit saves her life, delivers up the real bandits dreaded by all Venice, ensnares conspirators and performs many notable services. In his real character of Flodoardo he has already won Rosabella's love.

Pointing out French influence on 'Monk' Lewis, Maurice Heine notes : " We see this young man [M. G. Lewis] during the journey which he made to Paris in 1792, acquiring a copy of ' Justine '." De Sade considered " *The Monk* superior in all respects to the exotic outbursts of Radcliffe's brilliant imagination ". He added : " this genre . . . is certainly not without merit ; it was the inevitable outcome of the revolutionary upheavals experienced throughout the whole of Europe. . . ." De Sade further thought that " the appearance of this novel was truly a literary event. It answered the need for strong emotions following great social upheavals, flattered sensualism with its voluptuous pictures and irreligion by the boldness with which it treated sacred things."

But one must not neglect the strong English influences on Lewis. In his foreword to *The Monk*, the author mentions that his main idea came from Addison's " Santon Barsisa " in *The Guardians* (1714). Lewis was especially attracted by Mrs. Radcliffe's *The Mysteries of Udolpho*, and his imagination was enkindled by the lone castle amid the far Apennines, those awful halls of dread, and fascinated by Montoni's flashing eyes, dark countenance, and sombre nature. Ambrosio inherits some of his qualities from Montoni, and later influences the creation of Radcliffe's Schedoni.

In English literature Lewis must have known the dark dramas and the old ballads rediscovered by Percy, Watson, and Allan Ramsay. " He had certainly studied secrets of magic and sorcery." The theme of incest may have been suggested by similar morbid themes in the plays of Beaumont and Fletcher, Middleton, Massinger, Ford, and the Restoration theatre.

There has already been much discussion about his various German sources, but the influence of Elizabethan melodrama, and especially of Shakespeare's plays, is probably more deep on Lewis. *Romeo and Juliet* contains the whole gamut of the romanticism of graveyards and death. " The palace of dim night ", and " the nest of death, contagion, and unnatural sleep " described in the last scene of *Romeo and Juliet*, may have suggested to Lewis the picture of the subterranean charnel vaults of convents. Chapter X of *The Monk*, where Lorenzo adventures to discover Agnes, is pictured in the same deep gloom, where in the faint rays of a dim lamp we discern the shadow of mighty pillars bearing up the roof, and where the eye sees nothing but the most repulsive objects : skulls, bones, graves, and effigies of saints seeming to stare in horror and amaze. It is *Romeo and Juliet* again, when to effect his lustful purpose, Ambrosio administers a soporific draught to the beautiful Antonia, who, being taken as dead, has been conveyed to the vaults of the sepulchre. " The distilled liquor " which makes " a cold and drowsy humour " run through the veins, produces a " borrowed likeness of shrunk death ", the vial which Friar Lawrence handed over to Juliet, may have suggested the " juice extracted from certain herbs known but to few, which brings on the person who drinks it the exact image of death ", which was administered to Antonia. The power of silver myrtle which makes gates and doors fly open at its touch and charms every eye into

sleep, has something of Shakespeare's *A Midsummer Night's Dream*.
Again, in some of the situations and in the voluptuous nature of descriptions, *The Monk* is reminiscent of Shakespeare. One is reminded of
The Rape of Lucrece, when Ambrosio, " with Tarquin-like strides ",
goes to ravish Antonia :

> He now ventured to cast a glance upon the sleeping beauty. A single
> lamp, burning before the statue of Saint Rosolia, shed a faint light through
> the room, and permitted him to examine all the charms of the lovely object
> before him. The heat of the weather had obliged her to throw off a part of the
> bedclothes : those which still covered her Ambrosio's insolent hand hastened
> to remove. She lay with her cheek reclining upon an ivory arm ; the other
> rested on the side of the bed with graceful indolence. A few tresses of her
> hair had escaped from beneath the muslin which confined the rest, and fell
> carelessly over her bosom, as it heaved with slow and regular respiration.
> The warm air had spread her cheek with higher colour than usual. A smile
> inexpressibly sweet played round her ripe and coral lips, from which, every
> now and then, escaped a gentle sigh or an half-pronounced sentence. An
> air of enchanting innocence and candour pervaded her whole form, and
> there was a sort of modesty in her very nakedness, which added fresh stings
> to the desires of the lustful monk.

The same voluptuous sensuousness of Shakespeare's description is evident
in :

> Ambrosio no longer possessed himself ; wild with desire, he clasped the
> blushing trembler in his arms. He fastened his lips greedily upon her's,
> sucked in her pure delicious breath, violated with his bold hand the treasures
> of her bosom, and wound around him her soft and yielding limbs.

The picture of still midnight is reminiscent of *Macbeth* :

> Guided by the moonbeams, he proceeded up the staircase with slow and
> cautious steps. He looked round him every moment with apprehension and
> anxiety. He saw a spy in every shadow, and heard a voice in every murmur
> of the night-breeze. . . . Yet still he proceeded. He reached the door of
> Antonia's chamber. He stopped, and listened. All was hushed within. . . .

When Ambrosio gazes at the lovely form of Antonia in the magic mirror,
one is reminded of Shakespeare's depiction of Lucrece :

> Antonia . . . was undressing to bathe herself. The long tresses of her hair
> were already bound up. The amorous monk had full opportunity to observe
> the voluptuous contours and admirable symmetry of her person. She threw
> off her last garment, and advancing to the bath prepared for her, put her foot

into the water. It struck cold, and she drew it back again. Though unconscious of being observed, an inbred sense of modesty induced her to veil
her charms ; and she stood hesitating upon the brink, in the attitude of the
Venus de Medicis. . . .

The powerful and moving description towards the end of *The Monk*
recalls Marlowe's *Dr. Faustus* :

> Will you be mine, body and soul ? Are you prepared to renounce Him
> who made you, and Him who died for you ? Answer but "yes"! and Lucifer
> is your slave.

The description of Lucifer as he appears to Ambrosio in his cell is almost
Miltonic. Announced by thunders and earthquakes, the Devil appears
enveloped in blue fires that increase the cold of the dungeon. The
suggestion of Milton in "fallen angel" is very much heightened, for
the fiend appears not in his seraphic radiance but as a much-blackened
rebel from the infernal regions, with a voice "that sulphurous fogs had
damped to hoarseness" :

> He appeared in all that ugliness which, since his fall from heaven, had been
> his portion. His blasted limbs still bore marks of the Almighty thunder. A
> swarthy darkness spread itself over his gigantic form : his hands and feet
> were armed with long talons. Fury glared in his eyes, which might have
> struck the bravest heart with terror. Over his huge shoulders waved two
> enormous sable wings ; and his hair was supplied by living snakes, which
> twined themselves round his brows with frightful hissings. In one hand he
> held a roll of parchment, and in the other an iron pen. Still the lightning
> flashed around him, and the thunder with repeated bursts seemed to announce
> the dissolution of Nature.

Maturin, commenting on this particular picture, declared that "few
scenes of supernatural agency have more power than that in which the
apostate spirit appears in all the beauty and despair of a fallen angel to
Ambrosio in the vault".

The Monk not only contains, most concisely, the idiosyncracies of
its kind, which gave a forcible stimulus to the manufacture of horror
novels, but it also marks a new phase in romanticism inherent in tragedies
of the soul, revealing deep, human conflicts, the struggle between
good and evil for ultimate mastery in human life. It revived the old
Marlovian theme of temptation and league with the Devil. The character
of the monk inaugurated a series of sombre, tragic phantoms of his type.
It set the fashion for writers such as Charlotte Dacre, who assumed the

name of Rosa Matilda, and penned novel after novel with would-be piquant titles, *The Libertine*, *The Passions*, *The Confessions of the Nun of St. Omar*, which latter is dedicated to Lewis himself in admiring terms. Charlotte Dacre remains a professed disciple of the Monk. Montague Summers observes, " the influence of *The Monk* upon *Zofloya* is extremely marked. Not only incidents, but even occasionally dialogue and description are reproduced with an almost startling fidelity."

By his verses Lewis participated in the revival of interest in the ballad form, and Scott ascribes to his friendship with Lewis a great influence on his own poetry. The enthusiasm of Lewis also inspired Shelley, Byron, and Coleridge, although the last was ungenerous enough to gird at the very poetry to which he owed not a little of his own stimulation.

Probably Dickens was much indebted to Lewis for his technique of representing a quick dramatic succession of incidents towards the close of his novels. André Breton thinks " the first novels of Victor Hugo (*Bug-Jargal*, *Han d'Islande*), as well as those of Balzac (*l'Héritière de Birague*, *le Centenaire ou les deux Béringheld*, etc.), are directly inspired by *The Monk* ".

His mystery and horror and German sensationalism for many years permeated English romance. E. T. W. Hoffmann (1776–1822), in Germany " the arch-priest of ultra-German romanticism ", shows the influence of Lewis in his *Die Elixiere des Teufels* (1816), translated in English as *The Devil's Elixir* (1824).

The publication of *The Monk* firmly established the " School of Horror ". The violent machinery for sensational effects came to be unstintedly used by the future writers of Gothic romance. Many employ ventriloquism or magic ; but almost all make use of the actual presence of real ghosts, not explained away, which remains the distinguishing feature of the Schauer-Romantik.

Mary Shelley's *Frankenstein* (1818) is another Gothic novel which falls within the orbit of the Schauer-Romantik, not so much for her treatment of horror, as for the individuality of her theme. While not the inventor of the scientific romance, she was the first to adapt its methods to the peculiar purposes of the novel of horror. *Frankenstein* carried horror into the pseudo-scientific : a proof that the Schauer-Romantiks carefully sought their inspiration in a succession of unfamiliar themes capable of being given a ' Gothic ' tone.

Mary Shelley's handling of her theme is different from the prurient

nightmares of the halls of Eblis, or the midnight diablerie of ' Monk '
Lewis, or the physical realistic horrors of Godwin. " The event on which
the interest of the story depends is exempt from the disadvantages of a
mere tale of spectres or enchantment. It was recommended by the
novelty of the situations which it develops." Frightful is the effect thus
produced by a human endeavour to mock the stupendous mechanism of
the Creator of the World. Eino Railo says, " Frankenstein enriched the
stage-setting of terror-romanticism by making its mysterious centre,
hitherto the haunted room, the laboratory of a cabbalistic seeker after
knowledge . . . a laboratory in which the deepest of all secrets, the skill
to awaken life in inorganic matter, is ultimately discovered ".

The circumstances leading to the birth of this tale of pseudo-scientific
horror date back to the summer of 1816, when Lewis, Byron, Shelley,
and Polidori were staying at the Villa Diodati, in the environs of Geneva.
It was a wet, ungenial summer, and the incessant rain often confined
their evenings around a blazing wood fire, where they amused themselves
with some German stories of ghosts, which happened to fall into their
hands. Night waned upon these tales, and even the witching hour had
gone by before they retired to rest, their heads filled with necromancy
and the supernatural. Each of them planned to emulate German
romanticism by writing unearthly tales. " I busied myself to think of a
story—a story to rival those which had excited us to this task. One
which would speak to the mysterious fears of our nature, and awaken
thrilling horror—one to make the reader dread to look round, to curdle
the blood, and quicken the beatings of the heart," says Mary Shelley in
her introduction, and she adds in her preface to Frankenstein : " Oh !
if I could only contrive one [story] which would frighten my readers as
I myself had been frightened that night."

Then Mary Shelley had a dream, and the dream was born of a passage
she had read in Erasmus Darwin, who was experimenting in the artificial
production of life. " When I placed my head on my pillow, I did not
sleep, nor could I be said to think. My imagination, unbidden, possessed
and guided me, gifting the successive images that arose in my mind with
a vividness far beyond the usual bounds of reverie." In her dream she
beheld the artificial monster coming to consciousness under the operations
of Frankenstein, " the modern Prometheus", " the pale student of
unhallowed arts kneeling beside the thing he had put together", which
began to " stir with an uneasy, half-vital motion ".

As the story unfolds, we find Frankenstein gathering mouldering cerements, skulls and bones, from churchyards, and putting them together, breathing into its nostrils the breath of life by means of scientific experiments :

> . . . the moon gazed on my midnight labours . . . who shall conceive the horrors of my secret toil, as I dabbled among the unhallowed damps of the grave, or tortured the living animal to animate the lifeless clay ? My limbs now tremble, and my eyes swim with the remembrance. . . .
>
> In a solitary chamber . . . I kept my workshop of filthy creation : my eyeballs were starting from their sockets in attending to the details of my employment.

And the result was the creation of

> a form which I cannot find words to describe ; gigantic in stature, yet uncouth and distorted in its proportions . . . his face concealed by long locks of ragged hair . . . in colour and apparent texture like that of a mummy . . . of such loathsome, yet appalling hideousness.

Frankenstein, after his unhallowed labours, falls asleep, but the horror of the scene when he wakens is vividly depicted. He opens his eyes and beholds the horrid thing stand at his bedside, opening his curtains, and looking on him with yellow, watery, but speculative eyes :

> I started from my sleep with horror ; a cold dew covered my forehead, my teeth chattered, and every limb became convulsed : when, by the dim and yellow light of the moon, as it forced its way through the window shutters, I beheld . . . the miserable monster. . . . He held up the curtain of the bed ; and his eyes, if eyes they may be called, were fixed on me. His jaws opened, and he muttered some inarticulate sounds, while a grin wrinkled his cheeks. . . . Oh ! no mortal could support the horror of that countenance. A mummy again endued with animation could not be so hideous as that wretch. . . .

Like the fabled fisherman who broke open a sealed jar and released a genie, Frankenstein is appalled at the result of his creation. " All the forces of Gothic terror are let loose when the monster, endued with superhuman strength and stature, not merely breathes and moves, but shows himself in possession of individual consciousness and a will of his own, which presently is roused to indignation, fierce sentiment, and thirst for revenge," says E. A. Baker. The narrative proceeds with the crimes of the giant, who strangles women and children. And in a mood of breathless excitement the reader is driven forward with feverish apprehension.

The plot of *Frankenstein* is fantastic, crude, and disjointed, having an insequence very dream-like, yet in spite of this bewildering confusion of incidents Mary Shelley vivifies the grotesque skeleton of the plot with scenes of tension and pathos. Sylva Norman, in a study of Mary Shelley, says : " Her passions are as incredible as her situations. . . . There is strength in her intellect, but it bows to her truly feminine invention which prefers to dive into a glade of detached fancy rather than face the responsibility of truth and living portraiture."

Her impetuous imagination pictures some strenuous scenes : the demon relates his own sensations at his birth, his delight in nature, his agony when the world hounds him away in horror, and his rage to punish mankind when Frankenstein refuses to conjure a female mate, a monstrous Eve, for his consolation. There is pathos in the monster's words :

> . . . no Eve soothed my sorrows, nor shared my thoughts ; I was alone, I remembered Adam's supplication to his Creator.

He implores further :

> I am alone, and miserable ; man will not associate with me ; but one as deformed and horrible as myself would not deny herself to me. My companion must be of the same species, and have the same defects. This being you must create.

This novel has a number of passages which make a profound impression on sensitive minds. These contain not only terrifying incidents, but also depict in fullness the mental and emotional states of the principal characters.

In the fateful inn, the monster revenges upon Frankenstein's beloved, his own lack of a female companion :

> . . . Suddenly I heard a shrill and dreadful scream. . . . She was there, lifeless and inanimate, thrown across the bed, her head hanging down, and her pale distorted features half-covered by her hair. . . .

And then is pictured the horror of the subsequent scene :

> . . . I felt a kind of panic on seeing the pale yellow light of the moon illuminate the chamber. The shutters had been thrown back ; and with a sensation of horror not to be described, I saw at the open window a figure the most hideous and abhorred. A grin was on the face of the monster ; he seemed to jeer, as with his fiendish finger he pointed towards the corpse of my wife. I rushed towards the window, and drawing a pistol from my bosom, fired ; but he eluded me, leaped from his station, and, running with the swiftness of lightning, plunged into the lake.

Certain fearful atmospheric effects are conveyed in the scene when
Frankenstein goes to the cemetery to vow the death of the monster :

> As night approached, I found myself at the entrance of the cemetery. . . .
> Everything was silent, except the leaves of the trees, which were gently
> agitated by the wind ; the night was nearly dark. . . .
> . . . I was answered through the stillness of the night by a loud and fiendish
> laugh. It rung on my ears long and heavily ; the mountains re-echoed it,
> and I felt as if all hell surrounded me with mockery and laughter. . . .
> The laughter died away ; when a well-known and abhorred voice,
> apparently close to my ear, addressed me in an audible whisper. . . .
> Suddenly the broad disc of the moon arose, and shone upon his ghastly
> and distorted shape. . . .

As the story closes, a fine scene of emotion and pathos is depicted
when the monster feels remorse over the corpse of Frankenstein, and
seeks his own death, under a grim arctic light, on a solitary ' ice-craft '
—borne away by the waves, and lost in the mists of darkness and distance.

Mary Shelley's other works, like *Transformation* and *The Mortal
Immortal*, are weaker treatments in evoking horror, but the dreadful
experiments by which Frankenstein's monster was created resemble the
revolting vivisections of Wells's Dr. Moreau, or the operation described
by Arthur Machen whereby human beings lose their souls and become
diabolized, given over utterly to unspeakable evil. Wells's fantasia, *The
Shape of Things to Come*, is reminiscent of Mary Shelley's *The Last Man*
(1825), a romance of the distant future.

Yet another species of the Schauer-Romantik is *The Vampyre : A
Tale* (1819), from the pen of Dr. John Polidori, " who travelled with
Lord Byron, as physician ". Stories of the dead arising from their
graves and feeding upon the blood of the young and beautiful were
current in Illyria, and Polidori's tale draws upon much legendary lore.
" The superstition upon which this tale is founded is very general in the
East. Among the Arabians it appears to be common : it did not, however,
extend itself to the Greeks until after the establishment of Christianity."
In an exhaustive study of the subject, Montague Summers has declared
that " cases of vampirism may be said to be in our time a rare occult
phenomenon . . . not that they do not occur but that they are carefully
hushed up and stifled ".

A vampire is a person whose spirit does not depart from his body
when organic life has ceased, but remains there, preventing it from
decaying and making the body return at night to the living to suck their

blood. The belief still exists that " vampyres nightly imbibed a certain portion of the blood of their victims, who became emaciated, lost their strength, and speedily died of consumptions ; whilst these human blood-suckers fattened—and their veins became distended to such a state of repletion, as to cause the blood to flow from all the passages of their bodies, and even from the pores of their skins." A person sucked by a vampire becomes a vampire himself, and sucks in his turn.

When a vampire's grave is opened the body is found fresh " and entirely free from corruption, and emitting at the mouth, nose, and ears, pure and florid blood ". The face is tinted with warmth of life, eyes open, and no cadaverous smell exhales from the coffin ; even a faint, appreciable respiration, and a corresponding action of the heart may be seen. The limbs are perfectly flexible and the flesh elastic. The coffin floats with blood, in which even up to a depth of seven inches, the body may lie immersed.

When a sharp stake is driven through the heart of the vampire, in accordance with the ancient practice, it utters a piercing shriek, as might escape from a living person in the last agony. And when the head is struck off, a fountain of blood gushes from the severed neck. The body is burned, and then the ashes thrown in his grave.

Polidori's inspiration comes from such a ghastly subject-matter. " The idea of a material and astral body led naturally to that of a double existence in a new sense " : themes relating to somnambulism and hypnotism and deeds committed under such influences now emerge on the romantic horizon.

The hero of Polidori's macabre tale is a sinister young Lord Ruthven, who is killed in Greece and reappears as a vampire feeding on the blood of women. He seduces the sister of his friend Aubrey and suffocates her during the night which follows their wedding.

The story is narrated in a restrained manner, and the author leaves us to form our own conclusions. Had Lewis handled such a pregnant theme, he would have revelled in gory details, expatiating on the agonies of the victims. But Polidori had not that genius for horror. He keeps the story in a quiet key for he " was so discreet in eschewing the sensational ". Montague Summers has confessed himself puzzled as to " how it was that such writers as Monk Lewis . . . and Charles Robert Maturin . . . the two lords of macabre romance, should neither of them have sent some hideous vampire ghost ravening through their sepulchral pages ". He adds that " until we come to Polidori's novel . . . nowhere . . . do we meet with the Vampire in the realm of Gothic fancy ". However, one should not assert too emphatically that this theme was entirely unexploited. Perhaps in an obscure, dusty library the Vampire even now stalks unseen through the dark pages of some neglected volumes. The lesser novelists who, in their passion for horrid phantasmagoria, deftly plundered the German charnels might have found a place for the Vampire in some funereal episode.

Polidori's tale, none the less, set a fashion for vampire stories. The prince of vampires is Bram Stoker's *Dracula*, round whom centres probably the greatest horror tale of modern times.

" The greatest as well as the last of the goths " of the Schauer-Romantik phase of the Gothic novel was Charles Robert Maturin (1782–1824), an eccentric Irish clergyman, who beguiled his time by weaving romances, and produced " the most remarkably constructed shockers " of his time. *Blackwood's Magazine* comments : " He walks almost without a rival, whether dead or living, in many of the darkest, but at the same time the most majestic, circles of romance." When the high summer of the Schauer-Romantik was on its wane, Maturin produced some fine and vigorous works stamped with a distinct individuality, power, and subtlety of thought. He wrote " the epitaph on the extinction of a school of writers which had become decadent and diseased ". Gifted with a psychological insight he can sound every note of fear arising from objects of invisible terror and gruesome horror.

Two different and distinctly separate currents of Gothic novel : the poetic exuberance of Mrs. Radcliffe, " the first poetess of romantic fiction ", and the lurid horrors of ' Monk ' Lewis, fuse together in the white heat of Maturin's imagination. His acute insight into character, vivid descriptive faculty, and sensitive style of writing, are in the tradition of Mrs. Radcliffe ; but by his unabashed free use of the supernatural he treads in the footsteps of Lewis, yet outstrips him in the force and skill of his attacks upon the reader's nerves. " Lewis's horrors, his crypts and smell of rotting corpses, pale beside Maturin's gruesome realism and suggestive power."

His eerie atmosphere is evoked not by crude whiffs from the church-yard ; rather he insinuates horror by the adroit Radcliffian device of reticence and suggestion. Maturin was intimately acquainted with the dim and dusky corners of Radcliffe's Gothic abbeys ; he had viewed with trepidation their blood-stained staircases, their skeletons and corpses ;

his vigilant eye had noticed each rusty lock and creaking hinge ; and he had carefully calculated the effect of these properties. The lurid horrors of ' Monk ' Lewis also left deep impressions on Maturin's treatment of the supernatural.

This connoisseur of sensations analyses his effects with the precision of a psychologist. " Emotions ", Maturin declares, " are my events," and he delineates not only physical but mental torture. He paints life in extremes : the gloom is darker, the sadness deeper. He is careful to represent those struggles of passion when the soul trembles on the verge of the unlawful and the unhallowed, and he strives " by means of his philosophical problem-themes to awaken feelings of moral horror ".

During the formative period of his genius he wrote three novels : *The Fatal Revenge or The Family of Montorio* (1807), *The Wild Irish Boy* (1808), and *The Milesian Chief* (1812), of which only the first is a horror story ; the third being an historical novel, now chiefly remembered because of the striking resemblance it bears in the opening chapters to Scott's *The Bride of Lammermoor* (1819).

His first novel, *The Fatal Revenge or The Family of Montorio*, is perhaps the most frightful romance, uniting physical and mental agony in a manner developed in his later *Melmoth the Wanderer* (1820). " I have allowed myself ", he says, " to base the interest of my novel entirely on the passion of supernatural terror."

Set in the gloomy Castle of Muralto, near Naples, in 1690, the story unfolds the dark crimes and mysterious deeds of an Italian family. The Count of Montorio has usurped the castle from his elder brother Orazio, and the latter resolves upon revenge. Having wandered over the earth for fifteen years learning black magic and other conjuring tricks, under the name of Schemoli he becomes confessor in the Castle of Muralto, where he awakens fright and horror by his mysterious doings. By his occult powers he begins to tempt Annibal and Ippolito, the two sons of Count Montorio, at the same time, in two different places, to murder their father. He conducts Ippolito to a vast subterranean region, and in a mirror of black marble shows him to himself in the act of murdering his father. Eventually under Schemoli's hypnotic suggestion, the two brothers murder the Count. In the end Schemoli is condemned to death by the Inquisition, but while in prison dies of a burst blood-vessel. The two sons are exiled and Montorio's name erased from the records of the country.

Other threads are interwoven : the love of Annibal and the beautiful

novice Ildefonsa ; the love of Rosalia di Valozzi for Ippolito—but all
these pale into insignificance before the picture of fiend-like temptations
and scenes of the occult. Schemoli behaves like a fiend in human shape,
who appears and disappears at will, is always and never present. His
ghastly, fiendish pursuits to this end fill three large volumes.

This clumsily constructed novel borrows its crude materials from
' Monk ' Lewis : the corpses and spectres circulate so freely that they
are scarcely to be distinguished from the living ; yet in his use of
suggestive terror Maturin is indebted to the technique of Mrs. Radcliffe :

> " Something is near," said the old man, " I feel the ground near me
> pressed, as if by feet."—" Hush," said I, " all is silent, a body cannot move
> without a sound."—" There is something near," whispered he again, " for I
> feel the air driven to my face, as if some one passed me."—" 'tis the bat,"
> said I, " that whizzes past you, or the wind that waves the ivy ; I have heard,
> or felt nothing yet."—" Oh no, Signor, there is a strange motion in the air ;
> a rank and stifling chillness, as if something that was not good, breathed
> upon us."
>
> There came indeed a blast across us, not like the blasts of that night, loud
> and feverish ; but cold and noisome, like a charnel stream. We shuddered
> as it passed ; I felt some effort necessary, to resist the palsied feeling that was
> stealing over me : " Michelo, let us not be baffled a second time. This form,
> whatever it be, is probably approaching ; before it oppress us with some
> strange influence, I will rush forth and meet it : and be they favourable and
> malignant, I will know its powers and purposes. . . ." I sought the aisle
> again. The moon poured a light as broad as day through the windows. I
> saw the tomb of Count Orazio. I beheld a figure seated on it ; I advanced
> in hope and fear. It was Michelo—he sat like a mariner, who leans on a bare
> and single crag, after the tempest and the wreck ; he was haggard, spent, and
> gasping.—I rushed to him, but he appeared not to hear my moving ; his
> head was raised, and his look fixed on the arched passage ; the moonlight
> poured a ghastly and yellow paleness on his still features. I looked in his
> eyes, they were hollow and glazed ; I touched his hand, it was cold and
> dropped from mine. I shuddered, and scarcely thought him an earthly man.
> A moment reproached my fears, and I tried to address some words of comfort
> and inquiry to him, but I was repelled by an awe in which I scarce thought
> Michelo an agent. . . .

Also the portrayal of Schemoli's character recalls the design of Mrs.
Radcliffe's Schedoni. There is the same sallow visage furrowed with
traces of bygone passions ; the same love of solitude, the same daunting
glance and flash of piercing eyes, inspiring dread all around. Indeed,
Maturin crowds into this story nearly every character and incident that

had been employed in earlier Gothic romances. And the setting, too, oscillates between the robbers' den and ruined chapel, castle vaults, and dungeons of the Inquisition, while each scene is admirably adapted to the situation contrived and emotion displayed.

In power of construction, *Melmoth the Wanderer* (1820), his masterpiece, marks a distinct advance on *Montorio*. This novel has a haunting quality, and it equals *The Monk*, if not in talent at least in extravagant frenzy. Maturin works on the same general theme as Godwin's *St. Leon*, and makes a striking use of physical immortality as a means of spiritual torture. *Melmoth* is a story of great angelic sin, a boundless aspiration after forbidden knowledge.

Maturin invests his horror with startling realism and great suggestive power. We are compelled to linger in the haunting atmosphere of desolation in the opening chapters of the book where the picture of a lonely and decaying farm, cold and gloomy weather, leafless trees, and a luxuriant crop of weeds and nettles, create an inexplicable feeling of paralysing dread and some impending disaster. It is verdure of the churchyard, the garden of death. The rising voice of the stormy night seems to make wild and dreary harmony with the tone of the listener's feeling, when young John Melmoth reads a manuscript telling of fearful matters as the demoniac portrait of his ancestor stares at him. The atmosphere is meetly filled by the deep rushing of the rain falling in torrents, while the sighs of the wind, and now and then a faint, distant, but long-continued peal of thunder, " sounds like the chidings of the spirits, that their secrets are disclosed ". The whole is bathed in an awful half-light reminiscent of Dante's *Inferno*.

The pages that follow sustain this nightmarish sensation. The narrative consists of a series of tales, intricately strung together. Although the structure is involved, there is an interior connection between the six stories, and the powerful narrative leads up to a grand final catastrophe. In each tale the Wanderer, who has bartered his soul in return for prolonged life, youth, and boundless power, is desirous to prevail upon some other mortal, to take the infernal lease, with all its consequences, off his hands. But none can hear without loss of reason the secret of Melmoth's command of supernatural powers. He wanders in search of individuals who, having fallen into utter distress, to escape further suffering, may be willing to exchange fates with him   This provides situations for Maturin to depict dreadful suffering, for before Melmoth appears with his offer, the fate of his prospective victims must be dire in the extreme.   These pictures are drawn with a remarkable command of detail.

In every episode of the disconnected narratives, whether in the mad-house, the subterranean vault of the convent, or the dungeon of the Inquisition, Melmoth's appearance is awaited with tingling nerves. " To the pressure from without is added the pressure from within. Maturin possessed a knowledge of human nature which belonged to no other writer of his school.   With acute analysis he traces the workings of the mind as it passes from resistance to apathy and on towards the verge of insanity.   The climax of agony which preludes the approach of Melmoth is internal as well as external."   His approach is heralded by strange music, and his eyes have a preternatural lustre that terrifies his victims.   None agree to his *incommunicable condition*.   His

> prayer falls parched and hissing on the fires that burn for ever, like a wandering drop of dew on the burning sands of the desert.

Melmoth says :

> I have traversed the world in the search, and no one, to gain that world, would lose his own soul.

Melmoth has been assigned a definite term of a hundred and fifty years.   The Wanderer is an ancestor of John Melmoth of Dublin. Monçada, a Spanish monk shipwrecked near Melmoth's house, relates to John the story of three other victims of Melmoth, which he had found in a manuscript owned by Adonijah, an aged Madrid Jew. Just as he is preparing to narrate several other stories, they are terrified by the apparition of Melmoth himself.   The latter tells them that they have nothing to fear since his wanderings are over, and no one knows his destiny for *none have consented* : Stanton in the London madhouse, Guzman, seeing his children starve, Elinor Morton, cruelly wronged, and last of all Immalee " the lovely child of nature ", the passionately adoring young bride, mother of his demon babe, deserted by all and dying in the prison of the Inquisition—all have refused to accept his *Terrible Condition*.

Melmoth sleeps, and in a fearful dream, where he overlooks an ocean of fire with an agonized soul on every wave, he sees the clock of eternity strike a hundred and fifty years—his allotted span.   On waking, John Melmoth and Monçada are horrified to see that he has utterly changed and presents the appearance of extreme old age.   The Wanderer tells them to leave him and not return, no matter what they see or hear ; that he must be left alone, and if they disobey their lives will be forfeit. Soon after midnight they hear sounds which grow more and more awful until it is impossible to discern whether it is the shriek of supplication or the yell of blasphemy. Suddenly all is silent ; they go into the room but no one is there ; a window is open to a back staircase and they see damp footprints which they trace to a cliff overlooking the sea :

> . . . there was a kind of track as if a person had dragged his way through it —a down-trodden track, over which no footsteps but those of one impelled by force had ever passed. . . . The ocean was beneath—the wide, waste, engulphing ocean ! On a crag beneath . . . something hung as floating to the blast. . . . It was the handkerchief the Wanderer had worn about his neck the preceding night—that was the last trace of the Wanderer.

The closing scene is especially reminiscent of the powerfully written last act of Marlowe's tragedy.

Thus the dominating figure in the novel is the terrible Melmoth. An ineffaceable portrait of this sombre and mysterious Wanderer is given by Melmoth himself :

> I have been on earth a terror, but not an evil to its inhabitants. None can participate in my destiny but with his own consent. . . . No one has ever exchanged destinies with Melmoth the Wanderer.

The reader senses behind him another being, from whom the deepest tragedy of human existence emanates :

> Where he treads, the earth is parched ! Where he breathes, the air is fire ! —Where he feeds, the food is poison!—Where he turns his glance is lightning.

This is like the *Tandava* or Dance of Destruction of Lord Siva.

We shrink back appalled before

> . . . the ominous lustre of those eyes which never rose on human destiny but as planets of woe.

The strange glare of his piercing eyes, and his smile, at once malignant, mocking and pathetic, burn themselves into the memory :

> . . . the mountain whose lava of internal fire has stifled, and undurated and inclosed for ever, all that was the joy of earth, the felicity of life, and the hope of futurity.

His eyes, lustrous with the brilliancy of hell, cast an enthralling, preternatural glare :

> . . . Accustomed to look on and converse with all things revolting to
> nature and to man,—for ever exploring the mad-house, the jail, or the
> Inquisition,—the den of famine, the dungeon of crime, or the death-bed of
> despair,—his eyes had acquired a light and a language of their own—a light
> that none could gaze on, and a language that few dare understand.

The fascinating personality of this restless traveller is indeed a creation
of genius ; his wanderings and endless persecution of mankind, his
tragic, endless migration from one continent to another, undeterred by
considerations of time and space, and his sudden appearance at fateful
moments recall to mind the Wandering Jew. " Faust and Mephistopheles
seem to be combined, in his person, for he has studied both the lawful
and unlawful sciences, achieved contact with the Devil, and at the price
of his soul purchased a term of youth, and now, in the part of Mephistopheles, seeks new victims." The theme of demoniac temptation finds
its highest expression in Mephistopheles, the most insidious agent of the
philosophy of evil—the same that tempted *The Monk*, appeared in Rosa
Matilda's *Zofloya*, or in James Hogg's *The Wool-gatherer* and *Confessions
of a Justified Sinner*. Unlike Milton, who elevates his Satan into a hero
by degrading his deity to a vulgar bully, Maturin never fails to evoke
his reader's sympathy with characters who resist evil.

In *Melmoth the Wanderer* we mark the culmination of the Schauer-
Romantik phase. All the machinery of the Gothic school is here : the
mysterious portrait, the decaying parchment, ruins and storms, Inquisition
and convent cells, entombed lovers, dead bride and insane bridegroom,
idyllic nature in the Indian islands—indeed the apotheosis of the whole
cult. The *Edinburgh Review* (July 1821) summed it up : " To complete
this phantasmagoric exhibition, we are presented with sybils and misers,
parricides, maniacs in abundance, monks with scourges pursuing a naked
youth streaming with blood ; subterranean Jews surrounded by the
skeletons of their wives and children ; lovers blasted by lightning,
Irish hags, Spanish grandees, shipwrecks, caverns, Donna Claras and
Donna Isidoras—all exposed to each other in violent and gloomy
contrast." Maturin has a much deeper, clearer, and more organized
vision of the place of evil and horror in the world than his predecessors,
and *Melmoth* of all novels of horror comes nearest to artistic greatness.

It has already been stated that Maturin's methods are subtler than

those of Lewis, for he seeks to communicate the presence of something
supernatural by a sense of haunting dread :

> It was one of those dismal nights . . . he perceived the miserable light that
> burned in the hearth was obscured by the intervention of some dark object.
> . . . Between him and the light stood the figure of Melmoth . . . the figure
> was the same ; the expression of the face was the same—cold, stony, and
> rigid ; the eyes with their infernal and dazzling lustre, were still the same.

He uses with great power Mrs. Radcliffe's method of suggestion :

> The wind was high that night, and as the creaking door swung on its
> hinges, every noise seemed like the sound of a hand struggling with the
> lock, or of a foot pausing on the threshold. . . . He saw the figure of his
> ancestor appear at the door . . . saw him enter the room, approach his bed,
> and heard him whisper, " You have burned me, then ; but those are flames
> I can survive—I am alive,—I am beside you " . . . [John] started from his
> bed,—it was broad day light. He looked round,—there was no human
> being in the room but himself. He felt a slight pain in the wrist of his right
> arm. He looked at it, it was black and blue, as from the recent grip of a
> strong hand.

At one place we are reminded of Mrs. Radcliffe's description of the
Castle of Udolpho :

> As they approached the Castle, the scene became glorious beyond the
> imagination of a painter, whose eye had dreamed of sun-set in foreign climes.
> The vast edifice lay buried in shade,—all its varied and strongly charactered
> features of tower and pinnacle, bartizan and battlement, were melted into
> one dense and sombre mass. The distant hills, with their conical summits,
> were still clearly defined in the dark-blue heaven, and their peaks still retained
> a hue of purple so brilliant and lovely, that it seemed as if the light had loved
> to linger there, and, parting, had left that tint as the promise of a glorious
> morning. The woods that surrounded the Castle stood as dark, and apparently
> as solid as itself.

Yet at times his use of ghastly realism goes beyond Lewis's :

> It was on the fourth night that I heard the shriek of the wretched female,
> —her lover, in the agony of hunger, had fastened his teeth in her shoulder ;
> —that bosom on which he had so often luxuriated, became a meal to him
> now.

Or :

> They dashed him to the earth—tore him up again—flung him into the
> air—tossed him from hand to hand, as the bull gores a howling mastiff with
> horns right and left. Bloody, defaced, blackened with earth, and battered

with stones . . . with his tongue hanging from his lacerated mouth, like that
of a baited bull ; with one eye torn from the socket, and dangling on his
bloody cheek ; with a fracture in every limb, and a wound for every pore,
he still howled for " life—life—life—mercy ! " till a Stone . . . struck him
down. He fell, trodden in one moment into sanguine and discoloured mud
by a thousand feet. . . . The crowd, saturated with cruelty and blood, gave
way to grim silence. But they had not left a joint of his little finger—a hair
of his head—a slip of his skin.

Monçada's dream in prison depicts an excess of physical horror :

> The next moment I was chained to my chair again,—the fires were lit,
> the bells rang out, the litanies were sung ; —my feet were scorched to a
> cinder,—my muscles cracked, my blood and marrow hissed, my flesh
> consumed like shrinking leather,—the bones of my legs hung two black
> withering and moveless sticks in the ascending blaze ;—it ascended, caught
> my hair,—I was crowned with fire,—I closed it, the fire was within, . . . and
> we burned and burned ! I was a cinder body and soul in my dream.

Maturin can introduce horror on a cosmic scale :

> . . . voices accompanied and re-echoed by the thunders of ten thousand
> billows of fire, lashing against rocks. . . . They talk of the music of the
> spheres !—Dream of the music of those living orbs turning on their axis of
> fire for ever and ever, and ever singing as they shine.

There is almost a Miltonic grandeur and irony in the image of

> —the eternal roar of a sea of fire [that] . . . makes a profound bass to the
> chorus of millions of singers in torture.

In line with the poetic effusions of Mrs. Radcliffe, the works of
Maturin are distinguished by a powerful eloquence of style, and his
dignified and stately language is in tune with the grandeur and sublimity
of his theme. The impetuosity and profusion of his ideas are clothed in
suitable words and images, which are pregnant with intense, passionate
feeling. He ably analyses emotions, and appears to be swayed by the
feelings he describes. Even his extravagances come flaming hot from
his excited imagination. In a biographical note on the author prefixed
to the 1892 edition of *Melmoth the Wanderer*, we read : " He rouges his
roses, and pours perfume on his jasmine, though Maturin's flowers are
rather mandrakes and nightshades too fearful and venomous to flourish
even in Circe's garden."

His narrative is marked by its sense of variety. Sometimes it grows
biblical, as in Jew Adonijah's speeches ; often it rises to poetic and lyrical

heights. His descriptions of nature are infused with a sense of atmosphere
and local colour. He successfully recaptures the rich and balmy odour
that scents the Indian air by night, its lofty colonnades of tamarind and
banyan, its shedding blossoms, cocoa and picturesque palm trees, while a
series of pictures display the midnight darkness of the tropics, the clouds
of suffocating dust, and thunders which are like the trumpet of doom.

His sensuousness and romanticism reminds us of the more voluptuous
aspect of Keats :

> Below . . . there were flowers and fragrance ; colours, like veiled beauty,
> mellowed, not hid ; and dews that hung on every leaf, trembling and
> sparkling like the tears of spirits, that wept to take leave of the flowers. The
> breeze, indeed, though redolent of the breath of the orange blossom, the
> jasmine, and the rose. . . .

He indulges in poetic effusions while commenting on the meeting of
Isidora (Immalee) and her Demon Lover in the Spanish summer night,
when Melmoth leans against the trunk of a giant myrtle-tree which casts
a shade over his portentous expression, and they never utter a word to
each other till the dawn appears, when the breeze speaks to her in a voice
whose melody is borrowed from her own heart :

> Language is no longer necessary to those whose beating hearts converse
> audibly—whose eyes, even by moonlight, are more intelligible to each
> other's stolen and shadowed glances, than the broad converse of face to face
> in the brightest sunshine—to whom, in the exquisite inversion of earthly
> feeling and habit, darkness is light, and silence eloquence.

Speaking on love he says :

> To love, beautiful Isidora, is to live in a world of the heart's own creation
> —all whose forms and colours are as brilliant as they are deceptive and
> unreal. To those who love there is neither day or night, summer or winter,
> society or solitude. They have but two eras in their delicious but visionary
> existence,—and those are thus marked in the heart's calendar—*presence*—
> *absence*. These are the substitutes for all the distinctions of nature and society.
> The world to them contains but one individual,—and that individual is to
> them the world as well as its single inmate. The atmosphere of his presence
> is the only air they can breathe in,—and the light of his eye the only sun of
> their creation, in whose rays they bask and live.

Maturin's use of similes is explanatory as well as ornamental. The short
and quivering grasp of the hands of old Melmoth is

> like the claws of some bird that had died of hunger,—so meagre, so yellow,
> so spread.

The dark and heavy thunder-clouds are like

> shrouds of these spectres of departed greatness.

Some fine pictures of nature are embodied in his ornamental similes :

> There was a mild, inoppressive, but most seductive light in the dark-blue eyes that fell so softly on hers, like moonlight floating over a fine landscape.

or

> There beamed among them, an eye of dark and brilliant light, like a star amid the deepening shades of twilight.

On the wrinkled cheeks of Guzman was

> a gleam of joy, like the cold smile of a setting sun on a wintry landscape.

Happy tears are like

> those showers in a fine spring morning, which announce the increasing warmth and beauty of the day.

There is also a note of sensuousness in some of his images :

> The lovely valley of Valencia blushed and burned in all the glory of sunset, like a bride receiving the last glowing kiss of the bridegroom before the approach of night.

Immalee, referring to her shadow, says :

> There is not a rose-leaf that drops in the river so bright as its shadow. . . . My friend lives under the water. . . . It kisses me too but its lips are very cold.

Maturin can be very expressive :

> . . . the kiss of childhood that felt like velvet.

It is curious that Maturin, a priest, should have introduced in his works sentiments averse to Christianity. Certain specific charges of atheism and indecency may be levelled against him. Several passages from his novel easily spring to mind by force of especial indecency. There are some extremely detailed and lurid descriptions of what he conceived was monastic life in Spain. Monçada prays not to be made a monk :

> Let me embrace the meanest, but do not make me a monk. . . . Give me a sword,—send me into the armies of Spain to seek death,—death is all I ask, in preference to that life you doom me to.

There are particular descriptions of atrocities inside the convent and conventual life :

> . . . they spit in my face as they passed. I wiped it off, and thought how little of the spirit of Jesus was to be found in the house of his nominal brethren

Commenting further upon it he says :

> . . . the Christianity of these countries is diametrically opposite to the Christianity . . . recorded in the pages of your Bible.

and that

> . . . the infernal spirit is the hero, and in the disguise of a monk he appears in a convent, where he torments and persecutes the community with a mixture of malignity and mirth truly Satanic.

There are statements like the following :

> the virtues of nature are always deemed vices inside a convent.

Or

> I have heard much of the terrors of convents,—of their punishments, often carried till the infliction of death would have been a blessing. Dungeons, chains, and scourges, swam before my eyes in a fiery mist . . .—such is the sterility of humanity in a convent.

This element of anti-Catholic feeling in Gothic novels with an especial reference to Maturin may be the basis of a fruitful psychological study. The anti-Catholic note is struck again and again in the Gothic novels.

Maturin weaves an original romance out of many varied strands, and *Melmoth* is not merely an ingenious patchwork of previous stories. Although he frequently borrows scenes and incidents from other writers we have seen that his ideas and his characters are peculiarly individual. Immalee, the heroine in *Melmoth the Wanderer*, is a glorification of the Emily of Mrs. Radcliffe, while the monastic horrors, which form the scene of " The Spaniard's Tale," have their corresponding setting in *The Monk*.

In " The Tale of the Indians " he displays a close acquaintance with the Orient, its religions, and its literature. Shakespeare's tragedies may have suggested to him the idea of enhancing the interest of his story by dissecting human motive and describing passionate feeling. The phrase ". . . would lose his own soul " echoes the biblical text, which may have inspired Maturin with the idea of this romance. Marlowe's *Dr.*

Faustus, and the first part of Goethe's *Faust*, left a strong impression on this novel.

Melmoth the Wanderer fascinated Rossetti and Thackeray, and " had some influence on the French romantic school and was utilized, in some particulars, by Balzac ".   The genius of both Hugo and Baudelaire felt the spell.   This novel may be called " the swan-song of the ' roman-noir ' ; after it the fashion gradually died away ".

CHAPTER VII

'GOTHIC' DISTRIBUTARIES : THE RESIDUARY INFLUENCES

AFTER every tempest comes a calm, and at last the Gothic rage was to subside. The countless volumes that swarmed from the press, thick as Vallombrosan leaves, during those sixty years of the Gothic novel's heyday, at last became demoded and out of vogue. Exponents of Gothic romance extend well into the first quarter of the nineteenth century, as is evident from the works of Francis Lathom, Mrs. Meeke, Sarah Wilkinson, T. J. Horsley-Curties, W. C. Wren, Charles Lucas, Mrs. York, Catherine Ward, Jane Porter, William Child Green, Robert Huish, Hannah Jones, Eleanor Sleath, and very many more : but these were minor ' gothic' writers whose works were animated by the last flicker of enthusiasm for Gothic fiction. Reaction had set in ; the symptoms and process of disintegration were evident. Slowly and steadily the old and mighty pillars of ' Gothic' tottered and crumbled.

As far back as 1927, Michael Sadleir raised a pertinent question : " It remains to inquire where, when its great days were over, the Gothic romance took refuge." This question still remains unanswered. It is interesting therefore to pierce the haze that mantles the diffluent waters of Gothic fiction, and trace the course of its distributaries. The story of ' Gothic' disintegration and the obscure underground channels of Gothic romance, is by itself a subject for independent research.

The process of literary disintegration does not follow any law of physics. In natural science, when there is the destruction of cohesion or disintegration of ' matter', it separates into its component particles. When, however, a body of literature disintegrates, first its old forms decay and then they are transformed into something new and beautiful. Thus the florescent body of ' Gothic' fiction became desiccated, as dry as old river-beds, and its waters diverged into fresh channels, nourishing new forms of succeeding literature.

There seems to be difficulty in assigning limits to the period when Gothic fiction remained in vogue. Some date its declining interest from the year 1797, which saw in the publication of Mrs. Radcliffe's *The Italian* the zenith of the Gothic vogue, after which " The Mighty

Enchantress of Udolpho " retired from authorship in the full blaze of her glory. K. K. Mehrotra has termed later novelists, like Lewis and Maturin, " belated advocates " of an " outmoded genre ". Others find the efflorescence of Gothic fiction extending well into the second decade of the nineteenth century, until the publication of *The Heroine* (1813), *Waverley* (1814), or *Northanger Abbey* (1818) started eroding its established popularity. The evening sky is a diffused harmony of colours : the red stain of sunlight melting into a tint of glorious purple, then fading into a deep grey of darkening twilight ; nor can the eyes measure where one colour ends and the other begins. So it is with the disintegrating phase of Gothic romance.

Edith Birkhead asserts that between the years 1797 and 1820 the Gothic novel maintained only a " disreputable existence ". Writers who penned romances after 1800 may have written for a dwindling audience, but their works are far from being discreditable. There remain lingering traces of conscious artistry, and those forebodings of mystery, which were characteristic beauties of the works of Charlotte Smith and Mrs. Radcliffe. " By 1800 the Gothic novels were in high favour with the reading public," says Willard Thorp. Although ' Monk ' Lewis had written in 1801 that the " unheeded spell " of the tale of terror was growing feeble, he himself, far from being merely a " belated advocate " of Gothic romance, or resisting the undercurrent of popular disfavour, swam rather briskly with the popular current. Still there were a host of readers in England who thought with Catherine Morland that novels should be " all horrid ". The tale of terror was yet a living, vital thing.

Worlds do not pass away overnight and the transition from the Gothic world of *Otranto*, *Udolpho*, and *Frankenstein*, to that of Heathcliff and Oliver Twist, cannot be described briefly nor measured with geometrical instruments ; but the main lines of the change are apparent if the story of Gothic disintegration is viewed against the background of shifting popular taste.

Sensibility changes from age to age, and the eternal swing of the pendulum of literary history, the ebb and flow of fiction according to certain inexpressible literary laws, inevitably brings in a reaction against any extreme. Thus it happened with the Gothic novel. Its forces spent themselves, its charms lost potency, its glamour was dissipated, and the Gothic spell broken. The reading public fell in a torpor—characterized by the languor of an exhausted appetite.

It is perhaps rash to assert that *Waverley* either ' ousted ' Gothic romance from public favour or "rendered it obsolete". Mr. Sadleir's statement that "The Gothic novel *crashed* and became the *vulgar blood*", is only partly true. It did not 'crash' like a 'spent rocket' : rather its fall was like the slow collapse of a mighty empire, and the 'vulgar blood' was but a symptom of it. The phases of its decay are reflected in the changing tastes of the age, and in reviews that appeared in magazines and journals ; the process of disintegration is manifest in the satires, skits and parodies that followed in a trail during the period of 'Gothic' decline.

The opinion that the fame of Gothic romances was eclipsed by the Waverley novels is also erroneous. According to Robert D. Mayo, "twenty years of unimaginative repetition had already broken the hold of the tale of terror on the general reading public beyond Scott's power to weaken it further". Moreover, it is easy to perceive a close semblance between the novels of Scott and Gothic fiction since both draw inspiration from the same fount. *Waverley* and its successors drink deep from the waters of Gothic romance, and there is a perceptible organic relationship between the Gothic efflorescence and the tremendous popularity of Scott's works. The outmoded motifs and properties of Gothic romance were replaced by Scott in a manner that afforded similar excitement but added to it the colour and conviction of reality. The wicked Montonis, the scheming Schedonis, the savage banditti and spectres of Gothic romance, became in the works of Scott genuine outlaws, monks, highland chiefs, and phantoms of Scottish tradition. For the Salvator Rosa land-scapes were substituted real mountains, forest-vistas, valleys and caves, and the impregnable castles of Scotland. The appeal of Gothic romance still cast a fresh glow on the reader's mind, and (again quoting Mayo) "when Scott breathed new life into the old forms, the general audience returned with the same eagerness".

The causes of 'Gothic' disintegration are not far to seek. The first cause was psychological. Scott himself had an inkling : "Children when tired of admiring a new play-thing find a fresh and distinct pleasure in breaking it to pieces," he says. The finest flower of Gothic romance, which had afforded such general delight to the public, was destined to the common fate of neglect and contempt. Moreover, every new and original kind of literature produces a tribe of imitators, who undersell the first author with highly coloured copies, but "nothing so quickly exhausts the popularity of a work of art as its power of multiplying its kind".

The Gothic novel had become guilty of the excesses of the 'vulgar blood'; its atmosphere of crude sensationalism and violence was a logical outcome of the instinct for liberty which had inspired the whole movement. A soupçon of terror is enough to impart a strong flavour ; in excess the palate is deadened and nauseated. The Schauer-Romantik writers, by attempting to achieve their horror-effects through quantity rather than quality, gave a colouring of gross improbability to their themes. By becoming outrageous and too violent, they began to defeat their own object and failed to freeze the blood. Their methods out-stripped the limits of their reader's endurance. Emphasis and exaggera-tion, duels, murders, and blazing scenes of horror, even spectres and fiends could appal no more, just as the chords of a violin when over-stretched no longer yield musical notes. Continued and repeated feelings of suspense and awe quickly made the satiated public indifferent to the strongest stimuli of that kind.

The imitators of Mrs. Radcliffe and Lewis popularly misused the limited range of properties until familiarity turned into monotony. Peacock observes that the reader " had lived upon ghosts, goblins, and skeletons . . . till the devil himself . . . became too base, common, and popular ". George Colman wrote in the 'nineties :

> A novel now is nothing more
> Than an old castle and a creaking door,
>   A distant hovel,
> Clanking of chains, a gallery, a light,
> Old armour and a phantom all in white,
>   And there's a novel.

While the publication of *The Mysteries of Udolpho* (1794) fanned the enthusiasm for Gothic romance it also contributed factors which eventually precipitated the decline of the Gothic movement. Scott gives it expression : " It was the cry at the period . . . that the romances of Mrs. Radcliffe, and the applause with which they were received, were evil signs of the times, and argued a great and increasing degradation of the public taste, which, instead of banquetting as heretofore upon scenes of passion, like those of Richardson, or of life and manners, as in the pages of Smollett and Fielding, was now coming back to the fare of the nursery, and gorged upon the wild and improbable fictions of an overheated imagination."

The Radcliffian technique of " supernaturual expliqué " considerably distracted public interest from examining the credibility of her tales. Mysteries which were finally resolved in a natural manner were an insult to a reader's intelligence and reason. Again, to quote Scott, " the more imaginative class of readers resemble men who love to walk through a misty, moonlit landscape, more to be teazed than to be edified by the intrusive minuteness of a reasonable companion who may disturb the reveries by divesting every rock and stone of the shadowy semblances in which the fancy may have dressed them, by restoring to them the natural forms and commonplace tinge of reality ".

Finally, as the Gothic novel encompassed a wider range of human experience, it lost its individuality and merged into other forms. All these forces together engineered the disintegration of Gothic fiction.

As time drew on the type revealed a steady decline in popularity. The critical attitude which illustrates the first symptom of disintegration, is best reflected in the reviews of the *Critical* and the *Monthly*. " These critics . . . continued to emphasize the need for truthful characterization and careful motivation," says J. B. Heidler. As far back as 1765 both the *Critical* and the *Monthly* reviewers had sniffed scornfully at the marvels of the first Gothic novel The *Critical* referred to the ' monstrosities ' of *The Castle of Otranto* ; the *Monthly* noted " the absurdities of Gothic fiction ". The Gothic machinery in popular fiction had annoyed the reviewers, and when they learnt that *The Castle of Otranto* was not a translation (second edition), the *Monthly* reviewer was much irritated at the literary deception, and remarked :

> It is indeed more than strange, that an Author, of a refined and polished genius, should be an advocate for re-establishing the barbarous superstitions of Gothic devilism.

But slowly the ferocity which had characterized reviews of *The Castle of Otranto* subsided, as this species of fiction catered to the taste of a large reading public. Clara Reeve's *The Old English Baron* (1777), and Sophia Lee's *Recess* (1783), won the praise of reviewers.

The period between 1789 and 1800, which marks the efflorescence of Gothic romance, and the publication of Mrs. Radcliffe's novels, drew unhesitating praise and favour from the reviewers : however, " the closing years witnessed critical dissatisfaction with what they had so recently accepted," observes J. B. Heidler. Godwin, in the preface to *St. Leon* (1799) advocating the realistic portrayal of the strictly marvellous, wrote :

> The hearts and the curiosity of readers have been assailed in so many ways, that we, writers who bring up the rear of our illustrious predecessors, must be contented to arrive at novelty in whatever mode we are able.

The *Monthly* reviewer, while reviewing Mrs. Radcliffe's first work *The Castles of Athlin and Dunbayne* (1789), had not yet entirely overcome the prejudice against Gothic romance.   After having praised its wonders and marvels, he said :

> This kind of entertainment, however, can be little relished but by the young and unformed mind.

A Sicilian Romance (1790), despite its merit, had "numerous improbabilities", but *The Romance of the Forest* (1792), and *The Mysteries of Udolpho* (1794), drew favourable comments.   On the evidence of reviews, the year 1794 may be noted as the high-water mark of Gothic fiction. However, the tide turned once more when the *Monthly* reviewed *The Italian* (1797), and compared the Gothic romance to its disadvantage with the realistic novels of Richardson, Fielding, or Fanny Burney :

> This species of fiction is perhaps more imposing than the former, on the first perusal : but the characteristic which distinguishes it essentially from and shews its vast inferiority to, the genuine novel, is that, like a secret, it ceases to interest after it can no longer awaken our curiosity ; while the other, like truth, may be reconsidered and studied with increased satisfaction.

The merits of *The Italian* were well appreciated in the reviews, but the critics felt that the fortunes of the Gothic romance were careering downhill, and that it could not compete successfully with a realistic depiction of contemporary life as in the novels of Fielding, Smollett, and others. Time at last has proved its verdict a true one.

The *Critical Review*, dealing with Francis Lathom's *The Castle of Ollada* in 1795, wrote :

> Another haunted castle !   Surely the misses themselves must be tired of so many ghosts and murders.

The same year, this journal, while reviewing John Palmer's *The Haunted Cavern*, stated :

> In truth, we are almost weary of Gothic castles, mouldering turrets, and "cloud enveloped battlements ". . . . The tale of shrieking spectres, and bloody murders, has been repeated till it palls upon the sense.

And again they observe :

> We would wish that they would cease to build castles in the air, and return to *terra firma*, to common life, and common sense.

Such evidence of satiety with Gothic fiction can be found scattered in other journals and reviews.

Fielding had advocated a closely knit plot and the depiction of universal characters ; and for twenty years after 1740 the critics laid emphasis on characterization rather than on plot. The period between 1760 and 1789 marks a gradual acceptance of romantic novels which laid stress on careful plot development ; the years between 1789 and 1800 were a period synchronizing with the efflorescence of Gothic fiction, the finest flower being the works of Mrs. Radcliffe.

During the 'eighties, which saw the beginning of a craze for Gothic fiction, haunted castles acquired great popularity. The middle of the last decade of the eighteenth century marks the climax of the vogue, but " by the end of the century . . . the age proclaimed again the superiority of realistic depictions of contemporary life as written by Fielding, Smollett, and Fanny Burney ".

The reaction did not confine itself to periodicals, for by 1797 the symptoms of discontent definitely crystallize into a whole set of satires, parodies, and skits against the school of Gothic fiction.

There appeared in the *Monthly Mirror* an advertisement of *The Mountaineers : or The Maniac of the Cave*, wherein the advertiser stated that

> the fertility of the author's incomparable genius never appeared to greater advantage ; presenting an assemblage of all the beauties of *Desperation, Execration, Detestation, Perturbation, Humiliation,* and *Ostentation.* . . . The Piece is composed of MIRTH AND SORROW, JOY AND HORROR with Rage and Despair most pleasantly blended. Amidst a variety of scenery which is too numerous to be here inserted are the following : A picturesque view of a ship-wreck, A storm at Sun Rise. A Superb Banquet, interspersed with eating and drinking, singing and dancing. A dreary Cave, most beautifully decorated with Skulls, Skeletons, Bones and Monuments. . . . The piece to conclude with a pleasing view of the INFERNAL REGIONS. In which will be introduced an entire new Shower of Fire, and a grand COUNTRY DANCE BY DEAD BODIES, assisted by Furies, Imps and Devils of the whole company.

The *Magazine Encyclopedique* for 1797, cited by Ferdinand Balden-peiger in the *Journal of Comparative Literature*, printed " a recipe to obtain a good mixture of shudders and fright, in three volumes ", as follows :

> Recipe :
> An old castle, half of it crumbling down,
> A long corridor, with numerous doors many of which must be hidden,
> Three corpses still weltering in their blood,

Three skeletons carefully wrapped up,
An old woman hanged, stabbed several times in her throat,
Robbers and ruffians galore,
A sufficient dose of whispers, stifled moans and frightful din.

All those ingredients well mixed and divided into three parts or volumes give an excellent mixture which all those who have no black blood may take just before going to bed while having their baths. They will feel all the better for it. Probatum est.

In 1799 the same journal parodied the kind of romance people were devouring by advertising the mock title " *The English Knight*, or Adventures once somewhat extraordinary, but quite simple and common-place nowadays of *Mr. Babaud*, a shopkeeper of the Rue St. Honore . . . translated . . . by the R. S. Spectre Ruini, an Italian Monk (2 vols.). They take place in the ruins of Paluzzi, Tivoli, in the tombs of St. Claire, in the abbeys of Grasville, in the Castles of Udolpho, Mortymore, Montroir, Lindenberg ; in a word, in all the places where you find ghosts, monks, ruins, ruffians, underground passages, and a western tower and dungeons."

The romance had become a cheap mechanical thing, and the mind of the nation was turning away from it to reinstate those teachers of moral prudence whose influence had been impaired by the flood, but not destroyed. The frequent parodies and satires are symptomatic of the new sensibility which was manifesting itself in English prose fiction as the Gothic manner became exhausted. Winifred H. Rogers, who has examined nearly fifty such works, notes the marked change in the readers' sensibility during the years 1796–1830 and comments that these attacks hurled against the pseudo-sentimentalists and Gothic novelists " do not explain the change ; they are merely a factor in that change, but a factor worthy of note ".

As early as 1789, when Mrs. Radcliffe's *The Castles of Athlin and Dunbayne* appeared, James Cobb published his skit *The Haunted Tower*, which pokes fun at one of her favourite motifs : the idea of a haunted wing or chamber. He ridicules the Gothic sources of terror, by depicting certain stock situations.

More Ghosts! (1798) is a satire against the Gothic novel according to a contemporary reviewer.

A direct satire on the school of terror appeared in *The Anti-Jacobin* (1798), in the form of four acts of a burlesque *The Rovers, or the Double Arrangement*, with introductory discourse and notes. E. A. Baker called it

" the wittiest of all the attacks on both the sentimentality and the terrorism of those who learned from the German schools ".

In the *Monthly Mirror* (1800) was published a satirical parody " *St. Godwin, a Tale of the Sixteenth, Seventeenth, and Eighteenth Centuries*" by Count Reginald De St. Leon, which is obviously a hit at Godwin and his novel.

The best of these extravanganzas is *The Heroine, or The Adventures of Cherubina* (1813) by Eaton Stannard Barrett, which not only burlesques the ' Gothic' heroine, ' gothic' situations and machinery, but also travesties both the tale of terror and the language of sensibility. The author has fallen deeply under the spell of the literature he parodies, and his work is a clinging kind of tribute to the force of its original, and catches the soul as well as the form of Gothic fiction. Oliver Elton considers it " the most comprehensive skit upon the fiction that was ceasing to be in vogue ".

There were certain other precursors of this work. Maria Edgworth mocked the current heroine in *Angelina*, one of her *Moral Tales* (1801). Mary Charlton, in *Rosetta, or Modern Occurrences* (1799), and Benjamin Thompson in *The Florentines* (1808), turned seriousness inside out, while Sarah Green in *Romance Readers and Romance Writers* (1810) described the follies of a clergyman's daughter who lost her common sense through reading too much fiction.

Barrett parodies the romantic situations in the novels of Mrs. Radcliffe, Mrs. Roche, and ' Monk' Lewis, and achieves his effect by using actual phrases from the works against which he is hitting, and placing them in absurd, ridiculous positions, and by paralleling the situations, actions, events or sentiments expressed in Gothic novels. Throughout the book the author sustains a running fire of criticism, and yet provides abundant entertainment. He writes with great energy and unflagging zest. Jane Austen herself read *The Heroine*, and confessed the pleasure she derived from it. In 1816 *The Biographical Dictionary of the Living Authors of Great Britain and Ireland* concluded with the following eulogy :

> This work (*The Heroine*) has been pronounced not inferior in wit and humour to Tristram Shandy, and in point of plot and interest infinitely beyond Don Quixote.

Since it is perhaps the best work of the reactionary school it deserves a closer scrutiny. The story centres round the adventures of Cherry, a

country girl, who, inspired by Gothic romances, assumes the name of
Cherubina. She reaches such an imaginative tension that she feels she
is an heiress kept in unwarranted seclusion. She rummages her father's
desk for "ancient stolen documents" that may perhaps give some clue
regarding her birth, and chances upon a yellow scrap which she interprets
according to her own whim. She then escapes, leaving a note that she
is going "to wander over the convex earth in search of her parents",
and the story recounts her comic experiences. She faces tempests,
explores deserted houses, and finally thinks she has reached her ancestral
castle in London, which is revealed to her as Covent Garden Theatre.
After a series of adventures she takes possession of somebody else's castle
and orders it to be furnished in 'Gothic' style. At one place she finds
a blade-bone of mutton in some Gothic garbage and takes it for the bone
of a foully murdered ancestor.

The entire work is a more pronounced parody of Gothicism than
Northanger Abbey, and burlesques every feature of terror fiction : the
inflated language, the excited swearings, the feudal furniture, the medieval
architecture, the Gothic weather, the supernatural temper, the spectres
and phantoms.

The Gothic heroine had always been a beautiful shadow. Her
beauties and virtues turned to perfection, as the reality of her character
lessened. The Gothic novels had described her in lavish epithets : her
mind was "a rich jewel contained in a most beautiful casket", or her
"skin was white as the unsullied snow on the mountains, save where
the crimson of her lips, and the rosy hue of her cheeks, opposed a shining
contrast to the shining brightness of her bosom". There were exquisite
descriptions of the symmetry and proportion of her shape. There were
poetic ecstasies like "Her eyes were large and sparkling ; but mild as
the moon in the evening of summer, when she darts her trembling
beams through the intermingled branches of the forest, and gilds the
glittering stream that murmurs at their roots".

Barrett notes :

> A heroine is a young lady rather taller than usual, and often an orphan ;
> at all events, possessed of the finest eyes in the world. Though her frame is so
> fragile, that a breath of wind might scatter it like chaff, it is sometimes stouter
> than a statue of cast iron. She blushes to the tips of her fingers ; when other
> girls would laugh, she faints. Besides, she has tears, sighs, and half sighs, at
> command ; lives a month on a mouthful, and is addicted to the pale
> consumption.

He observes :

> I have read of some of them who were thrown among mountains, or into cells, and desolate chambers, and caverns ; full of slime, mud, vermin, dust, and cobwebs, where they remained whole months without clean linen, soap, brush, towel, or comb ; and at last, when rescued from. captivity, forth they walked, glittering like the morning star, as fragrant as lily, and as fresh as an oyster.

The acquired accomplishments of the Gothic heroine were legion. She could paint and sew, and play either the lute, the harp, the guitar, or the oboe—the four plaintive instruments to soothe one's melancholy. She could compose ballads of unrequited love, and sing them melodiously to the pale moon floating upon the waters. The only initiative she ever displayed was in the unfailing courage to explore the dark recesses of castles and convents.

Barrett writes :

> when a heroine is reduced to extremities, she always does one of the two things, either faints on the spot, or exhibits energies almost superhuman.

Or even performs

> journies on foot that would founder fifty horses.

He remarks on the conventual smile of the heroine in all the silence of despair, something between Niobe, patience, and a broken lily.

Cherubina says :

> Tears are my sole consolation. Oft times I sit and weep, I know not why ; and then I weep to find myself weeping. Then, when I can weep, I weep at having nothing to weep at ; and then, when I have something to weep at, I weep that I cannot weep at it.

Macaulay, who was a great lover of cheap Gothic romances, found twenty swoons distributed among four ladies in the course of a five-volume novel.

Barrett flings casual remarks on the stock 'gothic' atmosphere, " the rattling rain, and whistling wind ", " the horrid, horrible and horridest horror ! ", of " rusty daggers, mouldering bones, and ragged palls, that lie scattered in all the profusion of feudal plenty ". He comments upon the " blood on floors, and daggers, that looked as fresh as a daisy at the end of centuries ", and remarking on the supernatural says that " Indeed, ghosts keep such late hours, that 'tis no wonder they look pale and thin ".

Barret refers to *The Mysteries of Udolpho*, *The Italian*, and *The Bravo of Venice*, and praises them as being " often captivating and seldom detrimental ". At the close of the book he summarizes his indictment against the Gothic romances in general. Professor Raleigh remarks : " The prose romance was dead. It had fallen into its dotage, and the hand of Eaton Stannard Barrett had killed it. *The Heroine* seemed to mark the end of an age of romance, and the beginning of a new era of sententious prose."

The Hero : or The Adventures of a Night! A Romance, was published in 1817, and is jokingly dedicated to the authors of *The Mysteries of Udolpho*, *The Tomb*, *Grasville Abbey*, *The Monk*, *Hubert de Sevrac*, *Celestina*, and *The Heroine*.

An anonymous work, *Prodigious!!! or, Childe Paddie in London* (1818) makes fun of the " improbable-immoral-absurd-sentimental-gothic-fiction ". It caricatures the Gothic heroes and villains and dwells upon their impossible adventures. The author hurls a lengthy satire on 'Monk' Lewis and the element of pornography in his work.

The works of Thomas Love Peacock are parodies of fiction itself as a type of literature, but parodies utilized for satires of a more specific kind. His *Nightmare Abbey* (1818) is a satire against the romantic poets as well as against Gothic novels. Writing on the reading public of his time, he says :

> That part of the reading public which shuns the solid food of reason for the light diet of fiction requires a perpetual adhibition of sauce piquante to the palate of its depraved imagination.

Jane Austen's *Northanger Abbey* (1818), begun in 1797–98 and " completed in 1803, when Mrs. Radcliffe's popular dominion was still unchallenged, was published at least half a dozen years too late to affect the general taste ", says Robert D. Mayo. This is proved by the contrast between the market value of Mrs. Radcliffe's work and Austen's *Northanger Abbey*. Whereas *The Mysteries of Udolpho* fetched £500 and *The Italian* £800 from the publishers, an ungenerous sum of £10 only was paid for the manuscript of *Northanger Abbey*. E. A. Baker suggests that " the cautious publisher held up the book out of fear of affronting the thousands of readers who idolized Mrs. Radcliffe ". Jane Austen writes in her advertisement prefixed to *Northanger Abbey* :

> This little work was finished in the year 1803, and intended for im-mediate publication. It was disposed of to a bookseller, it was even advertised,

and why the business proceeded no farther, the author has never been able to learn. That any bookseller should think it worthwhile to purchase what he did not think it worthwhile to publish, seems extraordinary. . . .

According to Baker " the burlesque of Udolpho was clearly part of the original design ", for *The Mysteries of Udolpho* is closely parodied in certain chapters. Although there are a great many delicately tipped shafts of ridicule against Mrs. Radcliffe, Jane Austen practises a nice sense of artistic restraint. The satire hurled at the Gothic romances was rather subtle and fine, rather delicately mischievous, and it never did seriously disturb the popularity of Gothic tales. This novel is directed particularly against those feminine readers whose minds were coloured with them and who confused Gothic fiction with the realities of life. Thomas Hervey Lister's *Granby* (1826), is another satire of this type.

In *Northanger Abbey* the ' heroine ' is a young lady whose head is turned by romances which " address the imagination alone, and act upon the mind like inebriating stimulants ". The story narrates the burlesque of Gothic experiences which Catherine undergoes during her visit to Northanger Abbey. Her imagination is excited because of an excessive dose of Gothic romances, and she explores the secret wings in search for horrors, but finds herself only in sunny chambers. Nor does she chance upon any imprisoned wives, nor skeletons of immured nuns. Opening a black chest at midnight, she excitedly grasps a time-yellowed manuscript, which is eventually revealed as an old laundry list ! Mr. Tilney's ironic jests satirically comment on all the elements of Gothic romance. Austin Dobson says : " It is probable that *Northanger Abbey* was originally only a more serious and sustained attempt to do for the Radcliffe school what Cervantes had done for *Esplandian* and *Florismarte of Hyrcania*, and Mrs. Lennox for *Cassandra* and *Cleopatra*."

During the first phase of ' Gothic ' disintegration, the diffluent waters were channelled into Gothic serials, tales, fragments, and shockers, but the first great distributary was the Gothic drama whose current bore all the extravaganzas and improbabilities, the mystery and terror of Gothic fiction. An adequate study of the subject is attempted by Bertrand Evans in his *Gothic Drama from Walpole to Shelley*, to which is appended a list of Gothic plays.

" The first dramatisation of a ' tale of terror ' was an adaptation of Walpole's *Castle of Otranto*, entitled *The Count of Narbonne* in 1781 . . . by Robert Jephson." Mrs. Radcliffe's *A Sicilian Romance* and *A Romance of the Forest* were acted on the stage in 1794, the latter under the title of

Fountainville Forest. The Italian reached the stage as *The Italian Monk* (1797), and in 1798 Boaden produced at Drury Lane a dramatic version of Lewis's *The Monk*, with the title of *Aurelio and Miranda.* Thorp has pointed out that all these stage versions were tame, denuded of most of the supernatural effects. " Thus at the very end of the century the critics were still insisting that the theatre was no place for the creations of a romantic imagination."

The potent spell of Gothic romance had been losing its force and vigour for some years before 1820, yet in a new guise it continued to appeal to a minority audience down to the middle of the nineteenth century and beyond. The periodical press quickly responded to the vogue of Gothic romance. Serialized works like *The Monk and the Robbers* (1794–1805) in the *Lady's Magazine*, or *The Ruins of St. Oswald* (1800) and *The Banditti of the Forest ; or the Mysterious Dagger* (1811–12) in the *Lady's Monthly Museum*, are full-length Gothic novels. Between the years 1791 and 1812 the *Lady's Magazine* had printed twenty-one Gothic romances in serialized form.

Two distinct types, *Gothic tales* and *Gothic fragments*, mark the first cleavage in Gothic fiction. The former differs from the serialized romance only in point of length, seeking to achieve the same effects within a shorter compass of several hundred words, such as were spread over twenty to thirty instalments of the serialized novel. The elaborate romance first gave rise to shorter ' *tales* ' with a pronounced undercurrent of ' Gothic ' properties—with remote settings, idealized character-creations, and violent or erotic incidents set in an atmosphere of terror. Robert D. Mayo points out that " the presence of short tales of terror in the magazines from 1792 to 1820, along with Gothic novelettes and serialized romances, shows that the publishers of *Blackwood's* and the *London Magazine* were no innovators in offering sensational fiction to the reading public, but were adhering to an established precedent in periodical literature ".

A typical example of this kind of fiction is *The Clock Has Struck ! ! !* a ' *Legendary Tale* ' from the *Lady's Magazine* of 1809. The writer has abbreviated the entire apparatus of a full-length Gothic romance : here are abductions, rescues, villainy, and murder ; the background is medieval, with its usual castle, chapel, and burial vaults, and there are concentrated attempts to evoke an atmosphere of suspense, but all is compressed to less than twenty-five hundred words, with its focus on one single episode of terror. It is truly a Gothic romance in miniature such as might easily be extended to several instalments in serial form or into the usual four volumes by any skilled writer. Mayo gives figures : " In 1805, in fact, the high-water year for Gothic fiction in the *Lady's Magazine*, three of the four continued stories offered (or eighty-four per cent in quantitative terms) are tales of terror. After 1806 a period of decline for this type of fiction appears to have set in. From 1807 to 1809 the proportion drops to forty-four per cent ; and during 1813 and 1814 Gothic stories disappear entirely." The periodicals offered a really fruitful period for Gothic short stories. " The editors of English magazines had enlivened their pages with sensational fiction in both serial and short-story form, and . . . by 1810 the Gothic short story was a well-defined and familiar species of fiction."

The *Lady's Magazine* provides us with a " sensitive barometer for the taste of its audience ". As the very name suggests, it fed the fancies of leisured middle-class feminine readers, and was published for nearly fifty years after 1770, reaching a circulation of sixteen thousand. " Terror became the regular ingredient of the *Lady's Magazine*, every volume of which until 1813 was to feed in some form or other the general taste for imaginative horrors."

During the first decade of the nineteenth century the *Lady's Magazine* published several ' gothic ' tales of which the following are noteworthy : *Edeliza, A Gothic Tale* (1802), *Adelaide* (1806), *The Mysterious Admonition* (1807), *The Vale of Avignon, a Tragic Romance* (1807), *The Castle of Almeyda* (1810). Yet none of these extend beyond five thousand words, the shortest one limiting itself to six hundred. Towards the close of the eighteenth and beginning of the nineteenth century, the short stories and novels in instalment had become a popular and regular feature of the then respectable publications, such as the *Scots Magazine* (1789–1803), the *Town and Country Magazine* (1769–96), the *Lady's Magazine* (1770–1837), the *Monthly Mirror* (1795–1811), the *Lady's Monthly Museum* (1798–1832), to name only a few.

Montague Summers has remarked that the Gothic novel is by nature committed to " a certain leisure " and " long drawn suspense ", and that it " does not permit of any abbreviation ". Yet the writers of Gothic tales in the periodicals made a bold attempt in that direction, and very nearly achieved success.

Gothic *fragments* strike a nicer balance between form and content, and are patterned after *Sir Bertrand* of the *Miscellaneous Pieces in Prose* (1773), or Nathan Drake's *Montmorenci, a Fragment*, from his *Literary*

Hours (1798), and his *Sir Egbert* and *Henry Fitzowen* in the *Monthly Literary Recreations* (1807). *Sir Bertrand* was reprinted in the *Monthly Mirror*, Vol. XIII (January 1802), *Sir Egbert* and *Henry Fitzowen* appeared in the *Monthly Literary Recreations*, Vol. II (January 1807), and Vol. III (October–December 1807) respectively.

Most of the Gothic fragments are of a kindred species without any attempt at the construction of a thrilling plot sequence, having neither exposition, nor resolution of events, nor any accounting for mysterious horrors. Such patch-work is an exercise in evoking atmosphere, comprising disconnected episodes of terror, and " divorced from the novelesque elements which encumber the Gothic tale ". Some examples of the type are *The Vision of Ismena; Raymond, a fragment; Malvina,* and *Sir Edwin.*

The Vision of Ismena (1792), is a fantasy of terror, set in the framework of a dream-vision where one scene melts away swiftly into another in a nightmarish sequence, and the author tries to evoke feelings of suspense, wonder, strangeness, and fear in succession. *Raymond, a fragment* (1799) contains a wealth of Gothic details, and the narrative abruptly ends at the very moment of crisis—a distinguishing characteristic of the writers of this genre.

Another distinguishing feature of the Gothic fragment was its readiness to exploit the supernatural. Whereas the Gothic *tales* were a progeny of the Radcliffe school, explaining away mysteries, the *fragments* made extensive use of natural terrors. They abound in thunders, violent tempests, gloomy landscapes, caverns, howling winds, the tolling of distant bells, moping owls, spectral effects—in fact all the paraphernalia of Walpole's *Otranto.*

A further corrupted form of the Gothic novel were the garishly crude sixpenny books, and the *shilling shockers,* of which W. W. Watt, writing for the Harvard University Press, says : " The stories varied in length from mere anecdotes to tales of thirty thousand words, but many of the publishers specialized in two definite lengths, dealing out thirty-six pages for sixpence and seventy-two for a shilling." These shilling shockers were bound under a captivating title-page, and the frontispiece depicted an etching of the most sensational incident of the story : a dark phantom before the distraught heroine in a deserted castle wing, or a gloomy hero bound in ropes against a tree by a group of banditti, or a frowning villain hurling his victim over a Gothic precipice into the yawning chasm below. These ' blue-books ' had such attractive multiple titles as : *The Secret Oath, or Blood-Stained Dagger; The Miseries of*

Miranda, or The Cavern of Horror; The Abbot of Montserrat, or The Pool of Blood, thundering " the maintitle at their readers through two barrels. . . . Often the first of the two titles suggested the ' love-interest ', and the second represented the ' horrid ' element ". The more ambitious title-page inscribed an exciting synopsis of the entire tale.

How many of the shilling shockers were true abridgments of Gothic novels is not possible to determine, although Watt has pointed out that *The Old English Baron, The Italian,* and *The Monk* were abridged and published under various titles in this category as shilling shockers : also " many of the shilling shockers were abridgments and translations from the German ". The stories provided nothing original. The ' love-interest ' was subordinated to the thrill-producing machinery ; they clung to certain conventions of Gothic plot ; and the characters were exaggerated to an astonishing degree. The shockers not only set forth medieval legends of " The Wandering Jew ", the " Demon Frigate " or " Dr. Faustus ", but also concentrated on Gothic anecdotes of freaks, monsters, and murderers, and thus catered to the perverted taste for excitement among degenerate readers.

Since the writers of the shockers were restricted by limitations of space, the intricacies of plot could not be detailed in a leisurely fashion, nor could the atmosphere be invoked in slow intricate detail. The author laid the setting of his scene in a single paragraph, and switched to a quick succession of incidents at once. Their publication and commercial value stand as an index of the sensation-craze into which the Gothic vogue degenerated in its declining years.

The Gothic novelists contributed some vital components of romanticism. The matter, style, and spirit of Gothic romance, its images, themes, characters, and settings, sloughed their gross husk and emerged transformed into the finer elements of Romantic poetry. No attempt has been made so far to isolate the actual process of transformation, or span the artistic distance between the finished product and its raw material. The intermediate stages of evolution have received no attention.

At the outset one notices certain startling resemblances between Gothic fiction and the canon of Romantic poetry : the philosophy of composition, the portrayal of the chief character in the story and the treatment of external nature, are all alike. There may well be a connection between the Romantic philosophy of composition as embodied in the *Lyrical Ballads* (1798) and the Gothic philosophy set down by Walpole thirty-four years before. In both Gothic and Romantic creeds there is a marked tendency to slip imperceptibly from the real into the other world, to demolish the barriers between the physical and the psychic or spiritual. See Keats's *Ode to Psyche*, last stanza, and Shelley's *The Sensitive Plant*. Compare the animated inanimate in *Otranto*, and the animated dead in *Montorio*. We notice in both the novels and the poems the same utilitarianism of art as reflected in the philosophic prefaces and appended morals ; the same defiant anti-authoritarian note ; the same handling of grotesque and repellent themes ; the same nuances of style —the use of close wrought suspense, and vast, cataclysmic piling up of details for the final hurtling climax. Compare the narrative method of *The Giaour* and *Lara* with *Udolpho* and *Montorio*. All are mystery tales, unrolled backwards by the explanation at the end.

Gothic villain and Romantic hero come of the same lineage. Bertrand Evans notes that " the villains Manfred, Montoni, and Schedoni, in the novels of Walpole and Mrs. Radcliffe . . . after leaping the gap between the ages . . . show us the Byronic hero. Resemblances are obvious : yet the one is a villain and the other a hero." These figures move in a similar world : the panoramic landscape settings, the Gothic interiors evoking terror and fear—in fact the whole machinery of Mrs. Radcliffe and the authors of her school furnished the pattern and set the style for poets of the succeeding generation.

The Romantic poets hark back to the sources of terror, and once again revive the latent feelings of awe, wonder, and fear. *La Belle Dame Sans Merci, Alastor, The Thorn, Darkness,* rely wholly or in part on the terror-motif for their impressiveness. Also the streak of morbid-grotesque, the use of horrible and gruesome detail—lingers as an inherit-ance of Gothic in the second generation of romantic poets. The unpleasant and diseased realism of the Schauer-Romantiks, their veritable mania for worms and reptiles, the element of the gory, which had quickened the appetite of jaded sensation eventually inspired the pathologic and ghastly in Romantic poetry.

In both Gothic novels and romantic literature the conception of the titanic in character is paralleled by the conception of the titanic in nature. The storm-racked atmosphere tinged with prevailing misty melancholy, a romantic richness of colour and a persistent suggestion of dim and sweeping vastness—all derive from Gothic settings. The charm of Mrs. Radcliffe's arcadia, where in the shadow of exalted mountains repose vast woods, their gloomy grandeur diffusing a sacred enthusiasm over the mind, and where the scent of orange blossoms pervades the dewy air mingled with a fragrance of spicy myrtle far among the cliffs, preludes the enchantment Nature held for the Romantics. " In more than one way, the prose of Mrs. Radcliffe anticipated and guided the poetry of the Romantic revival. Prose like hers could not hope to remain prose long," says Raleigh, and before his time T. S. Perry had registered the same possibility : " The poets of the Romantic school were indebted for far more than moonlight and roaring wind to this curious story (i.e. *Otranto*)."

The Gothic novel and Romantic poetry were in constant interaction, many writers of each making frequent sallies into the domain of the other. The average Gothic novelist was a poet too. The verses that intersperse their novels are romantic in tone and atmosphere. Besides, Mrs. Radcliffe, Lewis, and Maturin wrote Gothic ballads and versified many Gothic incidents.

While the Gothic romancers tried their hands at fragments of Romantic poetry, the Romantic poets experimented with Gothic fiction in the novel and drama. The first generation of Romantic poets drew their inspiration from contemporary romance, a debt too great but little reckoned, the legacy of boyhood Gothic fiction. J. C. Jeaffreson, in *The Real Shelley* (1885), says : " It is something to the honor of prose fiction that the two greatest poets of the nineteenth century (i.e. Shelley and Byron) may be said to have been mentally suckled and reared on novels . . . taught by novels how to feel and think and how to make others feel and think."

The Gothic villain who had evolved from Manfred in *The Castle of Otranto*, through Lord Lovel in *The Old English Baron*, and through Malcolm, Mazzini, the Marquis Montoni, and Schedoni of Mrs. Radcliffe, finally taking on various traits in Eblis of Beckford, or Falkland of Godwin, or Maturin's Montorio and Melmoth was transformed into the stalwart Romantic figure who finally became " the Byronic hero ", an evolving, changing concept, although individual and distinctive in each of his manifestations.

Byron's narrative heroes are cast in the true Gothic mould, verging on the metaphysical superman, victims of Destiny, fired by vengeance and suffering from remorse. Childe Harold bears faint traces of the Wandering Jew, and is a victim of Destiny ; the Giaour is veiled in mystery and aloofness ; the Corsair is another misanthropic figure, whose superman qualities recall Montoni ; Lara belongs to the metaphysical superman group ; while Manfred, a mysterious magician, is an apotheosis of all that has gone before, and represents the climax of Byron's Gothic achievement.

All are aristocratic, moody, self-tortured, driven to an eccentric philosophy and way of life by disillusion—Harold, to aimless wandering ; the Giaour, to a total retreat from the world ; Lara, to contemptuous and passive toleration ; and Manfred, to a plunge into the oblivious maze of supernatural science. All are marked by the same haunting sense of pathological melancholy ; exiles from society, burning with a flaming desire to penetrate occult mysteries ; or brooding, crafty princes who, fired by consuming ambition, sacrifice friend and foe alike to their dark and mysterious ends. They move amid wild and gloomy settings : in dusky moors, lonely heaths, castles of luxury or decay, staring over bleak landscapes.

Another Gothic character was the ' villainess ' who may have inspired the theme of ' fatal women ' in Romantic poetry. The ' Gothic ' villainess was violent in emotion, ambitious and unscrupulous, and never shrinking from the use of poisoned goblets if need be. Countess Mazzini in *A Sicilian Romance*, Countess Villefort and Laurentini in Christabel where Lady Geraldine is a wilful power of evil incarnate in a contrast to the elegant Antonias and fair Emelies, the angelic heroines of Gothic fiction. These ' fatal women ' may have inspired Coleridge's *Christabel* where Lady Geraldine is a wilful power of evil incarnate in a tempting body, a queer mixture of Matilda and the Bleeding Nun. Keats's Lamia, the serpent woman who tramples men under feet and ruins them by her deadly charms, or Byron's Gulnare, a combination of violence and sweetness derive their inspiration from the same ' Gothic ' source.

An outstanding Gothic motif—the Wandering Jew—first enters Romantic poetry in Wordsworth's *Borderers*. " A wanderer must I go . . . " says Marmaduke at the end of Act V. It also occurs in the third book of Keats's *Endymion* ; Coleridge's Ancient Mariner is a wanderer over uncharted seas ; Shelley's *Alastor* is the St. Leon type of Wandering Jew.

At this stage it may be worth while to examine the ' Gothic ' influence on individual poets ; Wordsworth modelled his blank verse tragedy, *The Borderers* (1795–96), partly on *The Robbers* of Schiller, and more on current Gothic fiction. He often uses Radcliffe's panoramic method with the human touch inset, evoking fear by means of natural description. Two of his poems, *Guilt and Sorrow* and *Peter Bell*, have a Gothic flavour.

In the former the Gothic atmosphere is obtained by description, and from the terror of a murderer who is flying from the scene of his crime, alone in a storm on Salisbury plain. The landscape terrifies him. See stanzas 9, 10, 12 and 13. Wordsworth's ravens, gallows, shrieks, phantoms, darkness and storm, the red sun and ruined building, are reminiscent of *The Mysteries of Udolpho*.

Peter Bell reveals a similar use of landscape to evoke fear, and the poet consequently explains away the supernatural terrors. Peter, lost in a fearsome wood, comes upon a glade bathed in moonlight (lines 356–60), in which stands an immovable, lonely ass. All is ghostly silent ; Peter suspects witchcraft, grows afraid, looks into the pool, and drops into a swoon before an inexplicable thing of horror. Wordsworth does not hold us on tenterhooks long enough like Mrs. Radcliffe. He explains that Peter had only seen the face of the owner of the ass, drowned by accident. The second and the third part of *Peter Bell* accumulates a set of Radcliffian terrors. Peter, while riding home on the ass, is frightened by a scream emanating from a cave. Looking back Peter finds a stain of blood, which is explained away as coming from the wounded ear of the ass. Peter sees the ghost of his betrayed wife on the road, which the poet explains to be an optical illusion. Lane Cooper describes the poem as " Wordsworth's Ancient Mariner ".

Wordsworth is at certain times and in certain moods Radcliffian. In a number of fragments of the *Prelude*, external nature is in consonance with moods of terror. He " paints the visionary dreariness " of scenes in " colours and words that are unknown to man ". There are descriptions of days " tempestuous, dark, and wild ", and of rising crags

> That, from the meeting-point of two highways
> Ascending, overlooked them both, far-stretched.

In the same poem, *The Prelude*, he pictures an open place that

> overlooked
> From high, the sullen water far beneath
> On which a dull red image of the moon
> Lay bedded, changing often times its form
> Like an uneasy snake. From hour to hour
> We sate and sate, wondering if the night
> Had been ensnar'd by witchcraft.

The last two lines have a typically Gothic tinge. The Radcliffian method and effect is obvious in the lines :

> I heard among the solitary hills
> Low breathings, coming after me, and sounds
> Of indistinguishable motion,—steps
> Almost as silent as the turf they trod.

Then the titanic in Nature is portrayed :

> When, from behind that craggy steep till then
> The horizon's bound, a huge peak, black and huge,
> As if with voluntary power instinct
> Upreared its head. I struck and struck again,
> And growing still in stature the grim shape
> Towered up between me and the stars, and still,
> For so it seemed, with purpose of its own
> And measured motion like a living thing,
> Strode after me.

Coleridge bases his play *Remorse* (1813) on the Sicilian's tale in Schiller's *Ghost-Seer* ; his *Christabel* (1816) is a supernatural ballad, and, says Eino Railo, " even as a fragment, is a masterpiece of the poetry of terror ". He successfully creates a ' Gothic ' atmosphere in the opening lines of this poem, and displays a complete mastery over Gothic materials, while every subtle detail of the descriptive background evokes a sense of eeriness and fear as we float dreamily through scenes of unearthly misty moonlight. The poem, with its sense of foreboding and horror of the serpent-maiden, narrates a true Gothic tale. The Gothic details make an imposing array : " 'Tis middle of night by the castle clock ", " the night is chilly, but not dark " ; a small full moon is half-veiled by broken clouds ; a haunted castle stands near a rock. The fiend quality of Geraldine, the Gothic description of the castle interior " carved with figures strange and sweet ", the moan in the forest, the magic bells—are such stuff as Gothic romance is made of.

The delicacy and subtlety of the poetic genius of Coleridge produced the weirdness of *The Ancient Mariner* (1798), who is akin to the Wandering Jew, a man haunted by his crime. The poet uses the dream as a device for revealing the future, and piles up a number of Gothic conventions rather than horror. The sinking of the fearful skeleton ship, the seven nights spent in company with the dead, the re-animated spectre-corpses, all are reminiscent of Gothic tradition. The setting of the wedding-scene recalls Lewis's *Alonzo* and Schiller's *Ghost-Seer*, and like most Gothic novels the poem ends in a moral.

Some descriptions in *Kubla Khan* (1816) recall Maturin and Lewis.

> A savage place !—as holy and enchanted
> As e'er beneath a waning moon was haunted
> By woman wailing for her demon-lover,

reminds us of Immallee and her demon-lover Melmoth. The Wandering Jew, who had appeared in Lewis's *The Monk*, with flashing eyes and floating hair, had visited the spectre-ridden Raymond, drawn a circle about himself while exorcizing the phantom, and bade the hero close his eyes and refrain from gazing upon him during incantation. Coleridge, who had bitterly criticized *The Monk*, uses the same ingredients in :

> Beware ! Beware !
> His flashing eyes, his floating hair !
> Weave a circle round him thrice
> And close your eyes with holy dread
> For he on honey-dew hath fed
> And drank the milk of paradise.

The poetry of Keats touches the mysterious springs of suggestive terror. The famous *La Belle Dame Sans Merci*, which so exquisitely evokes the Renascence of Wonder, has echoes of the unknown lady who touches the shield in Mrs. Radcliffe's *Gaston de Blondeville* :

> Her beauty was faded, yet she seemed young, and she had a look of sorrow and of wildness, too, that touched the hearts of many, that beheld her.

Martha L. Shackford has, in *Modern Language Notes* (XXVI—1921), traced the influence of *The Mysteries of Udolpho* on *The Eve of St. Agnes*. Keats was familiar with Mrs. Radcliffe. He writes to Reynolds on 14 March 1818 :

> I intend to tip you the Damosel Radcliffe—I'll cavern you, and grotto you, and waterfall you, and wood you, and water you, and immense-rock you, and tremendous-sound you, and solitude you.

Some passages in *Endymion* recall Mrs. Radcliffe. Keats had a leaning towards ruined castles, and the interior description of a poem like *The Eve of St. Agnes* yields an impression strongly Radcliffian. The picture of its Gothic hall shows a similar feeling for atmosphere :

> In all the house was heard no human sound ;
> A chain-dropped lamp was flickering by each door ;
> The arras, rich with horseman, hawk and hound,
> Fluttered in the besieging wind's uproar ;
> And the long carpets rose along the gusty floor.

He writes to a friend, speaking of *St. Agnes Eve* and *The Eve of St. Mark* :
" You see what fine mother Radcliffe names I have." The grim story in
Isabella of Lorenzo's ghost, who

> Moaned a ghostly undersong
> Like hoarse night-gusts sepulchral briers along,

is surely inspired by ' Gothic '.

The Oriental luxury and abundance in his descriptive matter, style,
and material resemble Beckford. Keats knew *Vathek*. It contributed a
few detailed devices in other phases of his verse. The burning heart of
Eblis reappears twice in *Hyperion, a Vision* :

> One hand she pressed upon that aching spot
> Where beats the human heart, as if just then,
> Though an immortal, she felt cruel pain.

Or from *Cap and Bells* :

> Annoy'd
> Her tender heart, and its warm ardours fann'd
> To such a dreadful blaze, her side would scorch her hand.

The following from the banquet scene in *Lamia* smacks of *Vathek* :

> Of wealthy lustre was the banquet-room,
> Filled with pervading brilliance and perfume :
> Before each lucid panel fuming stood
> A censer fed with myrrh, and spiced wood,
> Each by a sacred tripod held aloft.
> Whose slender feet wide-swerved upon the soft
> Wool-woofed carpets : fifty wreaths of smoke
> From fifty censers their light voyage took
> To the high roof. . . .

The following extract from *Hyperion : A Vision* has resemblances to
Vathek's approach towards the valley of Eblis :

> I looked around upon the curved sides
> Of an august sanctuary, with roof august,
> Builded so high, it seem'd that filmed clouds
> Might spread beneath as o'er the stars of heaven. . . .
> The embossed roof, the silent massy range
> Of columns north and south, ending in mist
> Of nothing.

Byron acknowledges his debt to Gothic romance :

> Otway, Radcliffe, Schiller, Shakespeare's art,
> Had stamped her image in me.

The nature description of *Childe Harold*, in style, tone, and material is reminiscent of Mrs. Radcliffe. The poet pictures the elemental phases of nature, mountain, sea, and storm. The description of Venice in Canto IV, stanza 18, strikes a close correspondence between Radcliffe's prose and Byron's poetry. Also some passages in *The Giaour*, including one of a deserted palace, are of a Radcliffian turn.

Blessington reports, in *Conversations*, that Byron had a mild preposses-sion for worms and special predilection towards vampires. "Do you know ", said Byron, "that when I have looked on some face that I love, imagination has often figured the changes that death must one day produce in it—the worm rioting on lips now smiling, the features and hues of health changed to the livid and ghastly tints of putrefaction . . . this is one of my pleasures of imagination."

Byron's *Lines Inscribed upon a Cup formed of a Scull*, his *Siege of Corinth*, some passages in *The Giaour*, and *The Bride of Abydos* abound in gory details.

This last is very much a versified Gothic romance. Giaffir kills his brother to gain power, and proposes to marry his daughter to a villain to gain still more power. In *The Siege of Corinth*, the Gothic spectre of a damsel appears to her lover after her death, though he thinks it is she in person. She chills him with a touch. In *Lara*, Byron makes use of a Gothic situation in which the terror is not explained away. Attendants rush in and discover Lara stretched on the ground in a semi-conscious state with his sabre half drawn ; what has happened we are never told. *Manfred* abounds in Gothic machinery : a curse, remorse, large Gothic halls, a fiery star, an attempted suicide, spots of blood on the goblet, a hall filled with demons, a phantom, a tower with a secret chamber, a warning abbot, terror-stricken and chattering domestic servants, and a mysterious death by blasting.

But of all the Romantic poets the mind of Percy Bysshe Shelley was most deeply saturated with Gothic diablerie. Shelley as a youth was an ardent disciple of Gothic romances. He read them omnivorously, and his pen assayed the style of the most haggard spectre-monger of Lane's Minerva Press. He retained far into his years of splendid and imaginative poetry the tricks of Gothic style, and the flavour of Gothic

material.   The effect of this riot of imagination exercised a potent spell
on the impetuous spirit of Shelley, who, during his adolescence, revelled
in moon-illumined castles, saturnine monks, scowling desperadoes and
obtrusive spectres.   Urged by a restless desire, in quest of the supernatural,
he haunted cemeteries in expectation of " high talk with the departed
dead " ;   dabbled in chemical experiments and read ancient books of
magic by candle-light.   Under the influence of ' Monk' Lewis and
Charlotte Dacre, he wrote two Gothic novels :   *Zastrozzi* (1810) and
St. Irvyne (1811).   These, says Lord Ernle, are " curiosities of literature
of the melodramatic and blue-fire type ".   Shelley also wrote a Gothic
fragment :   *The Assassin* (1814).
     Shelley's most striking Gothic description is to be found in *Alastor*.
These are descriptions of

> Rocks, which, in unimaginable forms,
> Lifted their black and barren pinnacles
> In the light of evening. . . .

Its precipice, obscuring the ravine, disclosed above

> Mid toppling stones, black gulphs and yawning caves,
> Whose windings gave ten thousand various tongues
> To the loud scream. . . .

And then finally " the howl of thunder " and " the hiss of homeless
streams ", mingle in solemn song with

> the broad river,
> Foaming and hurrying o'er its rugged path

which

> Fell into the immeasurable void
> Scattering its waters to the passing winds.

Similar Gothic descriptions abound in *The Witch of Atlas*, and also in
The Cenci, where, " beneath the crag ", " the melancholy mountain
yawns " and

> Below
> You hear but see not an impetuous torrent
> Raging among the caverns.

     Horror was passion with Shelley.   His verse is coloured throughout
with a morbid relish for the ghastly, and " death's-head " allusions ;
charnel-house metaphors and fragments of cadavers are scattered throughout his work in consequence of his Gothic romance reading and writing.
His vocabulary consists of a profusion of words like ' ghosts ', ' shades ',

'tombs', 'torture', 'charnel', and 'agony'. His similes too have a supernatural tint. In *Alastor* the poet is

> an inspired and desperate alchymist
> Staking his very life on some dark hope.

In *Ode to the West Wind* the dead leaves are compared to " ghosts from an enchanter fleeing ". Shelley often attempted to work on the ' gothic ' emotion of fear ; the lurid patches in *The Revolt of Islam*, the decaying garden in *The Sensitive Plant*, the tortures of Prometheus, or the agonized soul of Beatrice in *The Cenci*—all are captured in words of anguish and despair. In *The Cenci* the fierceness of algolagnic sensibility is clearly marked, while streaks of it gleam in, and animate many of his other poems.

Thus the Gothic novel left an indelible stamp on the romantic characters and nature painting ; ' gothic ' threads of horror were inextricably woven into the new romantic material. The currents of influence are most widely diffused, and vital to the spirit and method of treatment in Romantic composition.

The contribution of the Gothic novel to nineteenth-century fiction was not merely a sense of structure, but also a certain spirit of curiosity and awe before the mystery of things. In structure the ' Gothic ' method of dramatic suspense was combined with the picaresque type, and in theme the romantic spirit was made to blend with the spirit of realism. The Victorian writers are indebted to the technique and devices of Gothic fiction : most of their works were patterned and modelled after the demoded species. The interesting plots in Victorian novels bear impress of the widespread and long enduring vogue of Gothic romance, and reveal that notable writers were conscious of the power of the weird and eerie.

W. C. Phillips has emphatically asserted that Dickens " was more indebted to that waning romance than criticism has generally indicated ", and indeed there is no want of continuity between the Gothic romance and the mid-nineteenth-century novels. " Dickens, the plot-maker, as opposed to Dickens the delineator of human oddities, brought down to date the essential appeal of *The Romance of the Forest*, and adapted it to the prejudices, credulity, and taste of the audience for which he wrote." From the final scene in *Oliver Twist*, where Bill Sykes brutally murders his mistress, through the opium-tainted atmosphere of *Edwin Drood*, there is no complete story lacking in the most brutal stimulants of fear.

Although Dickens, in his realism, treads in the footsteps of Fielding and Smollett, in *Great Expectations* he portrays a scene where we find Miss Havisham standing by her dressing-table which is covered with dust—in a room displaying traces of former splendour, faded tapestries and heavy tables of marble. Her satin slippers have faded and turned yellow with age ; the wedding cake stands mouldering in the centre of the old banqueting table. The whole effect resembles the feeling of dread created in Chateau le Blanc in *The Mysteries of Udolpho*, where Emily and Dorothée explore the chamber of the dead Marchioness, where hangs the black veil, and on the dressing-table a pair of gloves dropping to pieces with age.

The Brontë sisters create striking effects by utilizing the devices of Mrs. Ann Radcliffe. Emily Brontë presents the amazing and terrific character of Heathcliff in *Wuthering Heights*. The picture of the wind-swept Yorkshire moors provides a background for the expression of tense human feelings. The shadow of Heathcliff's personality has a demonic power. Andrew Lang, in an entertaining article, *Mrs. Radcliffe's Novels*, which appeared in *The Cornhill Magazine*, July, 1900, pointed out that Charlotte Brontë borrowed the idea of the hidden mad wife in *Jane Eyre* from a similar incident in *A Sicilian Romance*. In *Jane Eyre* she comes very near to the conception of the Gothic villain in her portrayal of Rochester. The Brontës never trifled with emotion nor made use of supernatural elements to heighten the tension. They present the terrors of actual reality and life.

Popular interest in sensational fiction could be revived only by exploring new themes which might exert a fresh appeal. Away from the outmoded conventions of Gothicism in history and legends, writers like Sir Walter Scott, Allan Cunningham, and James Hogg sought real-life equivalents in their quest for new materials. Later ingenious writers like Bulwer Lytton, Wilkie Collins or Stevenson experimented with new themes in quest of ingenious sources of mystery and terror.

George Edward Bulwer Lytton once more tried to elevate the novel of terror. His writings reveal a strong love of the mysterious. His *Ernest Maltravers*, *Alice*, and *Strange Story*, focus interest on some dark mystery which is revealed only at the end of the book. While invading the orbit of supernatural romance, he outstrips the realm of Gothic terrors, and soars into more exalted regions, inspiring awe rather than horror. According to him the exercise of reticence and leaving things unsaid should be the integral characteristic of a supernatural tale. He smoothes away the crudities of Gothic romance and strips off the vulgar blatancy of conventional spectral tales.

Zanoni was published in 1842. *The Haunted and the Haunters, or The House and the Brain* in the *Blackwood's Magazine* for 1859. The latter story centres round a mysterious personality, who exercises a strange power over the life and personality of other individuals. He appears, no man knows whence nor why, and disappears as strangely, and his entire career is shrouded in mystery. Lytton here works on the nightmare motif, and endows inanimate objects with supernatural powers. The atmosphere imparts a ghostly chill, and in the darkness one feels the intolerable oppression of a shameless evil. At one place a woman's hand, without a body, rises up to clutch some ancient documents, and then withdraws.

In *A Strange Story* Lytton introduces the elixir of life, and with other 'gothic' properties like magic, mesmerism, spectres, bodiless Eyes, and even a gigantic Foot. Margrave mixes certain chemicals and prepares to drink the elixir of life, but at the crucial juncture a stampede of beasts frightened by a dreadful Foot, dashes the beaker from his lips. The powerful liquid wastes its potentialities on the desert sands. A magic richness of foliage and green instantly springs up on the spot in the barren desert. The blooming flowers and colourful butterflies indicate life all around, but the body of the individual who so laboriously manufactured the elixir lies dead. Lytton hints at a symbolic meaning : that the laboratory of the scientist holds several elixirs of life, and that the growth of life is magical, and existence itself is a miracle. At one place the supernatural manifests itself : a vast Eye is seen in the distance, which moves nearer and nearer. Then other Eyes appear : " Those Eyes ! those terrible Eyes ! legions on legions ! And that tramp of numberless feet ! *they* are not seen, but the hollows of the earth echo to their tread."

In James Hogg's *The Wool-Gatherer*, a man of vicious life is haunted by the wraiths of those he has wronged, and as he lies in the throes of death he hears the doleful voices of women in torment and the pitiful wailing of infants, though nothing is visible. After the man is dead, the supernatural howlings become so dreadful that " the corpse sits up in the bed, pawls wi' its hands and stares round wi' its dead face ". When the watchers leave the room for a few seconds, the body mysteriously disappears never to be found again.

In *The Private Memoirs and Confessions of a Justified Sinner*, Hogg writes a tale of spiritual horror in a realistic setting. He handles the theme of temptation by the Devil, in the semblance of a duplicate personality. The tale without ever becoming mere parable keeps suggesting its inner meaning to us.

De Quincey wrote *Klosterheim* in 1832. In the *Blackwood's Magazine* for January 1838 was published his *The Household Wreck*, which conveys a strange sense of foreboding, and exemplifies how the anticipation of horror, a period of psychic dread, is often more harrowing than actual reality. He published another tale of terror, *The Avenger*, in 1838.

William Harrison Ainsworth attempted to revive the " feeble and fluttering pulses of old romance ". He fashioned his early tales in Gothic manner, and remains a professed disciple of Mrs. Radcliffe. Montague Summers expresses appreciation in *The Supernatural Omnibus*: " His sense of the supernatural, and the truly admirable way in which he utilized awe and mystery in his romances, have at least culled one, and that not the least green, laurel in the stephane of immortality which crowns Ainsworth's brow."

In the *European Magazine* for 1822 had appeared his *The Test of Affection*, wherein a wealthy person uses Mrs. Radcliffe's supernatural tricks to test the devotion of his friends. There are scenes of alarming noises and skeleton apparitions. In *Arliss's Pocket Magazine* (1822) appeared his *The Spectre Bride*, but his *Rookwood* (1834), a novel, is probably the best in his manner. There is in it a profuse use of Gothic properties, like skeleton hands, flickering candles, and sepulchral vaults.

Marryat, said *The Times Literary Supplement* (5 April 1941),"certainly, if only by virtue of *Snarleyyow* and *The Phantom Ship* is in the Gothic tradition ". The tales of Mrs. Riddell are dank with ' gothic ' shadows and doom. Her *Uninhabited House*, *The Haunted River*, *The Nun's Curse* are sufficient to show her lineage. Montague Summers has rightly recognized " the Gothic tradition in Wilkie Collins and Le Fanu . . . two great masters of the mysterious and macabre, who . . . will remain, unsurpassed and unapproached ".

Sheridan La Fanu, the master of the horrific genre, loves to paint the ghastly and the macabre, and is gifted with a melodramatic and sombre power. Like Poe he can invest the most mechanical of plots with an atmosphere of weird and eerie horror. His works have a grimness and power derived from the Gothic romance.

Joseph Conrad could touch the innermost springs of ' fear '. His romantic imagination displays a fine command over the possibilities and powers of 'terror'. A note of inexpressible mystery and unknown dread is struck in his novels : *The Nigger of the Narcissus, The Secret Agent, Typhoon,* and *The Shadow Line.* The voyage of the schooner, doomed by the evil influence of her deceased captain, recalls the awe and horror of Coleridge's *The Ancient Mariner.*

In modern times the marvellous has become more scientific and for this reason even more frightening. The fantasy of H. G. Wells, as also of C. S. Lewis, shows us worlds unknown, monstrous and horrible.

Charles Brockden Brown, the first Gothic novelist of America, penned stories of sleep-walkers and ventriloquists, and shows an unmistakable resemblance to Mrs. Radcliffe and her technique. Brown has a deep interest in morbid psychology, and his novels illustrate the workings of the human brain under great emotional stress. Psychological interest produces a hypnotic effect, and creates in the readers a mood of awestruck horror.

Among other American writers, Hawthorne and Poe are 'Gothic' in their treatment of the supernatural and mysterious. These writers show that the walls dividing the seen and the unseen world are often very thin. Hawthorne creates a mysterious atmosphere of foreboding and evokes the terrors of an invisible world, utilizing soul-shaking embodiments of mortal dread. The mystery of Death exerts a strong fascination over his mind, yet on the whole he is melancholic, not morbid. He does not extend his art to the domain of physical horrors. His pictures are neither crude nor harsh, rather they are shadowy and subdued.

Edgar Allen Poe exploited the 'gothic' power of suggestion, and cast a hypnotic spell over his readers to comply with his fantastical themes. He made full use of the power of words and tricks of style. In an article published in 1845, James Russell Lowell wrote :

> In raising images of horror, he (Poe) has a strange success, conveying to us sometimes a dusky hint, some terrible doubt, which is the secret of all horror. He leaves to imagination the task of finishing the picture, a task to which only he is competent.

Poe, an avowed apostle of the morbid and grotesque, made excursions into the world of preternatural wonders, while a finer realization of the mysticism and sinister beauty underlies the darker movements of thought. "And what a mental chamber of terrors that mind was ! Horror piles on horror in his early and later tales ; blood, unnatural lust, madness, death—always death—fill his pages and the 'haunted palace' of his brain," says Howard Haycroft in *Murder for Pleasure, the Life and Times of the Detective Story* (1942).

Poe raised terror to tragic heights, and produced dramatic and powerful effects by a rigid economy of effort without any extravagant or superfluous touches. The successfully diffused atmosphere of creepiness in *The Cask of Amontillado* and *The Masque of Red Death*, or the dreary pictorial effects in *The Fall of the House of Usher*, were definitely inspired by Mrs. Radcliffe's deserted abbeys and the opening of Maturin's *Melmoth the Wanderer*. The outline of Poe's tales is distinct, the impressions swift and deep. He added ' psychology ' to the old ' gothic ' raw material, and captured the airy, gossamer filaments of sensations by touching upon obscure feelings of psychic dread.

E. F. Benson's *Image in the Sand* and *The Angel of Pain* are of Gothic lineage ; the stories of " Geoffrey Crayon " abound in situations of awe and dread ; and Irving (writing under his own name) sometimes strikes a note of horror. The subtle and recondite short stories of Henry James have a capacity to sway the feelings in a far more potent manner than the raw sensations of ' Monk ' Lewis and Maturin. The author of *The Turn of the Screw* has a consummate scientific insight into the hidden springs of fear, and can thrill the reader by only a slight touch on the nerve.

Thus the shadow of ' Gothic ' fell on both sides of the Atlantic in Victorian times.

The influence of the Gothic novel on modern detective fiction and ' thrillers ' is by itself a fruitful topic for independent research.

Miss Dorothy Scarborough has made a wide survey of the mass of fiction introducing the ghastly and psychic elements in modern literature, and has stated that " the real precursor of supernaturalism in modern English literature was the Gothic novel ". Montague Summers, in his learned introduction to *The Supernatural Omnibus*, makes a historical approach to the long series of spectral tales and studies in phantom lore, and proves that certain supernatural themes—witchcraft, fairies, vampires, werewolfs, ghosts friendly and unfriendly, wraiths of the living—such macabre tales for thrills, curiosity and awe of invisible powers that continue to pour in till today, all drink deep at the old fount of Gothic fiction. In modern tales of the eerie and weird, we trace the same themes, rationalized and semi-rationalized, to suit our altered conceptions of the relation between flesh and spirit.

The symbols of dread and the ghostly were used effectively in the

Gothic novel : the triple veil of night, desolation, and silence aided the cumulative effect of supernatural awe. The gruesome accompaniments and suggestions conditioned an uncanny psychosis. Modern ghost stories work up to much the same effect.

Each piece of crude and creaking machinery of Gothic romance has been brought to perfection by the individual writers of modern ghost stories : by E. F. Benson, Bram Stoker, M. R. James, Algernon Blackwood, and others. The portrait that walked out of its frame in Walpole's *Otranto* may have appeared ridiculous, but the same motif becomes in Bram Stoker's *The Judge's House* a thing of menace and horror. The stage coach that carries Raymond and the spectre of the Bleeding Nun so fantastically at a tremendous speed in Lewis's *The Monk*, takes on a more artistic and terrible form in Amelia B. Edwards's *The Phantom Coach*.

M. R. James, whose hauntings are real, where ghosts and demons have actual reality ; E. F. Benson and Marion Crawford with their vampires visibly and carnally sucking the blood of their victims ; or Algernon Blackwood and Robert Hichens, with tales of macabre and elemental spirits—all stand in the Gothic tradition.

Thus, like the golden and red-plumed Phoenix, the fabulous bird of Arabia, which at the close of his long life builds himself a funeral pyre of the twigs of cassia, frankincense, and other aromatic woods, which he sets alight by the fanning of his wings to immolate himself, thus magically renewing his youth, so also the Gothic romance even from its ashes rose in a new splendour, lit with new glories, rejuvenated and purified. Although its old garments have been cast aside, the same spirit is reincarnate in new forms. The Gothic novel remains a vital thing, a potential force in the literature of today.

CHAPTER VIII

QUEST OF THE NUMINOUS : THE GOTHIC FLAME

THE main stream of Gothic Romance which issued from Walpole's *Otranto* diverged into three parallel channels : first, the Gothic-Historical type developed by Clara Reeve and the Lee sisters, finally culminating in the Waverley Novels of Sir Walter Scott, where historic supernatural agents disport themselves against an authentic background of chivalrous pageantry ; secondly, the School of Terror initiated by Mrs. Radcliffe and maintained by a host of imitators, perhaps the most extensive Gothic type in which superstitious dread is aroused by constant, dim suggestions of the supernatural—as constantly explained away ; and lastly, the works of the Schauer-Romantiks or The School of Horror, distinguished by lurid violence and crudity. Walpole adumbrated the machinery and characters of a Gothic story ; Miss Reeve designed the characteristic Gothic ghost in an English setting ; while Mrs. Radcliffe spread over all the warm colours of her romantic imagination. The later Schauer-Romantik writers were less concerned with atmosphere and suggestion than the bold machinery of animated corpses. Eventually the two Gothic streams of ' terror ' and ' horror ' met in the genius of Charles Robert Maturin.

Readers of the Gothic novel were able to consume increasing quantities of sensation as their appetite for terror demanded a succession of grosser stimulants. The later Gothic phase traverses a whole spectrum of horror : the Oriental and exotic horror of Beckford's *Vathek*, the throbbing physical horror of Godwin's *Caleb Williams* and *St. Leon*, the dismal charnel house horrors of ' Monk ' Lewis, the weird quasi-scientific horror of Mary Shelley's *Frankenstein*, and the carnal vampire horror of Polidori. But inevitably a point was reached when there were no new worlds of the macabre to conquer, and the Gothic novelist had perforce to indulge in an unwholesome profusion of ghastly and decadent realistic detail. The pullulating horror of the Schauer-Romantik phase was not a mere excrescence or pathological accident, but consequent upon laws of literary psychology. Thus literary Gothic describes a full circle from realism verging on romance in Smollett's *Ferdinand Count Fathom*, through the sustained romances of Walpole and Mrs. Radcliffe, gradually returning to realism in Lewis, Godwin, and other Schauer-Romantiks.

The Gothic novel was animated by the spirit of Gothic art. Ruskin, in *The Stones of Venice*, enumerated various characteristics that make up the soul of the Gothic. Placed in order of their importance, they are, as he described them : Savageness, Changefulness, Naturalism, Grotesqueness, Rigidity, and Redundance. These may be applied to fiction thus : ' savageness ' is in its broadest sense manifest in Walpole's *Otranto* ; ' changefulness ' indicates the variety and intricate structure of plots in the Gothic novel ; ' naturalism ' was evident in the pastoral settings of Mrs. Radcliffe, and ' grotesqueness ', or the tendency to delight in the fantastic and morbid, was a feature of Schauer-Romantiks like Lewis and Maturin.

Walpole's novel supplied an impetus and vigour to the commencement of the Gothic revival, and gave its literature a form and fashion. The acorn planted by him grew and proliferated, until the thickly intertwining branches overarched a large expanse. One limb of this mighty tree is Mrs. Ann Radcliffe, whose genius, despite changing literary fashions, continues to preserve her masterpieces alive. *The Romance of the Forest* still gives unfailing delight ; *The Italian* is no mean example of a forceful psychological study ; whilst the very title, *The Mysteries of Udolpho*, has passed into proverb. Another branch, luxuriant with churchyard ivy, is Matthew Gregory Lewis whose macabre talents gave *The Monk* such enduring notoriety that it ran into several editions. Maturin's *Melmoth the Wanderer*, at the apex of all these branches, is vigorous even today. Other lesser, crowding branches, once quick and green, have become dead wood and fallen away, to be gathered only by collectors of such curios.

The Gothic novel was at its comeliest and best during the 1790's, after which it was handicapped by popular prejudice, by the pedantry of reviewers, and the vagaries of its producers themselves. By 1840 the vogue of the serial novel was finally established, as appears from the generally increased dependence of the magazines upon serial fiction. The Gothic Romance was not a hasty mushroom that sprang up out of a reactionary desire for fetid sensation. It decayed, but only after a normal cycle of literary growth ; its ripeness was exotic, but the result of a gradual maturing ; and in its florescent period it bloomed in works of intrinsic merit and beauty.

The full-blown Gothic novel is distinguished by three individual qualities : the subjectivity of the writer ; a love of the picturesque later turning into a passion for the supernatural and horrible ; and thirdly, it is also a barometer of reaction against the preceding age of literature, not proudly and fiercely rebellious as in France, but recording a gentle and unconscious revulsion.

Like the collapse of many mighty empires the realm of Gothic fiction crumbled away, yet it exercised an enormously potent sway over the realm of English literature. It coloured English poetry, shaped the succeeding dramas, and fashioned the technique of English prose. Out of a ' gothic ' mould came succeeding melancholic literature, with its pleasantly harrowing tales of ill-starred love, and death, and deserted souls grieving eternally ; drama which was pitifully tragic, and lyrics that were despairing ; lengthy novels stuffed out with disasters and bespattered with the bleeding fragments of warm hearts.

Gothic literature to a great extent shaped the style, material, and spirit of early nineteenth-century romantic poetry, the gruesome and grotesque elements in its stage-setting, its depiction of character and external nature. The Gothic novel left its mark on that enormous school of sensational fiction which flourished roughly from 1830 to 1880, or perhaps one might even venture on a later date. The sensational novel of the Victorian era, which relied primarily on an appeal to fear, and whose narrative texture of villainy, violence, and crime included the delineation of much that was abnormal, terrible, and hideous, is a direct lineal descendant of the Gothic novel. The Gothic manner was inherited essentially unchanged in the works of Bulwer Lytton, Harrison Ainsworth, and the far finer artistic productions of Le Fanu and other writers of macabre tales. Thus one may say that the Gothic romance had a tonic influence on English literature.

Previously scant attention had been paid to the scenery in the novel. Mrs. Radcliffe set the style for morose landscapes, as Walpole had for gloomy castles. The writers of ' Gothic ' gave to the English novel the technique of a dark impressionistic portrayal of Nature and the power of harmonizing tempests of the soul with external storms.

The Gothic novel had a good historical and psychological justification for its origin : it was neither a sudden bursting wave nor a spontaneous revolution ; rather it was the outcome of an organic development with wide-spreading roots penetrating deep into the past. Romance, born out of a spark of reaction, glowed with a steady numinous flame, fanned by the interplay of forces within and without, by the speculations and philosophies of Germany and France, countries to which English minds gave as much as they took, and all were enriched in the exchange. The revival of interest in heroic romances, Shakespeare, Spenser, and Milton, provided a fit vessel, and dissatisfaction with the realistic novels of the mid-eighteenth century supplied the fuel.

The last four decades of the eighteenth century record the upsurge of a " Renascence of Wonder " that affected Poetry, Painting, Gardening, and Architecture. The Gothic novel was an early expression of that movement which carried all Europe into a century of new thoughts and new strivings. " Many qualities in eighteenth-century art and life ", says Oswald Doughty, " combined with the great renaissance of imagination to form the romantic revival."

Romanticism insists upon aspiration, yearning desire, mystery and wonder, and from those essential elements spring the colour and characteristics of the Gothic novel. It drew attention to new aspects of reality, and offered a fuller vision of life. Its yearning for the loveliness of the past was born out of a passionate desire for the beautiful, and it struck an entrancing note of wonder and mystery, mingling themes of night, moonlight and dreams, seeking in the strange, mysterious Middle Ages an atmosphere remote and ideal. The ages of chivalry and strange, incredible adventures, were a domain which fancy created and imagination ruled. And in this enchanted land of mystery, beauty lay hid and wonder lurked. It initiated a new interest in medieval literature, in myths, folk-tales, ballads, and medieval romances of chivalry. The enlightened age, tired of too much light, was being attracted by the soothing and alluring mystery of the " Dark Ages ".

The nucleus of any art form has been explained by Nietzsche as the interaction of two impulses, the Apollonian and the Dionysian. The Apollonian spirit embodies the artistic instinct for order and individuation, the Dionysian urge restores man's communion with nature and irrational primitive forces. If from the benign smile of Apollo sprang Augustan classicism, from the frenzied tears of Dionysus originated the romantic beauties of literature. From out of the desolation and languor of Augustan culture, where the vigorously branching roots lay covered in dust, sand, torpid and languishing, the Gothic novelists struck a magic Dionysian spring and literature sprouted full and green and luxuriantly alive. " Having been shut up for a century in a cage of sceptical indifference," says Edmund Gosse, " the spirit of man was blinded by the light and staggered, bewildered by such strange phenomena." The Gothic novelists touched the concealed, glorious, intrinsically healthy, primeval power that lay restlessly palpitating under the sophistications and form of the Augustan age.

During the earlier decades of the eighteenth century a stiff and starched formality had been more and more definitely imposed upon both poetry and prose. Those influences which had taught a flamboyant but none the less untidy literature a certain decorum and restraint, had in their turn become paralysed in a deathlike rigour. The Gothic novel was a symptom of general reaction against the forces of an exhausted Augustanism, and part of the movement which relaxed the classical restraints and widened the range of human sympathies, inciting literary minds to original, creative activity. Occasionally tinged with whimsicality and passion, often chaotic yet full of wonders, these novels are a key to the imaginative vision of a thrilling world and the exciting revelations of the unconscious. Immensely stimulating to the cramped fancy of the age, these fictions alone were strong enough to break the limitations of polished intellectual poetry and restore the fanciful, the terrible, and the sublime.

The rise of the Gothic novel may be connected with depravity, and a decline of religion. The sense of guilt, psychologists tell us, is deeply rooted in man, and when a religion loses its hold upon men's hearts, they must find some other outlet for their sense of guilt. It may be that the Gothic novelist experienced a sort of catharsis or mithridatic purging of his fears and self-questionings in the portrayal of horrors which proceeded from the frenzy of the creative brain, and perhaps comforted himself by suggesting that life is a mystery which death solves, and whose horrors fade away as a tale that is told. Perhaps his animal faculties of fear and inquisitiveness demanded a vent. But undoubtedly the Gothic romances were never born out of pure perversity, nor were they the mere titillation of jaded senses.

It remains to ascertain why horror so forcibly invaded literature just at this period. The late seventeenth and early eighteenth centuries have been recognized as, in all essentials, dominated by a strict concept of reason, that banished the emotional aura of religion and reduced the Deity to a clockwork Prime Mover of the Universe. The late eighteenth and early nineteenth centuries saw a new recognition of the heart's emotions and a reassertion of the numinous. It was these factors that produced the 'Gothic' horror. Like Love, Horror is an individual, primal emotion ; and it was a revival of pure emotion that these authors essayed within the isolated framework of the frowning castle and smiling meadow, with plots designed solely for emotional effect. Their hankering for emotion after an ultra-reasonable age demanded the crudest, most violently contrasted expression : it resembles the exaggerated, spontaneous reaction of children to the horror of the obscure and inexplicable, to giants and goblins.

In particular, these novels indicate a new, tentative apprehension of the Divine. Monastic life was no longer believed in, but at least it recalled the Ages of Faith and the alluring mystery of their discipline. The ghosts and demons, the grotesque manifestations of the supernatural, aroused the emotions by which man had first discovered his soul and realized the presence of a Being greater far than he, one who created and destroyed at will. Man's first stirring of religious instinct was his acute horror of this powerful Deity—and it was to such primitive emotion that he reverted, emancipated from reason, but once again ignorant of God, his spiritual world in chaos.

Primarily the Gothic novels arose out of a quest for the numinous. They are characterized by an awestruck apprehension of Divine immanence penetrating diurnal reality. This sense of the numinous is an almost archetypal impulse inherited from primitive magic. The Gothic quest was not merely after horror—a simple succession of ghastly incidents could have satisfied that yearning—but after other-worldly gratification. These novelists were seeking a ' frisson nouveau ', a ' frisson ' of the supernatural. They were moving away from the arid glare of rationalism towards the beckoning shadows of a more intimate and mystical interpretation of life, and this they encountered in the profound sense of the numinous stamped upon the architecture, paintings, and fable of the Middle Ages. The consequent " renaissance of wonder " created a world of imaginative conjurings in which the Divine was not a theorem but a mystery filled with dread. The phantoms that prowl along the corridors of the haunted castle would have no more power to awe than the rats behind fluttering tapestries, did they not bear token of a realm that is revealed only to man's mystical apperception, his source of all absolute spiritual values.

Supernatural manifestations have the power to fascinate and appal, for they touch the secret springs of mortal apprehension which connects our earthly with our spiritual being. Superstitions like the appearance of the dead among the living are perhaps most touching, since they excite a cold and shuddering sympathy for the strange beings whom we

may ourselves resemble in a few short years. They are mute witnesses
of our alliance with a greater power and make us aware of our fleshly
infirmity and our higher destiny. As we listen with a tremulous eagerness
to the echoes from beyond the grave, our curiosity and awe assume the
immensity of passions. As Schopenhauer said, men are mere phantoms
and dream pictures ; " golden dreams hover over our cradle, and
shadows thicken round the natural descent of the aged into the grave ".
All that appears real about us is but the thinnest shadow of a dream : in
Nietzsche's words, " underneath this reality in which we live and have
our being, another and altogether different reality lies concealed ".

Man's spirit therefore feeds on mystery, and his soul is quickened by
the icy touch of fear, for he experiences pure terror only when confronted
by the dim, indestructible world of the supernatural. The quiverings of
spirit which are base when prompted by things sordid and earthly, become
sublime when inspired by a sense of the visionary and immortal. The
Gothic novelists strike a union between our spiritual curiosities and
venial terrors, and mediate between the world without us and the world
within us ; they make external nature redolent of noble associations and
clothe the affections of the human heart with a spiritual dignity.

The spirit world is not the illusion of a dreaming brain ; feelings of
belief in life after death give energy to virtue and stability to principle.
These novels enable us to comprehend, perhaps, the sublimity of that
Deity who first called us into being, and thus elevate us above the evils
of this world by granting us the sense of being the centre of powers more
than earthly. The Gothic novel appeals to the night-side of the soul. As
we close its pages we shudder at the horrifying tales of Satanic spirits
and accursed beings, of mortals endowed with diabolical powers, and we
recognize the evils of the soul that they represent. All the main ' gothic '
characters share the unreality and eeriness of ghosts. The same ' other-
worldliness ', the same terrifying aloofness from common mortality
exhales from Mary Shelley's ' Monster ' and the Wandering Jew of the
Ahasuerus legend.

The authors of these works stand in the same relation to the reality
of dreams as the philosopher to the reality of existence. We discover our
larger life in dreams, and the Gothic novel lifts us from the narrow rut
and enables us to join the unspaced firmament ; it adds eternity to our
trivial hours ; and gives a sense of infinity to our finite existence. In
short, it evokes in us the same feelings that the Gothic cathedrals evoked
in medieval man.

" Beneath the multifarious crotchets and pinnacles, with which the Gothic novelists adorned his fictional fantasies, lay certain general principles of structure," says Michael Sadleir. In texture and design these novels echo the intricate workmanship of Gothic cathedrals. These authors build their tales around suggestive hints and dim pictures ; their pastoral scenes and complicated adventures are deftly related to the final catastrophe. Their masterly ordering of incidents, their contribution to the structure of the novel as an art form, is distinctive and impressive. The Gothic novel was not a cul-de-sac, but an important arterial development of the novel.

These novelists were the first to perceive and emphasize the dramatic method which has since become a platitude of narrative theory. Their methods and technique inspired Scott's feelings for individual scenes, led to the use of dramatic methods by Victorian novelists, the use of suspense in short stories by Poe and his successors, and eventually the mystifications and solutions of the modern detective novels and thrillers.

To bring the supernatural palpably into a scene, requires a bold experiment on the part of the novelist, and necessitates a long note of preparation and a whole train of circumstances that may gradually and insensibly lull the mind to an implicit credence. A series of incidents alone is, however, not enough to evoke terror ; these have to make a strong impression on the mind. The Gothic novelist knew the potentialities of his art, and achieved his effects by one of two methods : the realistic or the poetic. The first attempted to produce a semblance of fact by means of detailed description or by pretence to a logical sequence of reasoning ; the second aimed at arousing a poetic faith of the kind that Coleridge called " a willing suspension of disbelief ". The Gothic novelists adopted either or both methods and reinforced effects by skilfully and powerfully agitating the reader's feelings.

One may justly assert that the true interest in story form came only with Gothic fiction. By bringing in new interest and excitement, it gave the novel an unprecedented popularity which has not waned even to this day. The very titles of novels published between 1740 and 1760 show how realistic fiction veered round the life of an individual personality, the chief source of interest, while all the authors laid a general emphasis on the truthful portrayal of contemporary life. Dr. Huffman considers the " four broad principles " governing English novelists of the eighteenth century. They are : the statement of a moral purpose, the truthful depiction of contemporary English life, the constant predominance of reason and common sense, and the observance of probability in plot, characters and machinery.

Smollett, in his dedication in *Ferdinand Count Fathom*, defines the scope of a novel and states that although a novel should achieve the realistic portrayal of life, it must provide for a leading character as a focal point of production : " A Novel is a large diffused picture, comprehending the characters of life . . . for the purposes of an uniform plan, and general occurrence, to which every human figure is subservient. But this plan cannot be executed with propriety, probability, or success, without a principal personage to attract the attention, unite the incidents, unwind the clue of the labyrinth." The picaresque novel had emphasized action in and for itself, but the Gothic novelists used ' action ' to contrive and resolve complications of plot. As Scott pointed out : " the force, therefore, of the production lies in the delineation of external incident, while the characters of the agents . . . are entirely subordinate to the scenes in which they are placed."

Now, when the force of production hinges upon external incident, there is a new emphasis upon a careful placing of the incidents, which are striking and impressive, so as to sustain the interest of the long narrative. According to Mrs. Barbauld : " the unpardonable sin in a novel is dullness : however grave or wise it may be, if its author possesses no powers of amusing, he has no business to write novels."

When Walpole added dramatic effects to the old fairy-tales, he evolved a new technique in fiction, based on the principle of suspense. These books were the first to establish ' suspense ' as the major ingredient in a novel, and their deliberate and artistic manipulation of this new tool of their craft is something quite different from the methods of Richardson and Fielding. Dr. A. C. Kettle emphasizes that " the works of great novelists of the eighteenth century never depended for effect on the unexpected, except in the sense of verbal wit and incongruous situation in comedy ". But the critics with their usual tardiness were not ready to accept the quality of suspense as a necessary concomitant of the novel : " The story of a novel should be formed of a variety of interesting incidents ; a knowledge of the world and of mankind are essential requisites of the writer. . . . Sentiments should be moral, chaste and delicate . . . language easy, correct, elegant," we read in the *Monthly Review* (1790). There is no mention here of suspense or excitement.

The artistic manipulation of suspense in the Gothic tales developed along various lines. First we meet with "the black veil" method of Mrs. Radcliffe : Emily in *The Mysteries of Udolpho* quivers in front of a dark velvet pall which uncannily sways in the nocturnal wind. She draws aside the veil to confront a hideous corpse, putrid and dropping to decay. Again in the chamber of the dead Marchioness she shivers before the inky curtains, and perceives the folds moving unaccountably, when suddenly a repulsive face peers out at her. Inexplicable music forms another common device for creating suspense. Mysterious disappearances likewise increase the tension. Lights that glimmer and fade away, doors which open and close without any mortal aid, and groans and wails of unexplained origin heighten the effect. Dread secrets half-revealed at the hour of death, and mysterious manuscripts half-deciphered in failing light, likewise stimulate intense curiosity.

The technique of spot-lighting individual scenes, another contribution of the Gothic novel, has already been touched upon. Certain pictures do stand out from the rest strongly enough, amidst all the eddies and whirlpool of incidents, for the reader's imagination to remain focused on them.

Indirectly, by tracing in fiction the progress and consequence of one strong, indulged passion, another trait adopted from the drama, they gave an impetus towards that science of psychology which was to turn into a craze and fashion a hundred years hence. They forecast the technique of the future novel by presenting certain subtle studies of character-physiognomy. Thus, by portraying mental states and emotions of characters, they enlarged the scope of the novel, and by sounding the whole gamut of fear, pointed towards the psychological novel of over a century later.

The Gothic villains are a prime example of their creator's instinctive feeling for psychologically interesting characters who yet merge with the pervading theme of the supernatural. We can distinguish three types of Gothic villain : the character of Manfred fashioned by Walpole in 1764, a type composed of ambitious tyranny and unbridled passion, who developed through Lord Lovel of Clara Reeve's *The Old English Baron* ; the early villains of Mrs. Radcliffe, culminating in Count Montorio of Maturin and the character of Guzman in *Melmoth the Wanderer*, and also another descended from *Karl Moor*, the chieftain of Schiller's *Robbers* (1781). The latter type presents an "imposing figure". He is an outlaw, a Rousseauistic sentimentalist, a humanitarian who combats life's injustices, follies, and hypocrisies. Haunted by a sense of loneliness, helplessness, and despair, similar Victims of Destiny are La

Motte in *The Romance of the Forest*, Falkland in *Caleb Williams*, and in *St. Leon*, the disfigured, misanthropic outlaw captain.

The third type of Gothic villain is the terrible ' superman ' whose ways lie in darkness and whose strength originates far beyond mortal thought. He is a new mintage of the Satan portrayed by Milton in *Paradise Lost*—the immortal outcast, a masterful, vaunting villain, his spirit unbroken even in defeat. He is the Rosicrucian, the Alchemist staking his very life on some dark hope, and behind him is all the mystery of Cabbala, Freemasonry, Medieval Satanism. This Miltonic superman appears in these novels for the first time in *Eblis*, ruler of the realm of despair in Beckford's *Vathek* (1786). Nine years later Lewis introduced Lucifer in *The Monk*. Schemoli, the villainous monk of Maturin's *Family of Montorio* (1807) is obviously modelled upon his formidable predecessor Schedoni, Mrs. Radcliffe's physical superman endowed with a ruined aristocratic past and mysterious intellectual power.

These three main types have been presented in order of increasing complexity. Manfred, a kind of wicked baron born out of fairy-tale, becomes the Victim of Destiny, a supersensitive being drawn to evil against his better will, impelled by blind Fate ; a character who sentimentalizes over bygone days. The superman combines the qualities of both—Manfred assumes a gigantic physique and overwhelming motive, and the Victim of Destiny is now presented as the victim of injustice. Like Satan or the Ghost-Seer he has tempted fate, or has a Faustian compact imposed on him like the Wandering Jew. Paying an outrageous price for enormous benefits, he usurps his powers, then wraps his suffering in proud and lonely gloom. These three main types are fluid concepts which continually interact, though not annihilating distinction, for the Gothic villain remains to the last not a bundle of characteristics, but a set of characters. For the most part he is all melodrama and extravagant emotion, designed to excite the last possible twinge of sensation. His gradual development illustrates increasing skill in the art of romance. In him we see also the emergence of the ' Romantic ' character—an alien soul solacing itself in occult experiments with forbidden sciences or unscrupulous deeds. Lastly, the Gothic villain, like Frankenstein's monster, destroyed its creator, the Gothic novel.

Interpreted in its social context, the Gothic novel is a subtle and complex aesthetic expression of the spirit of Europe in revolutionary ferment. It is the most characteristic literary expression of the orgy of mental and emotional excitement that accompanied the French Revolution and grew out of the Industrialization of Britain. Since it is an expression of the late eighteenth-century *zeitgeist*, aspiring towards a more individual, spiritual world, an examination of it illuminates certain important aspects of the period.

The ' fantastic ' in literature is the surrealistic expression of those historical and social factors which the ordinary chronicle of events in history does not consider significant. Such ' fantasia ' express the profoundest, repressed emotions of the individual and society. John Draper has observed that " the existence or the lack of social tranquillity . . . governs both the amount of literature producible and the types of literature produced ".

The Marquis de Sade, in his preface to *Les Crimes de l'Amour* (1800), expressed the following opinion on the Gothic novel : " Then there are the new novels, nearly whose whole merit lies in magic and phantasmagoria, with the *Monk* at their head, which are not entirely without merit ; they are the fruit of the revolution of which all Europe felt the shock." André Breton considers the Gothic novels pathognominic of the social turmoils which agitated the whole of Europe towards the end of the eighteenth century. Michael Sadleir finds the Gothic romance as much an expression of a deep subversive impulse as was the French Revolution.

Whether or not the principles underlying the French Revolution consciously affected the outlook of the Gothic novelists and widened their conception of life, is difficult to prove, yet one may say that these works are symptomatic of the confused feelings of nostalgia and terror awakened by the times, sublimated by a purely artistic impulse. It would perhaps not be wrong to state that Romanticism and Revolution are fundamentally manifestations of the same impulse. There is an unconscious indefinable relationship between the Terrors of the French Revolution and the Novel of Terror in England. The excitement and insecurity engendered by the French Revolution did quicken the nerves of literature, and the Gothic novelists were not immune from these tremors. Montague Summers shrewdly notes : " Readers, it is presumed, delighted in imaginary terrors whilst the horrors of the French Revolution were being enacted all about them."

Both in England and over the Continent dark shadows were lowering ; the times were difficult, full of anxiety at the tremendous energies which were seething. Wider vistas were opening, new ideas fermenting in literature as in life. In France, unrestrained licence, rapine, and deeds of violence prevailed. It was such a period that produced the Marquis de Sade whose abnormal genius found vent in the composition of such *romans noir* whose pages of flagrant obscenity express his wild, erotic dreams. Harriet Jones, in her Preface to *The Family of Santraila* (1809), defends horrors on the grounds that they are reflections of the horror of vice and depravity. Yet while the writers were conscious of the decadence of the old order, the future seemed to offer them no hope. Bewildered and desperate, caught in the vortex of an evolving social structure, their individual frustration emerged in scenes of violence and horror.

The prominent Gothic motif of the ' ruin ' may be explained as being symbolic of the collapse of the feudal period ; the phantom that wanders along the corridors of the haunted castle symbolizes the inexplicable fear of the return of bygone powers ; the subterranean passages are the dark alleys through which the individuals stumble as they move towards the light ; in the sound of thunder and in stormy settings there is the rumbling note of a distant cannon. As Michael Sadleir puts it : " A ruin expresses the triumph of chaos over order. . . . Creepers and weeds, as year by year they riot over sill and paving stone, defy a broken despotism ; every coping stone that crashes from a castle-battlement into the undergrowth beneath is a small victory for liberty, a snap of the fingers in the face of autocratic power." None the less the ' ruin ' motif was expressive of the Gothic cult of the picturesque. " I dote on ruins," says a character in Mrs. Parson's *Lucy*, " there is something sublime and awful in the sight of decayed grandeur, and large edifices tumbling to pieces."

The Gothic romance with its ruined abbeys, frowning castles, haunted galleries, and feudal halls, its pathless forests and lonely landscapes, records a revolt against the oppressive materialism of the time. Pictures of lofty and craggy hills, silent and solitary as the grave, stand as noble contrast to the bustling cities dark with smoke. This escape was a complete reaction against the unpleasant murkiness of industrial civilization. Everywhere there is a constant contrast presented between peasant simplicity and aristocratic decadence in the works of Mrs. Radcliffe. This idyllic pastoral society and love of mountains are interlinked in the Gothic novels : Godwin's hero indulges his melancholy among Welsh mountains, Mrs. Radcliffe sets her scenes of rustic simplicity on the heights of Alps and Pyrenees, while Frankenstein's monster seeks refuge in the lonely hills. Elizabeth Cullen Brown, in *The Sisters of St. Gothard*

(1819), says, "A short reflection seems to convince me that virtue, benevolence, and all social and moral good, have fled the higher orders of society, and taken refuge in these happy mountains." Their idealization of the simple life and rural community was a marked and direct influence of Rousseau. It is curious and interesting to note that most of the idealized peasant communities are set in the verdure of Switzerland, a small, pastoral, traditionally independent and democratic country.

The Gothic novel also partakes of the general trends of contemporary ethics and religious thought. In the eighteenth century the Roman Catholic Church made its last great attempt at universal domination. Religion had earlier allied itself with political despotism : in France under Louis XIV, and in England under the later Stuarts. Montague Summers, who has particular qualifications to comment on the subject, says, " in the eighteenth century in France, monastic life, tainted by the general corruption, was at its lowest ebb ". The religious quarrels of the Commonwealth period in England, consumed by their own violence, engendered a scepticism which took the form of deism. Deism sought to equate ' reason ' with ' nature ' as the basis of religious thought just as reason was the basis of that secular spirit of scientific inquiry which criticized prevailing dogma and questioned the authenticity of the supernatural : and since religion was to be justified by empirical natural reasoning, Deism found its first definite expression in England.

Although Catholicism alone is never used by Gothic novelists as a means of evoking terror, and although there are no direct theological attacks, the implication is always that religion when abused becomes a horrible and ghastly perversion. Thus it is the incidental vestments, not the doctrine of Catholicism, that serve as a source of terror.

There is a charm about the sweet seclusion of a Catholic monastery and pious convent life, but the tortures and atrocities behind its walls make the heroines resolute in rejecting the veil. They dread seclusion from the cheerful intercourse of society and pleasant views of nature, to be immured in silence to practise a life of rigid austerity, abstinence, and penance, condemned to forgo the delights of the world. The monastery has two visages : sweet and comforting is the angelic presence of the Abbess of St. Clair to Emily St. Aubert when her father is dead, but the face of Schedoni hidden under a dark cowl inspires dread in the heart of Ellena. The monastic garb often envelops the heart of an assassin ; the walls of a cloister enclose the sullen misery of its votaries.

These novels portray their favourite theme of the sufferings of the unwilling nun in her convent prison, pining in the mute anguish of despair. Common knowledge of the existence of immoral nuns began the fashion for the most violent of the anti-Catholic novels, so that the cloister and the convent became symbols of horror and immorality. In *The Monk*, Ambrosio dreams of his mistress and awakens to find she has the face of the Virgin Mary. *The Monk* thus illustrates religious perversion by the blasphemous associations of the Holy Virgin with the Monk's mistress. The Spaniard's tale in *Melmoth the Wanderer* is fundamentally a treatise against the omnipotence of the Catholic Church, the fount of all evils and misery—symbolizing all the sinister potentiality of Evil. Maturin, with an avowed atheism, hurls a wild and fiend-like acrimony of satire. The Inquisition remains one of the stock sources of horror in the Gothic novel, a tremendous monument of the power, crime, and gloom of the human mind.

This gothic movement towards fantasy and romance especially gave a fresh lease of life to the whole race of story-spinners and story-readers. The literate public of Addison's time had been small, closely limited both geographically and socially. Addison had been anxious " to bring philosophy out of closets, schools, and colleges, to dwell in clubs and assemblies, at tea-tables, and in coffee-houses ". Now " the novel . . . played a prominent part in developing the reading public ", says A. S. Collins. Better communications had broadened horizons both geographically and socially, while Romanticism and Humanitarianism discovered the need for education, and education created a more extensive reading public. Helen S. Hughes points out that " out of this combination of wealth, leisure, and education, emerged a new-reading public . . . not too sophisticated, ready to be entertained ".

At the end of Chapter 26, volume 8, of his *Popular History of England*, Charles Knight quotes an estimate by Burke that in the final decade of the eighteenth century habitual readers in England numbered from 80,000 to 90,000. Professor W. P. Trent, an acknowledged authority on the minutiae of eighteenth-century bibliography, has the opinion that the estimate is too small. By now the profession of letters was recognizably established, theoretically free from the whims of a patron, but more than ever dependent on the taste of a public. The novelists understandably tended to give the public what it wanted.

It would appear, therefore, that the development of a larger reading public determined the quality and standards of literature towards the close of the eighteenth century.

Gothic fiction was the mainstay and possibly the creator of the popular circulating library, which in its turn sustained Gothic fiction. Fashionable, they were in their day to be found on the shelves of every circulating library, in both town and country, and they were devoured with delicious thrills and exquisite dread by whole armies of enraptured readers, the ranks being filled with women and girls who had nothing else to do. These novels were read and reread on every side by school-boys, by prentices, by servant girls, by the whole of that vast population which longed to be in the fashion, to steep themselves in the Gothic romance.

They were admittedly popular fare ; thus one cannot argue that they lapsed into oblivion and are consequently unworthy of study because they are not interesting. Rather they consumed themselves in their own violence, and died not from ennui but exhaustion, their essence distilled in the Romantic Movement.

Certain modern myths have grown up around Gothic romance. Dr. Kettle says the Gothic School has become " an exotic laboratory for experiments in the darkest mysteries of human and superhuman evil ". It is significant that the leaders of the most modern—and not the least advertised—of modern movements, Surrealism, loudly announce their legitimate descent from the Gothic novelists, from whom, as they tell us, they derive their essential ideas, their symbolism and sentimental forms. Nevertheless, in the last chapter of *The Gothic Quest*, Montague Summers asserts that such a claim cannot be justified. " The claims put forward by the Surrealists that their new movement is influenced by and draws vital inspiration from the Gothic romance are sufficiently surprising to necessitate an inquiry into the significance and quality of this connexion —if indeed any such there be."

The surrealistic methods employed by Walpole have already been discussed. The Gothic novelists produced surrealistic effects by the extensive use of grotesque contrast. Walpole had introduced the tricks of light and shade, colour and line, in his novel. Mrs. Radcliffe juxtaposed sound and silence, a kind of surrealism of atmospheric suggestion : a dead calm precedes the horrors of her tempest, sounds of retreating steps are followed by a stillness as of the grave, the music sinks low and faint as the afar off castle gates close at night and all grows still as death, a profound stillness marks the pauses of the surge breaking loud and hollow on the shore, the windows of the great hall are dark and, the torch being gone, nothing glimmers in the pitchy night save a solitary star. Even the faint, intermittent susurrus of leaves deepens the solemnity of silence. In the works of the Schauer-Romantiks, scenes of entrancing sweetness are balanced against episodes of gruesome horror ; the macabre accompanies the voluptuous, as in the famous Dance of Death.

An important surrealistic technique of ' telescoping ' images is also employed by these authors. These novels are neither historical nor descriptive of ancient medieval manners, but essentially descriptive of the eighteenth century ; and the fantastic telescoping of the two may be called a surrealistic technique.

The main doctrine of the Surrealist school is that there exists a world more real than the normal world, and this is the world of the unconscious mind. Their aim is to achieve access to the repressed contents of the unconscious, and then to mingle these elements freely with the more conscious images. In fact they, like Freudian psychologists, find a key to the perplexities of life in the material of dreams.

Dreams do constitute a definite source of the macabre and undoubtedly they inspired a number of Gothic tales. *The Castle of Otranto* was, as Walpole tells us, the result of an architectural nightmare. Mary Shelley's *Frankenstein* was likewise born out of a dream. Lafcadio Hearn, in his *Interpretations of Literature*, has asserted that all the best plots of macabre tales originate in dreams. He advises the writers of supernatural thrillers to study the phases of dream life, for nightmares provide a fertile ground for such apprenticeship. He writes : " All the great effects produced by poets and story-writers and even by religious teachers, in the treatment of the supernatural, fear or mystery have been obtained directly or indirectly from dreams."

No doubt there is a strikingly close relationship between dreams and supernatural impressions. Mystical presences usually haunt one in nocturnal hours when one arises from slumber. A guilt-laden individual starting up from sleep, imagines himself confronted with the phantoms of those he has wronged. The lover beholds the spirit of his dead beloved, for perhaps in dreams his soul had gone in quest of her. Savages, primitive men and children cannot possibly distinguish between dream and reality. Dreams are to them just actualities of experience. And it is impossible to prove that our dream life is altogether baseless and non-material.

Yet the real ancestry of Surrealism should be sought not so much in the Gothic novel as in its disintegrated form : the Gothic *fragments* of the early nineteenth century. These *fragments* are patchwork exercises in evoking atmosphere by disconnected episodes of terror. Neither

accounting for their mysterious horrors nor attempting the construction
of a thrilling plot sequence, these evoke precisely the same feelings
through the medium of words as do the paintings of Picasso, Marc
Chagall, Chirico, Klee or Max Ernst.

There have been sporadic attempts to give a Freudian interpretation
to Gothic motif and machinery. The present writer has not fully
attempted this application, and therefore cannot judge of its validity ;
nevertheless it is necessary and interesting to note how the forces of
nature as painted by the Gothic novelists are capable of being given a
Freudian twist. The turbulent settings in which the tempter appears in
Gothic novels, combine " in the highest degree the struggle between
the instinct of death on the one hand, which, as Freud has shown, is also
an instinct of preservation, and, on the other, Eros, who exacts after
each human hecatomb the glorious restoration of life ". The thunder
itself, by its violence and loudness of pitch giving a profound physical
stimulus to the ear, and ' lightning ', often known as a ' thunderbolt '
which has a sudden and supremely devastating power, have been
associated with the most terrifying things possible : as Mr. Hugh Sykes
Davies puts it, " the magnified image of the enraged father ". An
angered father threatening punishment is the symbol of all power and
terror for a child ; for an adult ' thunder ' no longer evokes the image
of an angered father, but transforms itself into that of an angry God.
The terror of death and the grave are closely allied to the theological
representation of the divinity as the God of Wrath. Even the spiral
staircase has been called symbolic of neurotic sensibility.

Melancholy, gloom, rape, and spiritual sufferings have earned for
these works their Continental title of ' les romans noir '. They are in
English fiction the first manifestation of what Mario Praz has termed
" The Romantic Agony " of literature, and what Dr. Kettle refers to as
" that often terrible exploration of the darker sides of the human mind
and experience, which later finds expression in such a novel as Wuthering
Heights ".

Signor Praz has made a wide survey of French and English literature
in the Romantic period and advances the view that one of the most
characteristic aspects of this literature is a peculiar " erotic sensibility " :
a sensibility profoundly algolagnic, obsessed with the idea of pleasure
obtained through sadistic or masochistic cruelty. Commenting on
Algolagnia, the relation of the sex impulse to pain, Montague Summers
has remarked : " It is probable that something of this masochistic feeling

lies (perhaps quite unconsciously) at the root of the fascination so universally exercised by uncanny tales of ghosts and spectres, which send hearers or readers to bed shuddering and glancing over their shoulders with delicious apprehension of a supernatural visitant." Immalee says in *Melmoth the Wanderer* : " I never felt a pain that was not pleasure."

It is possible that such sentiments expressed in the Gothic novel reflect the neurotic and erotic features of the age, and were the harmless release of that innate spring of cruelty which is present in each of us ; an impulse mysterious and inextricably connected with the very forces of life and death. The persecution of innocent females, so much a feature of the Gothic novels, is at bottom an erotic impulse.

Horror-romanticism has often been equated with perverted religious craving. The imagination of a neuropath like Matthew Gregory Lewis and his lascivious phantasies have led critics to think that those who are victims of a debased religious craving are also subject to erotic disturbances. So persistently has the theme of incest—as in *The Monk*—invaded literature that one suspects the dread of this sin to be somehow deeply intertwined with the roots of primitive religion. In *The Castle of Otranto* there is a vague suggestion of incest ; Ambrosio ends by raping and murdering his sister in *The Monk*, and henceforward the incest theme seems to pass into the convention of the Gothic novel. Even Mrs. Radcliffe hovers around it in *The Romance of the Forest*, and this theme was used by Maturin in the Spaniard's tale of *Melmoth the Wanderer* to further heighten the shocking situation.

Professor Dobrée has called the eighteenth century " a century of passion ", which in spite of " its superficial garniture of exquisite refinement, its veneer ", was " a brutal age ". The literary obsession with erotic and psychological or sexual perversion may have been a fantastic and terrible reaction against the corrupt aristocratic society of the day. As Montague Summers notes : " The eighteenth century was preeminently the century of systematized licentiousness . . . corrupt to the core. . . . All social life was concentrated on the elegant accomplishment of the sexual act. Science, art, literature, fashion, conversation, lent their every aid to enhance and embellish physical desire. ' Pleasure, voluptuous pleasure, was the soul of the eighteenth century ' cries de Goncourt. Phallic ecstasy almost became a religion as in the days of decadent Rome. It was an era of subtle artificiality, of powder and patches, silk and perfume, when the silken petticoat, the lace ruffle, and essenced hair proved more provocative by candlelight than clean nudity in the golden noontide sun." The close of the eighteenth century is marked by a crisis of feeling, of human emotion which coincided with a great political crisis, the upsurge of a great revolutionary movement. It gave birth to the myths of fatal men and women, from which developed a magnificent iconography of melancholia and algolagnia.

The Gothic romance is not concerned with a realistic approach to life. Character study and the social emotion of humour did not appeal to its authors. They aimed at awakening the twin emotions of Pity and Fear, but mainly Fear, as being more sublime. It must be acknowledged that Fear exerts a potent spell upon the human mind : horrid stories do impart a fearful joy. Human nature craves not only for amusement and entertainment but also demands the more strenuous catharsis of pity and terror. The tale of terror appeals to some deeply rooted human instinct ; an irresistible, inexplicable impulse drives us towards the macabre. Man in the darkness of his ignorance is attracted mothlike by the fascination of weird and eerie themes pertaining to his own death. As is the glory of the flame for the moth, so " our instincts of love and terror are the foundations respectively of our sense of beauty and the sublime ", says Edward Niles.

The tempestuous loveliness of terror exerted a powerful fascination for the Gothic novelists. Alonso, the Spaniard, in *Melmoth the Wanderer*, remarks, in his description of the death of the parricide torn to pieces by the mob : " the drama of terror has the irresistible power of converting its audience into its victims ", and "Alas ! in what moment of success do we not feel a sensation of terror ! "

The attempt to achieve Beauty through the medium of Terror, was ultimately an experiment with Burke's theory that everything calculated to awaken mental images of agony, of danger, or of things giving the effect of fear, remains a profound source of the sublime. We feel that they practically demonstrated Burke's theory of Fear and Sublimity. In his *Inquiry into the Origin of our Ideas of the Sublime and Beautiful* (1757), Burke had already defined the range and scope of the " Novel of Terror ". Mrs. Radcliffe adhered to his doctrine of the equivalence of the obscure, the terrible, and the sublime when she invoked feelings of dread under the obscurity of the triple mantle of night, desolation, and gloom, and by not carrying the idea of pain and danger as far as violence sustained her sublimity, producing a delightful horror, a kind of tranquillity tinged with terror. In her introductory essay to *Sir Bertrand*, a fragment (1773), Mrs. Barbauld attempts to explain how and why scenes of terror excite pleasurable emotions. She also discriminates between the scene of natural horror in Smollett's *Ferdinand Count Fathom* and the marvellous and terrible incidents in Walpole's *Otranto*.

The Gothic novelists led the readers to an ultimate state of terror through slow degrees of mounting suspense. The sublime terrors excited by great passions and catastrophes, approximate to the tragic emotions of pity and exaltation. Around these works hovers a spirit akin to that of tragedy, at least in the medieval and commonly accepted sense of a fall from high estate to misery and a wretched end. We cannot but feel our emotion go out towards Schedoni, Montoni, or Ambrosio in their hour of death. Villains they may have been, but we have been the constant spectators of their crimes and motives, and at the time of retribution we feel a deepening of understanding and sympathy.

Other properties of Burke's *Inquiry*, the stern beauty of mountainous landscapes, cataracts, and soaring eagles, the grandeur of storms with clashing thunder and lightning, the conflict of mighty nature's elements, are used by the Gothic novelists to arouse the emotions of terror and horror. Threatening physical exposure to the harshness of Nature is purely agonizing, but when felt only by the imagination, the pain is overpowered by sublime pleasure.

This type of literature chiefly concerned with the primitive excitement born of danger, battle, pursuit, the supernatural, fearful events, and visions, and love, appeals to the widest circle and gratifies the desire of its readers for something greater than reality, something they may admire and in their dreams would emulate.

If a work of art is the complement of life and a compensation for reality, if it does satisfy the need for spiritual activity, which ordinary reality does not satisfy, and if its purpose be to purify language, then the Gothic novel is a legitimate art form. It revived our apprehension of life itself by enlarging our sensibility, making readers more conscious of the kinship of terror and beauty and renewing awestruck wonder at possible forms of being.

An extension of Burke's theory produced the Beauty of the Medusa, beloved of the Schauer-Romantiks, a leprous beauty tainted with pain, corruption, and death. Walter Pater wrote of the Medusa, remembering Shelley's verse : " What may be called the fascination of corruption penetrates in every touch its exquisitely finished beauty." With the group of Schauer-Romantik writers " the very objects which should induce a shudder—the livid face of the severed head, the squirming mass of vipers, the rigidity of death, the sinister light, the repulsive animals, the lizard, the bat—all these give rise to a new sense of beauty, a beauty imperilled and contaminated, a new thrill ", says Mario Praz.

There are scenes in the works of the Schauer-Romantiks that are worthy the pencil of a Murillo, a Rosa, a Goya, or any of those painters, who, inspired by the genius of suffering, delight in representing the most exquisite of human forms in the extremity of human agony. Perhaps, as in *Melmoth the Wanderer*, the light of the moon gives an effect of corpse-like beauty to such lurid paintings as depict

> a St. Bartholomew flayed, with his skin hanging about him in a drapery—a St. Lawrence, broiled on a gridiron, and exhibiting his finely-formed anatomy on its bars, while naked slaves are blowing the coals beneath it.

These works have been slightingly described as " not good books, whose vitality springs from an inner source, but poor books, on which the colour of life was reflected from their readers ". For Dr. Arnold Kettle the Gothic romances lack " depth and significance ", and were written " with the sole interest to give the public sensations ". Consequently he asks " whether this school . . . can in any valuable sense be taken seriously " ; their ' horror ' is " an escape, a titillation of often rather jaded senses ".

He finds the " uniformity of the type quite astonishing [and believes] that it is almost impossible to distinguish one author from another ". This statement may be valid for minor Gothic authors who reflect each other and make common use of stock situations and attitudes ; but the major ones were distinctive, their works represent different phases and types of Gothic fiction. Dr. Kettle has stated " it is foolish to try to see the reflection of outside serious influences ". Yet it is possible to trace a definite stream of German and French influences that converged with English Gothic tradition in the Schauer-Romantik School of Horror. Perhaps it is the torrential spate of Gothic fiction which leads Dr. Kettle to presume that " they were easier to write ". But the deft artistry of their works and qualities already enumerated would be by no means plain sailing for any novelist, past or present.

It has been a commonplace criticism to say that Gothic novels are tenuous productions that display no knowledge of human passions, nor observations of life and manners. A closer scrutiny reveals them as lovely and glorious fabrics of supernatural enchantment whose texture and dark hues are too delicate to have been woven upon the loom of ordinary life. We have hardly the right to dismiss them with a patronizing smile, and a joking reference to subterranean passages, long-suffering maidens, vanishing lights, and creaking doors, when they appeal to man's innate sense of the mysterious.

As a product of imagination and art the Gothic novel is by no means negligible, but it is important to realize that their appeal is emotional, not intellectual. Maturin writes in his *Melmoth* :

> Let those who smile at me, ask themselves whether they have been indebted most to imagination or reality for all they have enjoyed in life, if indeed they have ever enjoyed anything.

And Mrs. Radcliffe had written earlier :

> What ardent imagination ever was contented to trust to plain reasoning, or to the evidence of the senses ? It may not willingly confine itself to the dull truths of this earth, but, eager to expand its faculties, to fill its capacity, and to experience its own peculiar delights, soars after new wonders into a world of its own.

Arthur Machen has observed :

> Man is so made that all his true delight arises from the contemplation of mystery, and save by his own frantic and invincible folly, mystery is never taken from him ; it rises within his soul, a well of joy unending.

Fiction, like the Kingdom of Heaven, has many mansions, and considered as a separate and distinct species of writing, the Gothic novel possesses merit and affords pleasure, nor can we hope to find the qualities of a Fielding in the works of Mrs. Radcliffe ; it is as if one were to demand mangoes of the grape vine.

It is true that the machinery of Gothicism creaks at times, and its phantoms stalk too mechanically, that a tone and colour of unreality undermines its values. Yet one may still relish even the strangely attractive absurdities of the School, and find pleasure in its outmoded fantasies and stucco supernaturalism, its most bizarre intrigues and baroque adventures, its language which is sometimes queerly coloured and patterned. While we may laugh at the statue from whose nose three drops of blood fell, and may not get a shiver from the portrait that walked out of its frame, these novels met the need of their times, which had not been met by the polished intellectualism of the Augustan age.

These novels answered to a demand for something wild and primitive, exciting the primordial emotions.

Almost everyone at some time or other has felt strange forebodings agitating his soul, that have suggested to his fancy a presentiment of evil. His higher faculties have recalled images and feelings long buried in the depths of his mind, stalking like spectres from the past. The Gothic novelists took these vague spiritual disturbances, and with psychological intuition allied them to a love of the picturesque and renewed feeling for Nature. The resulting effect is that they leave the faculties of mind infinitely more elevated and enlarged.

During the period when the forces of Christianity were nearly spent, and materialism had dislodged spiritual values, the Gothic novelists planned their novels with an awareness of the Deity and the consciousness of a just Fate. Whether the hero and heroine clasp chaste hands at the altar or go together to the clay cold grave, the villains learn in due course that the wages of sin is death.

Mrs. Barbauld found that the Gothic novel " is always ready to enliven the gloom of solitude, to soothe the languor of debility and disease, to win the attention from pain or vexations . . . " ; and while the panorama of life passes before us, it makes us forget the ordinary turmoils of existence. " It is pleasant to the mind ", she adds, " to sport in the boundless regions of possibility ; to find relief from the sameness of every-day occurrences by expatiating amidst brighter skies and fairer fields ; to exhibit love that is always happy, valour that is always successful ; to feed the appetite for wonder by a quick succession of marvellous events ; and to distribute, like a ruling providence, rewards and punishments which fall just where they ought to fall."

The Gothic novel with its romantic unrealities, its strange and sensational beauties, its far flights of extravagance, was not only the Novel of Adventure but also the novel of Happy Escape for spirits uneasy or terrified before the menace of the future. If man had not his dreams the world would become hideously real, and man himself an intellectual automaton. We call our dreams Romance, and it was just this that the Gothic novelists gave to their readers. As Walpole wrote in one of his letters : " Visions, you know, have always been my pasture. . . . I almost think there is no wisdom comparable to that of exchanging what is called the realities of life for dreams. Old castles, old pictures, old histories, and the babble of old people, make one live back into centuries that cannot disappoint one." As a reward, the reader—if not too restless, too impatient, and too modern—will find that he is transported back many a long year from this atomic age to a realm of magic and marvels, of knight-errantry and adventure, of combat and love, and surely that in itself is praise enough.

We escape into a world where anything may happen so long as it is terrible, where flashes of lightning are more frequent than sunlight, and where, if we are not poisoned with a magic potion in the second volume, we are probably stabbed with a jewelled dagger in the third. It is a world, in fact, of ungoverned passions and hisses and swoons, a realm where laws and morals are consumed in a blaze of passion. Even the parodist of the Gothic school of fiction, Eaton Stannard Barrett, realized that " Romances such as *The Mysteries of Udolpho*, *The Italian*, and *The Bravo of Venice*, which address themselves to the imagination alone, are often captivating, and seldom detrimental ".

A work of art brings back to us the freshness and spontaneity of the emotions of childhood, and evokes in us a long obliterated primitive sensibility. These novels are in the nature of adult fairy-tales, and the reader feels like a traveller on enchanted grounds. Well has Madame de Chasteney, the French translator of *Udolpho*, remarked that " the menacing voices, the prolonged gloom, the fantastic effect of its [*Udolpho*'s] terrors overwhelmed me once more like a child without my being able to discover the cause ".

It is not intricacy or bafflement that causes the Gothic romances to be read and reread with a never-diminishing thrill when the slick novel of today is forgotten in an hour. It is the small boy in all of us sitting before an open fire, with the winter wind howling outside, while a diffused atmosphere of warmth lingers behind the drawn curtains, which sets imagination aflame and keeps company with Gothic romance. There remains a naive simplicity about these tales in spite of all complexity of incident : the villain and the hero and the exquisite heroine, virtue rewarded and vice punished.

It is impossible to deny the art and delicacy with which the writers of the Gothic school calculated thrills, the adroitness with which they utilized the devices of reticence and suggestion, and analysed the effects with the precision of a psychologist. And who can be oblivious to the sense of atmosphere they created ? The landscape, ruins, characters, costumes, light and shade, sound and silence ; all are subdued by delicate touches to the key of emotion ; everything lulling the reader into the state of mind most in harmony with the incidents to be enacted. The

231231231231

Gothic novel affects the hearts of its readers with an almost holy serenity : the pure tints of light upon an overspreading atmosphere and darkness are most touching and most eloquent. Sometimes it casts a spell. We are really possessed and enchanted by the melancholy winds and the voices of the days of old. The memory of the past times return, and the very accents of the deceased seem to murmur from the grave. These novels are of the nature of complex symphonies with the feeling of awe and fear among the dominant motives.

Having read them, they float in our memory, here and there freshly remembered in their better parts, the rest fading into the distance and half-forgotten ; on the whole, a pleasing pageant of gloomy castles and ruined abbeys—moon-illumined caves and forests—dance and Provençal song, and sun-burnt mirth, and aerial music floating over fairy-haunted meadows—or choral chant of monk or nun, borne to the ear over the still waters of the Adriatic or the placid Mediterranean.

These novels are works of great charm, and this they owe also to their apprehension of the numinous. These may be read and enjoyed in the fullness of their beauty—a beauty which is like that of some still night when the cypress point to heaven as burned-out torches against the dusky sky, when the sickle of the harvest moon rides high above, and as the ivy shimmers and trembles on the moonlit ruins, when the pause of solemn stillness is broken only by the hooting of a moping owl, or by the amorous notes of the nightingale—a constant reminder that there is Death as well as Love.

APPENDIX I

THE total effect of *The Castle of Otranto* may be compared with the effect aroused by the paintings of prominent surrealist artists. Picasso is the first that comes to mind, and half his fascination lies in his capacity for arousing our sense of wonder. His manner is terrific at times, but mostly sombre in its colouring, essentially tormented in its inspiration, and, according to Herbert Read, "embodying in its totality the Gothic or Germanic spirit ". Walpole's novel has the same cumulative effect.

In the fantasies of Marc Chagall (born in Russia 1887, of Jewish parents), the impossible mingles with the possible as in dream experience, embodying the " subversive tendencies " in everything unfamiliar. He expresses the repressed inquietude of his inner self in a lyrical and symbolistic manner and paints from the heart. His ' lyricism ' in painting requires some explanation. Lyricism in poetry is a certain *direct* manner of giving expression to an emotional state ; we do not attempt to rationalize the expression. We feel the emotional equivalence of the words, although their literal meaning may be absurd. If we transpose the poem " Go, and catch a falling star " in painting, we shall get something like the art of Chagall—an art in which harmony emerges from an iridescent shimmer of colours, colours which work upon our emotions as inexplicably as words in a lyric ; colours which belong, not to any scene in nature but to a world of un-conscious fantasy. It is such a world that Walpole evokes ; a world of images, capable of symbolizing the fertility of the artist's vision and of expressing his creative joy.

Chirico (born in Greece 1888, of Italian parents) paints dream landscapes and presents a disturbing and terrifying combination of objects. He is a master of emotive atmosphere, who wields his brush for an emotional use of colour, and whose art presents a new version of the " pleasing horror ". It is a world not far removed from that of Walpole's.

The art of Paul Klee (born in Switzerland 1879) is instinctive, fantastic, and naively objective. " At times it seems child-like, at times primitive, at times mad," says Herbert Read. He creates a world with its own strange flora and fauna, and which has its own laws of perspective and logic. At times he escapes to the world of residual memory, of disconnected images, for that is the world of fantasy, the world of fairy-tales and myth. The art of Klee borders on a " metaphysical art ", and he directs his energies through the inward eye towards another and a more marvellous world. Klee's world, in fact, is a fairy world, a world of spooks and goblins, called by Herbert Read " a Gothic world ". *The Castle of Otranto* has the same child-like spontaneity, the same portrayal of a " primitive and mad world ", a story of ghosts and fantasies.

Max Ernst (born near Cologne in 1891) has a symbolic vision, and as a true and enthusiastic super-realist, he breaks down the barriers, both physical and psychical, between the conscious and the unconscious, between the inner and the outer world, and attempts to create a super-reality in which the real and the unreal, meditation and action, meet and mingle and dominate. In Walpole's story, too, we can evidence all these.

The total cumulative effect of Walpole's story is like an impression of sur-realistic art and there are many similarities between his style and that of other sincere and determined surrealists like Joan Miró, Salvador Dali, or André Masson. These might also be compared with the earlier surrealism of Bosch, Goya, or Blake.

APPENDIX II

DURING the summer of 1955, with the kind assistance of Dr. S. G. Dunn, D.Litt., sometime Professor of English at Allahabad University, India, I was able to trace some more obscure Gothic works at an antiquarian bookshop in Stratford-upon-Avon. These included a diminutive Victorian edition of Clara Reeve's *The Old English Baron*. This volume also contains another short Gothic tale *The Hand of Clay*. The latter work is not mentioned in Montague Summers's extensive *A Gothic Bibliography*, and I have not yet been able to trace the authorship. One of the Gothic tales written by Clara Reeve is supposed to have been lost from the London coach in May 1787 and never recovered. Perhaps *The Hand of Clay* is from her pen. If Clara Reeve did write it, then it shadows forth some Radcliffian techniques ; if it is a much later work by somebody else, it is a poor imitation.

I hope in the near future to publish a paper undertaking a separate and fuller discussion of its authorship and implications.

APPENDIX III

THE disintegration or ruin of pure Gothic romance provided stones for the extensive building of 'detectives' and 'thrillers'. The sensational stuff that floods the market today reveals precisely the same crude romanticism, the same blend of recognizable probability and deliciously menacing horror which characterized the Gothic novel. The cheap illustrated 'mysteries' with their wide, lucrative circulation, and the shilling novel with its decent vesture, closely resemble the chap books and shilling shockers of the Gothic school. The tradition that once was Francis Lathom or J. Hortley-Curties, is now Edgar Wallace, Peter Cheyney, and others. The Gothic romance not only provided a pattern, but also inspired the 'sensational' writers of today with the dark incentive that first set them upon the sinister paths of crime fiction.

The "Roman Policier"—an unfailing anodyne in this modern world—and which according to G. K. Chesterton expresses "some sense of the poetry of modern life", parallels Gothic fiction in technique and popularity. First, it has seen more verdant days and created a vogue. It supplied to the youth of the early twentieth century the romance and excitement provided by Gothic fiction to feminine readers a century ago. The trickle of 'detectives' and 'thrillers' quickly grew into a flood ; the spate, the avalanche of mystery fiction, truly resembles the publication of Gothic novels that fell torrentially from Lane's Minerva Press. But the really first-rate practitioners are always few ; the branches grow so thick that one can't see the wood for the trees.

Secondly, it shares the narcotic quality of Gothic, with the emphasis on variation and excitement characteristic of this genre. Likewise their books are passports to another world, to realms not of gold, but of violence, shootings and stabbings, of wild chases by land, sea, and air. The settings in the Gothic novel were the frowning castles on the Apennines, and we moved in another world of villainous monks, imprisoned beauties, magic potions, and jewelled daggers. The 'mystery' writers take similar pleasure in their craft, play fair with their readers, and "eschew mysterious chinamen and poisons unknown to science". Here, says *The Times Literary Supplement* (25 February 1955), is "murder witnessed from the soft cushions of an evening train, murder lying quiet behind a glass of port and a cigar, murder under the eiderdown. . . . The dull life expands, the fingerprint on the poker takes a new significance."

Thirdly, there is a striking resemblance between the 'gothic' philosophy set forth by Walpole in his preface to *Otranto*, and the motive and method that fires the writers of 'detectives' and 'thrillers'. The juxtaposition of fantasy with reality—a judicious blending of possible and impossible—gives identity to this genre. "The detective novel", says Haycroft, "must seem real in the same sense that fairy-tales seem real to children."

There are two methods of approach open to the detective novelist : again quoting Haycroft " he can put unreal characters into realistic situations, or he can put realistic characters into fantastic situations. The former method produces the classical *roman policier* . . . [in the second] . . . the plot possesses the mad logic and extravagance of a dream, while the *dramatis personae* are roughed in with just enough solidity to stand out against the macabre and whirling background." And again, the detective fiction " pointing the eternal triumph of good over evil, a modern Morality eschewing scenes of unnecessary violence, of sadism, and other recent tendencies ", as emphasized in *The Times Literary Supplement* (25 February 1955), reminds us of the element of the doctrinaire in Gothic romances, where the evil, both for myth-making and entertainment, is volatilized by a certain measure of fantasy.

Fourthly, the manner of disintegration is common to both species of fiction. Just as the later ' gothic ' writers were driven to cruder attacks upon the reader's nerves, so also the gradual decline of detective fiction is marked by an increasing emphasis on the thrill rather than on ingenious treatment of plots. With the passing of time a new note creeps in, and on this *The Times Literary Supplement* observes, " since what has to be evoked is the thrill, the thrill must be stimulated, however recklessly. And so there has come into being . . . a degenerate school— the school of thriller pure and simple, of tough writing, of desperado prose." Whereas a detective story has a healthy severity of form, having a beginning, middle, and end, with a logical sequence of events, the thriller is more flexible, having a loosely concatenated series of episodes, absorbing, but lacking any organic interconnexion.

Thrillers find the lowest common denominator of detective writing and give the public plenty of blood and thunder with a mixture of sentiment—and all for (in the late 1940's and early 1950's) a shilling. Thrill is piled on thrill and mystification succeeds mystification. We are led on through a bewildering maze of incidents, till everything is explained in the last chapter. Strong in dramatic incident and atmosphere, its weakness is a tendency to confusion and a dropping of links—for its explanations do not always explain. It is seldom dull but it is mostly nonsense. Its sickening and highly unconvincing violence accompanied by semi-pornographic leering, has its linkage with ' Monk ' Lewis. Sapper's crudely violent sensation novels are examples of this school, which Montague Summers had in mind when he remarked that " the old sensation novel even at its slummiest and worst is infinitely superior, is far better written, far better contrived than the most recklessly puffed and panegyrised ' thriller ' of today ".

The machinery, settings, themes, and characters of these thrillers are deeply reminiscent of Gothic novels. The eccentric detective, the locked room con-vention, the stolen document, the pointing finger of unjust suspicion, the solution by surprise, the expansive and condescending explanation when the chase is done —all smack strongly of ' Gothic '. The weird old mansions and castles of Gothic mode had lost their power to astonish and excite. The thrillers now show terror lurking in the back streets of the reader's hometown, although they retain the ' gothic ' themes of desperate rage, jealousy, or revenge, and look upon death and mutilation with the diabolical pleasure of the sadist and pervert. Their plots are wrought upon " such subjects as hypnotism, catalepsy, somnambulism, lunacy, murder by the use of X-rays and hydrocyanic acid gas, and a variety of other medical and scientific discoveries and inventions ", says Dorothy Sayers. The subject ranges from enormous murderers in space-helmets to microscopic murderers from the stratosphere—in fact the whole universe is ransacked to provide a thrill.

Besides murders, and various kinds of known and obscure poisons, the ' thrillers ' have ingeniously elaborated and added to the ' gothic ' machinery. Dorothy Sayers gives us a survey : " Whereas, up to the present, there is only one known way of getting born, there are endless ways of getting killed. Here is a brief selection of handy short-cuts to the grave : poisoned tooth-stoppings ; licking poisoned stamps ; shaving-brushes inoculated with dread diseases ; poisoned boiled-eggs ; poison gas ; a cat with poisoned claws ; poisoned mattresses ; knives dropped through the ceiling ; stabbing with a sharp icicle ; electrocution by telephone ; biting by plague-rat and typhoid-carrying lice ; air-bubbles injected into the arteries . . . hanging head downwards . . . guns concealed in cameras ; a thermometer which explodes a bomb when the tempera-ture of the room reaches a certain height ; and so forth."

Besides incidents of plunder, fraud, and conspiracy—stock situations of the Gothic novels—characters like maniacs, poisoners, forgers, and spies also appear to have walked out of the pages of Gothic novels to inhabit modern ' thrillers '. The weeping fair-haired girl, the evil scientist with hypnotic eyes, in the mystery novels, resemble the Gothic heroine and Gothic villain. Haycroft notes, " the criminal of the thriller is often its hero and nearly always a romantic figure ". Remarking about the art of Edgar Wallace, Gilbert Thomas wrote : " His heroines are a little too blonde and sweet and blue-eyed, his detectives too hand-some and dashing and brave, and his villains over-villainous."

Sir Arthur Conan Doyle was the first to introduce the character of the detective, Sherlock Holmes, in A Study in Scarlet (1887). Holmes, with his lean figure, his twin obsessions—cocaine and the violin—his remarkable faculty of disguise, and his phenomenal powers of deduction, is a romantic and outstanding figure like a Gothic villain. The picturesque exploits of detectives that fill the extravagant pages of the police novel and thrillers, the pursuit of dangerous tasks with no other weapon than their own courage, achieving often the impossible, is very much in line with the characteristics of the Gothic hero.

In methods of treatment Mrs. Radcliffe has been a great inspiration to this emerging school of fiction. The fare of thrill and excitement provided in The Last of the Mohicans, The Pathfinder, and The Deerslayer by J. Fenimore Cooper harks back to Radcliffian method. The patient Indian tracker, skilful and intelli-gent, observes and reads from a fallen leaf, a broken twig or a half-obliterated footprint. Other writers of this school take a " devilish delight in playing tricks upon the reader. They will withhold a vital clue or gloss over its significance ; they will retain valuable information, to spring it upon the reader in the last chapter ; they will throw suspicion upon the most innocent of characters." All

these ingredients of the ' mystery ' novel : the ingenuity of plotting, characterization and background, the perennially fascinating situation of pursuit, coupled
with the chief detective ware of ' suspense ' are the gift of Gothic romance. The
detective novel developed " in the wake of a constant succession of sensations,
horrors, supernatural happenings and general skullduggery, in which action is
usually subordinated to the plot ". Actions strike us with the highest degree of
unexpectedness, and the sequence of incidents has a power to lead us breathlessly
on through chapter after chapter. Its endless adventures and turns of fate, its
spirit of melodrama and terror, grip the reader's attention and make him share in
the actual drama.

The study of ' Gothic ' influence on modern ' police novel ' and ' thrillers '
would be incomplete without a mention of the outstanding practitioners of the
art. In *The Times Literary Supplement* (25 February 1955) we read : " The best
and most ingenious detective story and the most exciting thriller were both
written by Wilkie Collins in the middle of the last century, long before the forms
had established themselves." *The Moonstone* anticipated Agatha Christie's most
sensational works. In " *The Woman in White*, he [Collins] established a record in
continuous suspense, heroine-persecution and frustrated sexuality, and mystery
within mystery, together with brilliant characterization, including a credible
master criminal, which stands unchallenged ". His fine sense of architectonics in
arranging the sequence of events is another of his contributions.

The crown of detective fiction settles on the worthy head of Agatha Christie,
who, with nearly sixty books to her name, continues her amazing output with no
diminution of her uncanny powers ; no less commendable is the suspense and
mystification in the writings of Dorothy Sayers. There has been a more generalized
trend towards an amalgamation of the detective story and the mystery-thriller in
which violent action, suspense and danger, with or without love-interest, is
projected against a shifting background. Such artists are those of the calibre of
" Nicholas Blake " and Ngaio Marsh.

Even earlier Conan Doyle had mixed ' horror ' and ' detection ' in *The
Speckled Band* and *The Engineer's Thumb*. His creaking ' flash-back ' device in
The Valley of Fear comes from Godwin's *Caleb Williams*. Conan Doyle's other
works relevant to our argument are *The Hound of the Baskervilles* and *The Sign
of Four*.

Mrs. Henry Wood represents the development of the ' sensation ' novel
towards the melodramatic and adventurous. She is an admirable spinner of plots
round ' gothic ' themes of a missing will, a vanished heir, a murder, or a family
curse. She unravels her mystery with a cautious workmanship without any loose
ends, and makes frequent use of supernatural thrills which are explained away in
the manner of Mrs. Radcliffe.

Edgar Wallace, so understandably popular, often uses supernatural effects.
He mixes ' horror ' and ' detection ' in *The Terror* and *The Black Abbot*, wherein
the ghostly visitor and the Clutching Hand are constantly invoked to be exorcized
by the acumen and common sense of the detective. The writer tells his stories
in terms of action, and carries the readers breathlessly through a perfect maze of

fantastic mystery. His plots are remarkably intricate and he springs his surprises upon the reader with the sure touch of a dramatist.

Peter Cheyney's *The Storms are Dark* is a superb thriller of which the first chapter is a brilliant example of the creation of sinister atmosphere. Other popular writers are : Freeman Wills Crofts, L. A. G. Strong, Gladys Mitchell, and Georges Simenon.

Finally, the declining phase of Gothic romance—the Schauer-Romantik school—is reincarnate in the shape of *Horror Comics*. The term ' comic ' is a misnomer, for the ingredient of humour is entirely absent in its pages. It is the element of ' horror ' in its realistic pictures, its nauseating verisimilitude, that fascinates millions of children, adolescents, and illiterates. Again, to quote *The Times Literary Supplement* of 25 February 1955, " The picture of a man just hanged, the noose still around his neck and only the whites of his eyes showing ; a man slaughtered, his tongue ripped out ; a woman's eye being pierced by an injection needle ; a nocturnal base-ball game where a man's internal organs are used for balls and his severed arms for bats . . .", such pictures of gross, hardened, brutal realism may claim their ancestry in the Gothic Schauer-Romantiks. These romanticize force and violence, and bring their pictorial tales to an end with a poetic justice. " But even justice, when the gangster's death in the electric chair or on the gallows is shown in agonizing detail, has only a further brutalizing effect."

Besides the many reprehensible features, these ' comics ' are thinly disguised pornography, the meaning of sex and violence becoming identical—a linkage with ' Monk ' Lewis. " Half-naked women, vamps, alluring blondes—their secondary sex characteristics over emphasized—populate these pages." These pictures abound in themes of cannibalism, necrophilia, and vampirism. Well has Dr. Wertham remarked : " Outside the forbidden pages of de Sade, you find draining of a girl's blood only in children's comics." Such scenes of violence bear a note of sadism and masochism, besides many scenes of flagellation, crushing faces under iron boots and torturing the fair sex tied against trees. A closer analysis of ' Gothic ' influence on ' Horror Comics ' will probably invite the attention of some future Mario Praz.

BIBLIOGRAPHY

I. BIBLIOGRAPHICAL AIDS

(IN ORDER OF IMPORTANCE)

1. Blakey, Dorothy. *The Minerva Press, 1790–1820.* 1939.
2. Summers, Montague. *A Gothic Bibliography.* 1941.
3. *English Literature* (1660–1800) : *A Bibliography of Modern Studies.* Edited by L. A. Landa and others. 2 vols. Princeton. 1950.
4. *The Cambridge Bibliography of English Literature.* Edited by F. W. Bateson. 4 vols. 1940.
5. *Years Work in English Studies.* 1921–55.
6. Lenrow, Elbert : *Reader's Guide to Prose Fiction.* 1940.
7. Nield, Jonathan. *Guide to the Best Historical Novels and Tales.* 1904.
8. Bowen, Courthorpe. *A Descriptive Catalogue of Historical Novels and Tales.* 1905.
9. Cust, L. *Third Annual Volume of the Walpole Society.* 1913–14.
10. Hazen, A. T. *A Bibliography of Horace Walpole.* Yale University Press. 1948.

II. ORIGINAL WORKS

(AS TREATED IN THE RESPECTIVE CHAPTERS)

CHAPTER I

Castle of Wolfenbach : A German Story. 1793. Mrs. Eliza Parsons.
Clermont. 1798. Regina Maria Roche.
The Mysterious Warning : A German Tale. 1796. Mrs. Eliza Parsons.
Necromancer : or the Tale of the Black Forest. 1794. Peter Teuthold. Translated by Lawrence Flammenburg.
The Midnight Bell : A German Story. 1798. Francis Lathom.
The Orphan of the Rhine : A Romance. 1799. Mrs. Sleath.
Horrid Mysteries : A Story. 1796. Marquis of Grosse. Translated by P. Will.

CHAPTER II

Ferdinand Count Fathom. 1753. Tobias Smollett.
Longsword, Earl of Salisbury : an Historical Romance. 1762. Thomas Leland.

CHAPTER III

The Castle of Otranto. 1764. Horace Walpole.

CHAPTER IV

The Champion of Virtue : A Gothic Story. (1777.) Published the following year as *The Old English Baron.* Clara Reeve.
The Recess : or A Tale of Other Times. 1783–86. Sophia Lee.
Canterbury Tales. 1797. Sophia and Harriet Lee.

CHAPTER V

The Castles of Athlin and Dunbayne. 1789. Ann Radcliffe.
A Sicilian Romance. 1790. Ann Radcliffe.
The Romance of the Forest. 1792. Ann Radcliffe.
The Mysteries of Udolpho. 1794. Ann Radcliffe.
The Italian. 1797. Ann Radcliffe.
Gaston de Blondeville. 1826. Ann Radcliffe.

CHAPTER VI

Vathek. 1786. William Beckford.
The Adventures of Caleb Williams. 1794. William Godwin.
Travels of St. Leon. 1799. William Godwin.
The Monk. 1795. Matthew Gregory Lewis.
The Bravo of Venice. 1804. Matthew Gregory Lewis.
Frankenstein. 1818. Mary Shelley.
The Vampyre : A Tale. 1819. Dr. John Polidori.
The Fatal Revenge of the Family of Montorio. 1807. Charles Robert Maturin.
Melmoth the Wanderer. 1820. Charles Robert Maturin.

CHAPTER VII

The Haunted Tower. 1789. James Cobb.
More Ghosts ! 1798.
The Rovers : or the Double Arrangement. 1798. In the *Anti-Jacobin.*
Rosetta : or Modern Occurrences. 1799. Mary Charlton.
St. Godwin : A Tale of the 16th, 17th and 18th centuries. 1800. Count Reginald De St. Leon in *Monthly Mirror.*

Angelina. 1801. Maria Edgworth in *Moral Tales.*
The Florentines. 1808. Benjamin Thompson.
Romance Readers and Romance Writers. 1810. Sarah Green.
The Heroine. 1813. Eaton S. Barrett.
The Hero : or Adventures of a Night ! A Romance. 1817.
Prodigious ! ! ! or Childe Paddie in London. 1818.
Nightmare Abbey. 1818. Thomas L. Peacock.
Northanger Abbey. 1818. Jane Austen.
Granby. 1826. Thomas Henry Lister.

III. GENERAL SURVEY

(On the English Novel)

Baker, E. A. *History of the English Novel.* Vol. V. 1934.
Church, Richard. *Growth of the English Novel.* 1951.
Cross, W. L. *The Development of the English Novel.* N.Y. 1899.
Dunlop, John Colin. *History of Prose Fiction.* 1911.
Forsyth, William. *The Novels and Novelists of the Eighteenth Century.* 1871.
Foster, E. M. *Aspects of the Novel.* 1927.
Huffman, C. F. *The Eighteenth-century Novel in Theory and Practice.* 1923.
Johnson, R. B. *The Women Novelists.* 1918.
Kettle, Arnold C. *An Introduction to the English Novel.* 1951.
Leavis, Q. D. *Fiction and the Reading Public.* 1932.
Liddell, Robert. *A Treatise on the Novel.* 1947.
Lovell, R. M., and Hughes, H. S. *The History of the Novel in England.* Boston. 1932.
Lubbock, P. *The Craft of Fiction.* 1922.
MacCarthy, B. G. *The Later Women Novelists* (1744–1818). 1947.
Muir, Edwin. *The Structure of the Novel.* 1928.
Pelham, Edgar. *The Art of the Novel from 1700 to the Present Time.* N.Y. 1933.
Phelps, W. L. *The Advance of the English Novel.* 1919.
Raleigh, Walter. *The English Novel.* 1894.
Reeve, Clara. *The Progress of Romance.* 1785.
Saintsbury, G. *The English Novel.* 1913.
Scott, Walter. *The Lives of the Novelists.* 1906.
Verschoyle, D. (ed.). *The English Novelists.* 1936.
Williams, H. *Two Centuries of the English Novel.* 1911.

(LITERARY MOVEMENT AND IDEAS)

Babcock, R. W.   *Genesis of Shakespeare Idolatry* (1766–99).   Chapel Hill.   N.C. 1931.

Beers, Henry A.   *A History of English Romanticism in the Eighteenth Century.*   1899.

Bernbaum, E.   *Guide through the Romantic Movement.*   N.Y.   1930.

Conant, Martha P.   *The Oriental Tale in England in the Eighteenth Century.*   N.Y. 1908.

Das, P. K.   *Evidences of a Growing Taste for Nature in the Age of Pope.*   Calcutta. 1928.

Draper, J. W.   *The Funeral Elegy and the Rise of English Romanticism.*   N.Y.   1929.

Dowden, E.   *The French Revolution and English Literature.*   1897.

Elton, O.   *A Survey of English Literature.*   2 vols.   (1730–80.)   1928.

Elton, O.   *The Augustan Ages.*   1899.

Fairchild, H. N.   *The Romantic Quest.*   1931.

Foster, James R.   *History of the Pre-Romantic Novel in England.*   1949.

Gosse, E.   *A History of Eighteenth-century Literature.*   1889.

Gregory, A.   *The French Revolution and the English Novel.*   1915.

Harder, J. B.   *Eighteen-century Tendency in Poetry and Essay.*   Amsterdam.   1933.

Hussey, C.   *The Picturesque.*   1927.

MacClintock, W. D.   *Some Paradoxes of the English Romantic Movement of the Eighteenth Century.*   Chicago.   1903.

Manwaring, E.   *Italian Landscape in Eighteenth-century England.*   N.Y.   1925.

Marshall, Roderick.   *Italy in English Literature* (1755–1815).   1934.

Millar, J. H.   *The Mid-eighteenth Century.*   1902.

Oliphant, M. O.   *The Literary History of England in the end of the eighteenth and beginning of the nineteenth century.*   3 vols.   1882.

Perry, T. S.   *English Literature in the Eighteenth Century.*   N.Y.   1883.

Phelps, W. L.   *The Beginnings of the English Romantic Movement.*   1893.

Price, L. M.   *The Reception of English Literature in Germany.*   University of California Press.   1932.

Proper, C. B. A.   *Social Elements in English Prose Fiction between 1700 and 1832.*   Amsterdam.   1929.

Reed, Amy L.   *The Background of Gray's Elegy.*   N.Y.   1924.

Reynolds, M.   *The Treatment of Nature in English Poetry between Pope and Wordsworth.*   Chicago.   1905.

Robertson, J. G.   *Studies in the Genesis of Romantic Theory in the Eighteenth Century.*   1923.

Saintsbury, G.   *A History of Nineteenth-century Literature* (1780–1895).   1896.

Saintsbury, G.   *The Peace of the Augustans.*   1916.

Smith, D. Nichol. *Shakespeare in the Eighteenth Century*. 1928.
Stephen, L. *English Literature and Society in the Eighteenth Century*. 1904.
Stephen, L. *History of English Thought in the Eighteenth Century*. 1926.
Stockley, V. *German Literature as known in England* (1750–1830). 1929.
Stokoe, F. W. *German Influence in the English Romantic Period*. 1926.
Tymms, Ralph. *German Romantic Literature*. 1955.
Vaughan, C. E. *The Romantic Revolt*. 1900.
Vines, S. *The Course of English Classicism*. 1930.
Walters, H. B. *The English Antiquaries of the Sixteenth, Seventeenth, and Eighteenth Centuries*. 1934.
Willey, B. *The Eighteenth-century Background*. 1939.
Wright, W. F. *Sensibility in English Prose Fiction* (1760–1814). Urbana. 1937.
Yost, Jr., Calvin Daniel. *The Poetry of the "Gentleman's Magazine": A Study in Eighteenth-century Literary Taste*. Philadelphia. 1936.

(ON THE NATURE OF GOTHIC)

Addison, Agnes. *Romanticism and the Gothic Revival*. N.Y. 1938.
Anonymous. *The Gothic Renaissance, Its Origin, Progress, and Principles*. 1860.
Burra, Peter. *Baroque and Gothic Sentimentalism*. 1931.
Clark, Kenneth. *The Gothic Revival*. 1950.
Coleridge, S. T. *General Character of the Gothic Mind in the Middle Ages*. (Reprinted in *Miscellaneous Criticism*.) 1936.
Coleridge, S. T. *General Character of the Gothic Literature and Art*. (Reprinted in *Miscellaneous Criticism*.) 1936.
Eastlake, C. L. *A History of the Gothic Revival in England*. 1872.
Essays on Gothic Architecture. By several hands. 1800.
Haferkorn, Reinhard. *Gotik und Ruine in der Englischen Dichtung Des Achtzehnten Jahrhunderts*. Leipzig. 1924.
Harvey, John. *Gothic England*. 1947.
Harvey, John. *The Gothic World*. 1950.
Ker, W. P. *The Literary Influence of the Middle Ages*. (CHEL. Vol. X.)
Ruskin, John. *The Nature of Gothic* (*The Stones of Venice*). 1851.
Smith, Warren H. *Architecture in English Fiction*. New Haven. 1934.
Summerson, John. *An Interpretation of Gothic*. Heavenly Mansions. 1948.
Worringer, Wilhelm. *Form in Gothic*. Translated by Herbert Read. 1927.
Yvon, P. *Le Gothique et la Renaissance Gothic en Angleterre* (1750–1880). Caen. 1931.

250 THE GOTHIC FLAME

IV. IMPORTANT PREFACES, ADDRESSES, MEMOIRS, AND LETTERS

(PREFACES)

A note on Charles Robert Maturin prefixed to *Melmoth the Wanderer*. 1892.

Barbauld's introduction on Mrs. Radcliffe prefixed to *The British Novelists*. Vol. XLIII. 1810.

Barbauld's note " On the Origin and Progress of Novel Writing " prefixed to *The British Novelists*. Vol. I. 1810.

Barbauld's preface to *The British Novelists*. Vol. XXII. 1810.

Breton, A. Preface on Maturin in *Melmoth the Wanderer*. Paris. 1954.

Dobson, Austin. Introduction to *Northanger Abbey*. 1897.

Dobrée, Bonamy. Introduction to *From Anne to Victoria*. 1937.

Doughty, Oswald. Preface to *The Castle of Otranto*. 1929.

Fearnside, C. S. Introduction to *Classic Tales*. 1906.

Johnson, Brimley. Introduction to *Northanger Abbey*. 1898.

Moore, John. A view of the Commencement and Progress of Romance, prefixed to the works of Smollett. 1872.

Raleigh, Walter. Introduction to Barrett's *The Heroine*. 1909.

Rose, D. Murray. Prefaces to E. A. Baker's edition of *Half Forgotten Books*. Vols. VII and VIII. 1903.

Saintsbury, G. Introduction to *Tales of Mystery*. Vol. I. 1891.

Sayers, D. L. Introduction to *Great Short Stories of Detection, Mystery, and Horror*. 1928.

Scott, Sir Walter. Introduction to *The Castle of Otranto*. Reprinted 1907.

Scott, Sir Walter. General Preface to *Waverley Novels*. 1895.

Summers, Montague. Introduction to *The Castle of Otranto* and *The Mysterious Mother*. 1924.

Summers, Montague. Introduction to *The Supernatural Omnibus*. 1931.

(ADDRESSES)

Dobrée, Bonamy. Horace Walpole. Unpublished.

Macaulay's Essay on Walpole. Published in *Edinburgh Review*, October 1833.

Sadleir, M. The Northanger Novels : a Footnote to Jane Austen. English Association Pamphlet No. 68. 1927.

Summers, Montague. " A Great Mistress of Romance : Ann Radcliffe (1764–1823)." *Transactions of the Royal Society of Literature*. Vol. XXXV. 1917.

Summers, Montague. "The Marquis de Sade : A Study in Algolagnia." Publication No. 6 of the British Society for the Study of Sex Psychology. 1920.

(MEMOIRS)

A Memoir to Mrs. Radcliffe prefixed to *Gaston de Blondeville.* 1826.

A Memoir of Walpole prefixed to *The Castle of Otranto.* 1840.

Memoirs of Mrs. Radcliffe prefixed to Limbird's *British Novelists.* Vol. XIII–XVII. 1824.

Redding, Cyrus. Memoirs of William Beckford of Fonthill. 1859.

Scott, Sir Walter. Memoir of the life of Mrs. Radcliffe prefixed to Ballantyne Novelist Library. Vol. X. 1824.

(LETTERS [EDITED BY])

Baron-Wilson, Margaret. *Life and Correspondence of Matthew Gregory Lewis.* 1839.

Lewis, W. S. *Horace Walpole's Correspondence.* Vol. I–XIX. 1937–55.

Marshall, F. A. *The Life and Letters of Mary Wollstonecraft Shelley.* 1889.

Morley, E. J. *Hurd's Letters on Chivalry and Romance.* 1911.

Tovey, Duncan. *Gray and his friends : letters and relics in great part hitherto un-published.* 1890.

Toynbee, P. *Letters of Horace Walpole.* Vol. I–XIII. 1903–05.

V. CRITICAL WORKS

(PUBLISHED AND UNPUBLISHED DISSERTATIONS
[CHRONOLOGICALLY ARRANGED])

1894. Müller Faureuth, C. *Die Ritter und Raüber Romane.* Halle.

1902. Freye, Walter. *The Influence of Gothic Literature on Walter Scott.* Rostock.

1902. Mobius, Hans. *The Gothic Romance.* Leipzig.

1911. Mobius, Hans. *Die Englischen Rosenkreuzerromane und ihre Vorläufer, während des 18 und 19 Jahrhunderts.* Hamburg.

1913. Church, Elizabeth. *The Gothic Romance : Its Origins and Development.* Harvard. Unpublished.

1915. Killen, Alice M. *Le Roman ' Terrifiant ' ou Roman ' noir ' de Walpole à Ann Radcliffe et son Influence jusqu'en* 1840. Paris.

1917. Scarborough, Dorothy. *The Supernatural in Modern Fiction.*

1920. Longueil, A. E. *Gothic Romance, Its Influence on the Romantic Poets Words-worth, Keats, Coleridge, Byron, and Shelley.* Harvard. Unpublished.

1921. Birkhead, Edith. *The Tale of Terror.*
1922. Husbands, Miss Winifred. *The Lesser English Novel, 1770–1800.* London. Unpublished.
1927. Railo, Eino. *The Haunted Castle.*
1927. Lord Ernle. *Light Reading of our Ancestors.*
1928. Brauchli, J. *Der Englische Schauerroman um 1800.* Weida.
1929. Dennis, L. A. *The Attitude of the Eighteenth Century towards the Medieval Romances.* Stanford University.
1930. Foster, James R. *The Minor English Novelists (1750–1800).* Harvard.
1932. Tompkins, J. M. S. *The Popular Novel in England.*
1932. Watt, W. W. *Shilling Shockers of the Gothic School.*
1933. Praz, Mario. *The Romantic Agony.*
1935. Murphy, Agnes. *Banditry and Chivalry in German Fiction (1790–1830).* University of Chicago Press.
1938. Summers, Montague. *The Gothic Quest.*
1941. Kettle, A. C. *Relation of Political and Social Ideas to the Novel of the English Romantic Revival.* Cambridge thesis. Unpublished.
1942. Richards, P. L. *The Italian Novel as Influenced by English Gothic Fiction, 1820–1840.* Harvard.
1946. Tarr, Sister Mary Muriel. *Catholicism in Gothic Fiction : A Study of the Nature and Function of Catholic Materials in Gothic Fiction in England.* Washington. Catholic University Press.

(IMPORTANT MONOGRAPHS, ARTICLES, ESSAYS, AND BIOGRAPHIES)

Church, R. *Mary Shelley.* 1928.
Dobson, Austin. *Horace Walpole.* 1927.
Draper, John. *William Mason : A Study in Eighteenth-century Culture.* N.Y. 1924.
Edge, J. H. *Horace Walpole, the Great Letter Writer.* Dublin. 1913. (Privately printed.)
Ellis, S. M. *Ann Radcliffe and her Literary Influence.* CONTEMPORARY REVIEW. CXXIII. 1923.
Fairfax, J. G. *Horace Walpole's Views on Literature.* 1909.
Fyvie, John. *Some Literary Eccentrics.* 1906.
Gorer, Geoffrey. *The Revolutionary Ideas of the Marquis de Sade.* 1934.
Gosse, E. *Horace Walpole.* SUNDAY TIMES, 2 November 1924.
Greenwood, A. D. *Horace Walpole's World.* 1913.
Greenwood, A. D. *Horace Walpole and Mme du Deffand.* 1929.
Grylls, R. G. *Mary Shelley.* 1938.

Gwynn, Stephen. *The Life of Horace Walpole.* 1932.

Havens, G. R. *L'Abbé Prévost and English Literature.* Princeton. 1921.

Havens, M. A. *Horace Walpole and the Strawberry Hill Press.* 1901.

Heine, Maurice. *The Marquis de Sade et Le Roman Noir.* Paris. 1933.

Hilbish, F. *Charlotte Smith.* Pennsylvania. 1941.

Idman, Nilo. *Charles Robert Maturin.* 1923.

Ker, W. P. *Horace Walpole. Collected Essays.* 1925.

Ketton-Cremer, R. W. *Horace Walpole.* 1940.

Lewis, Melville. *Horace Walpole.* 1930.

Lewis, Wilmarth. *Collectors Progress.* 1952.

McIntyre, Clara Francis. *Ann Radcliffe in Relation to Her Time.* 1920.

Mehrotra, K. K. *Horace Walpole and the English Novel.* 1934.

Meyer, G. *Les Romans de Mrs. Radcliffe.* Revue Germanique. 1909.

Moore, Helen. *Mary Wollstonecraft Shelley.* Philadelphia. 1886.

Norman, Sylva. *Mary Shelley, Novelist and Dramatist.* On Shelley. 1938.

Peck, Louis Francis. *The Life and Works of Matthew Gregory Lewis.* Harvard. 1942.

Phillips, W. C. *Dickens, Reade, and Collins.* 1919.

Rossetti, L. M. *Mrs. Shelley.* 1890.

Ruff, William. *Ann Radcliffe or the Hand of Taste.* The Age of Johnson. 1949.

Scholton, W. *Charles Robert Maturin, the Terror Novelist.* Amsterdam. 1933.

Seeley, L. B. *Horace Walpole and His World.* 1895.

Stephen, Leslie. *Horace Walpole.* Hours in a Library. 1909.

Strachey, L. *Horace Walpole and Mme du Deffand.* Books and Characters. 1922.

Strachey, L. *Horace Walpole.* Characters and Commentaries. 1933.

Wieten, A. A. S. *Mrs. Radcliffe, Her Relation towards Romanticism.* 1926.

Yvon, P. *Horace Walpole.* Paris. 1924.

Yvon, P. *Horace Walpole as a Poet.* Paris. 1924.

(OTHER WORKS)

Bucke, Charles. *On the Beauties, Harmonies, and Sublimities of Nature.* 1837.

Burke, Edmund. *A Philosophical Inquiry into the Origin of our Ideas of the Sublime and Beautiful.* 1899.

Coleridge, S. T. *Biographia Literaria.* 1817.

De Sade, Marquis. *Idée sur les Romans.* Paris. 1878.

D'Israeli, Isaac. *Calamities and Quarrels of Authors.* 1812.

THE GOTHIC FLAME

D'Israeli, Isaac. *Curiosities of Literature.* 1793.

Drake, Nathan. *Literary Hours.* 1800.

Gilfillan, G. *Galleries of Literary Portraits.* 1856.

Green, Thomas. *Diary of a Lover of Literature.* 1800.

Hauser, Arnold. *The Social History of Art.* 1951.

Haycroft, Howard. *Murder for Pleasure : the Life and Times of the Detective Story.* 1942.

Hazlitt, W. *Lectures on the English Poets and the English Comic Writers.* 1870.

Mathias, T. J. *The Pursuits of Literature.* 1794.

Murch, Jerome. *Mrs. Barbauld and her Contemporaries.* 1877.

Nichols, John. *Literary Anecdotes.* 1814.

Nietzsche. *The Birth of Tragedy.* 1923 edition.

Read, Herbert. *Surrealism.* 1936.

Read, Herbert. *Art Now.* 1948.

Read, Herbert. *Contemporary British Art.* 1950.

Read, Herbert. *The Philosophy of Modern Art.* 1951.

Read, Herbert. *The Meaning of Art.* 1951.

Summers, Montague. *The Vampire, his Kith and Kin.* 1928.

Summers, Montague. *The Vampire in Europe.* 1929.

Summers, Montague. *Essays in Petto.* 1941.

Thomas, Gilbert. *How to Enjoy Detective Fiction.* 1947.

Tompkins, J. M. S. *The Polite Marriage.* 1938.

VI. ARTICLES IN JOURNALS

ATLANTIC MONTHLY

Lewis, Wilmarth S. " Horace Walpole Reread." CLXXVI. 1945.

CONSERVATIVE REVIEW

Fiske, Christabel. " The Tales of Terror." Washington. March 1900.

CONNOISSEUR

Summers, Montague. " The illustrations of the Gothick novels." XCII. 1936.

ENGLISH LITERARY HISTORY, A JOURNAL OF

Williamson, George. " Mutability, decay, and seventeenth-century melancholy." II. 1935.

ENGLISH STUDIES

Doughty, Oswald. "Romanticism in eighteenth-century England." XII. 1930.

Flasdieck, H. "Reinhard Haferkorn's Gotik und Ruine in der englischen Dichtung des 18 Jahrhunderts." VII. 1925.

Moss, Walter. "M. G. Lewis and Mme de Stael." XXXIV. 1953.

Praz, Mario. "S. H. Monk's *The Sublime*." XVIII. 1936.

ESSAYS AND STUDIES OF THE ENGLISH ASSOCIATION

Birkhead, Edith. "Sentiment and sentimentality in the eighteenth-century novel." XI. 1925.

Macaulay, T. C. "French and English drama in the 17th century : some contrasts and parallels." XX. 1934.

Wilson, Mona. "The twilight of the Augustans." XX. 1934.

ENGLISH HISTORICAL REVIEW

Toynbee, P. "Horace Walpole's *Delanda est Oxonia*." XLII. 1927.

HARVARD STUDIES AND NOTES IN PHILOLOGY AND LITERATURE

Aubin, R. A. "Some Augustan Gothicists." XVII. 1935.

JOURNAL OF THE ROYAL INSTITUTE OF BRITISH ARCHITECTS

Richardson, A. E. "The Gothic Revival in the early eighteenth century." XLV. 1937.

JOURNAL OF ENGLISH AND GERMANIC PHILOLOGY

Hughes, Helen Sard. "The middle-class reader and the English novel." XXV. 1926.

Lovejoy, A. O. "The Chinese origin of a romanticism." XXXII. 1933.

McKillop, A. D. "Mrs. Radcliffe on the supernatural in poetry." XXXI. 1932.

LA CRITICA

Marshall, R. "Italy in English literature, 1755–1815." XXXIII. 1935.

MODERN LANGUAGE NOTES

Allen, B. Sprague. "Hussey's *The Picturesque*." XLIV. 1929.

Allen, Don Cameron. "Early eighteenth-century literary relations between England and Germany." XLIX. 1934.

Anderson, Paul Bunyan. "English drama transferred to Prevost's fiction." XLIX. 1934.

Bernbaum, Ernest. " Recent works on prose fiction before 1800." XLII. 1927. LV. 1940.

Blanchard, Rae. " The French source of two early English feminist tracts." XLIV. 1929.

Cooper, Lane. " Wordsworth's Ancient Mariner, ' Peter Bell '." XXII. 1907.

Emerson, O. F. " Monk Lewis and the *Tales of Horror*." XXXVIII. 1923.

Hill, Charles J. " The English translation of Werther." XLVII. 1932.

Holbrook, William C. " The adjective ' Gothique ' in the eighteenth century." November 1941.

Heilman, R. B. " Fielding and the first Gothic Revival." December 1941.

Kaufman, Paul. " Defining romanticism : a survey and a program." XL. 1925.

Lovejoy, A. O. " The first Gothic Revival and the Return to Nature." XLVII. 1932.

Longueil, A. E. " The word ' Gothic ' in eighteenth-century criticism. December 1923.

McKillop, A. D. " The first English translator of Werther." XLIII. 1928.

Mayo, Robert D. " How long was Gothic fiction in vogue ? " LVIII. 1943.

Raysor, Thomas M. " The study of Shakespeare's characters in the eighteenth century." XLII. 1927.

Smith, Horatio E. " Horace Walpole anticipates Victor Hugo." XLI. 1926.

Wary, Edith. " English adaptations of French drama between 1780 and 1815." XLIII. 1928.

Wector, Dixon. " Horace Walpole and Edmund Burke." LIV. 1939.

MODERN LANGUAGE REVIEW

Hughes, A. M. D. " Shelley's Zastrozzi and St. Irvyne." VII. 1912.

King, R. W. " Italian influence on English scholarship and literature during the Romantic Revival." XX. 1925. XXI. 1926.

Mayo, Robert D. " The Gothic short story in the magazines." XXXVII. 1942.

Thompson, L. F. " Ann Radcliffe's knowledge of German." XX. 1925.

Waterhouse, G. " Schiller's Räuber in England before 1800." XXX. 1935.

MODERN PHILOLOGY

Kliger, Samuel. " The Goths in England : an introduction to the Gothic vogue in eighteenth-century aesthetic discussion." XLIII. 1945.

Kliger, Samuel. " The Gothic Revival and the German translation." XLV. 1947.

Scheffer, John D. " The idea of decline in literature and the fine arts in the eighteenth-century England." XXXIV. 1936.

Modern Language Quarterly

Baker, Carlos. " Spenser, the eighteenth century, and Shelley's ' Queen Mab '."
II. 1941.
Brandenburg, Alice Stayert. " The theme of *The Mysterious Mother*." X. 1949.

Notes and Queries

Eastwood, Sidney K. " Horace Walpole." CLXXXIX. 1945.

Publications of the Modern Language Association of America

Anderson, G. K. " The neo-classical chronicle of the Wandering Jew." LXIII.
1948.
Babcock, R. W. " The idea of taste in the eighteenth century." L. 1935.
Foster, James R. " The Abbé Prevost and the English novel." XLII. 1927.
Foster, James R. " Charlotte Smith, Pre-Romantic novelist." XLIII. 1928.
Hamm, Victor M. " A seventeenth-century French source for Hurd's *Letters
on Chivalry and Romance*. LII. 1937.
Havens. " Romantic aspects of the Age of Pope." XXVII. 1912.
Lovejoy, A. O. " Optimism and romanticism." XLII. 1927.
McIntyre, Clara F. " The later career of the Elizabethan villain-hero." XL.
1925.
McIntyre, Clara F. " Were the Gothic novels Gothic ? " XXXVI. 1921.
Niles, Edward. " The discussion of taste from 1750 to 1770, and the new trends
in literary criticism." XLIX. 1934.
Rogers, W. H. " The reaction against melodramatic sentimentality in the
English novel, 1796–1830." XLIX. 1934.
Shackford, Martha Hale. " *The Eve of St. Agnes* and *The Mysteries of Udolpho*."
XXXVI. 1921.
Rolfe, Franklin P. " Seventeenth-century prose fiction." XLIX. 1934.
Thorp, William. " The stage adventures of some Gothic novels." XLIII.
1928.
Warner, James H. " Emile in eighteenth-century England." LIX. 1944.
Warner, James H. " Eighteenth-century English reactions to the *Nouvelle
Heloise*." LII. 1937.
Wallace, Cable Brown. " Prose fiction and English interest in the Near East."
LIII. 1938.
Trowbridge, Hoyt. " Bishop Hurd : A re-interpretation." LVIII. 1943.

Philological Quarterly

Babcock, R. W. " The attitude towards Shakespeare's learning in the late
eighteenth century." IX. 1930.

258 THE GOTHIC FLAME

Perkinson, R. H. " Walpole and a Dublin Pirate." XV. 1936.
Pottle, Frederick A. " The part played by Horace Walpole in the quarrel between Rousseau and Hume." IV. 1925.
Wallace, Cable Brown. " The popularity of English travel books about the Near East, 1775–1825." XV. 1936.

PARTIZAN REVIEW
Sypher, Wylie. " Social ambiguity in a Gothic novel." XII. 1945.

REVUE DE SYNTHÈSE HISTORIQUE
Van Tieghem, P. " Prinsen's De roman en de 18c in West Europe." XL. 1925.

REVUE DE LITTÉRATURE COMPARÉE
Review of Marshall's *Italy in English Literature*, 1755–1815. XV. 1935.

REVUE ANGLO-AMÉRICAINE
Draper, John W. " Social influences once more." VIII. 1931.

REVUE DES COURS ET CONFÉRENCES
Yvon, Paul. " En relisant Horace Walpole." XLIII. 1926.

REVIEW OF ENGLISH STUDIES
Collins, A. S. " The growth of the reading public during the eighteenth century." II. 1926.
Tompkins, J. M. S. " Ramond de Carbonnières, Grosley and Mrs. Radcliffe." V. 1929.

STUDIES IN PHILOLOGY
Aubin, R. A. " Three notes on graveyard poetry." XXXII. 1935.
Aubin, R. A. " Grottoes, geology and the Gothic Revival." XXXI. 1934.
Stein, Jess M. " Horace Walpole and Shakespeare." XXXI. 1934.
Williams, George G. " The beginnings of nature poetry in the eighteenth century." XXVII. 1930.

SOUTH ATLANTIC QUARTERLY
HolzKnecht, K. L. " Horace Walpole as Dramatist." XXVIII. 1929.
Martin, Abbott C. " The love of solitude in eighteenth-century poetry." XXIX. 1930.

SATURDAY REVIEW OF LITERATURE

Phelps, W. L. " Eino Railo's *The Haunted Castle.*" 15 October 1927.

THE TIMES LITERARY SUPPLEMENT

Anonymous. " Maturin and the novel of terror." 26 August 1920.

Esdaile, Katherine A. " Walpole's *Anecdotes of Painting.* 19 March 1931.

Fairchild, Hoxie N. " Byron and Monk Lewis." 11 May 1946.

Phelps. " The picturesque age." 1 December 1927.

Lewis, W. S. " Walpole's *Anecdotes.*" 7 May 1931.

Praz, M. " The prelude to romanticism." 13 August 1925.

Peck, Lewis F. " Lewis's *Monk* (7 March 1935) ; corr. by W. Roberts (14 March 1935) ; by E. G. Bayford (28 March 1935) ; by Frederick Coykendall (25 April 1935).

Sadleir, M. " Poems by Ann Radcliffe." 29 March 1928.

Review of Stockley's " German literature as known in England, 1750–1830." 13 March 1930.

Smith, W. H. " Strawberry Hill and Otranto." 23 May 1936.

Sadleir, M. " Tales of terror." 7 January 1939.

Toynbee, Paget. " Horace Walpole and Robert." 14 April 1932.

Special " Detection and terror supplement." 25 February 1955.

THE SEWANEE REVIEW

Turnell, Martin. " The novels of Prevost." Autumn 1953.

YALE REVIEW

Woolf, Virginia. " Two antiquaries : Walpole and Cole." XXVIII. 1939.

UNIVERSITY OF ILLINOIS STUDIES IN LANGUAGE AND LITERATURE

Heidler, Joseph B. " The history from 1700 to 1800 of English criticism of prose fiction." XIII. No. 2. 1928.

UNIVERSITY OF CALIFORNIA PUBLICATIONS IN ENGLISH

Evans, Bertrand. " Gothic drama from Walpole to Shelley." XVIII. 1947.

INDEX

(See also Classified Bibliography)